Scapegoats for a Profession

Scapegoats for a Profession

UNCOVERING PROCEDURAL INJUSTICE

Ann Daniel

University of New South Wales
Sydney, Australia

harwood academic publishers

Australia • Canada • France • Germany • India • Japan
Luxembourg • Malaysia • The Netherlands • Russia
Singapore • Switzerland

First published 1998
Second printing 2000

Amsteldijk 166
1st Floor
1079 LH Amsterdam
The Netherlands

British Library Cataloguing in Publication Data

A catalogue record for this book is available from the British Library.

ISBN 90-5702-277-X

Cover design by Jessica Cotterell.

CONTENTS

ACKNOWLEDGMENTS

This research has been made possible through the trusting cooperation of the people whose stories are told in the book. I hope I do justice to the candour and confidence of our discussions.

Family who work in the media and the systems of law and health counselled my interpretations of events. Their advice on things legal and medical and on the clarity of my writing was invaluable.

Dianne Burn joined forces with my first research assistant, Jaqueline Foyster; Dianne added to her field research an expert knowledge of the law governing professional conduct and practice and Jaqueline brought remarkable powers of investigation to the research task. Stefan Horarik searched the library for references. Janette Murdoch, who works with me in the School of Sociology, aided and abetted the production. I am deeply indebted to our family and these friends.

Others, who are not explicitly named, have assisted from their positions in the justice systems, the health department and the conduct divisions of law and medicine. The Health Care Complaints Commissioner, Merrilyn Walton, as well as the managers of the Conduct Division of the Law Society, first Fred Smith and, in recent years, Garry Still, have given me access to materials and advice.

Like all my colleagues at the University of New South Wales, I am indebted to the librarians at the university library for their continuing assistance. Their large part in the work of scholars in the humanities and social sciences calls for recognition.

This research and other work still in progress was assisted by a three-year grant from the Australian Research Council. The value of such financial assistance is readily recognised. The anonymous peer encouragement which such grants embody should be equally acknowledged. An ARC grant is a licence to work harder!

Amongst the scholars who advised on earlier papers I should count Professor Alan Kerckhoff of Duke University who arranged for me to present a paper which prompted lively discussions at a formative stage with his colleagues in Sociology at Duke. In Ireland Mr Justice O'Flaherty, James Nugent SC, former

President of the Bar Council and my friends Gail and Sean Freyne of Trinity College provided research leads and great conversations.

I am grateful to the editors at Harwood Academic Publishers, and to Professor Bouma and the other reviewers of early chapters of the book who urged its publication.

Throughout the research and writing of this book my husband, Ray Burn, prompted and supported its making. His critical intelligence and extensive knowledge of professional life guided and stimulated my enthusiasm for the inquiry and made possible its completion.

INTRODUCTION

*D*isciplinary *P*ractices

In 1993 I began a study of the discipline of professions, a path trodden by many researchers before me. Professions appear as self-important, self-regarding, moral communities tightly knit together. Their disciplinary practices are directed to an engagement with learning and skill. They value obligations to colleagues, and, beyond the collegiate, some care for the community where the profession is practised. My search was directed to those disciplinary practices governing learning and loyalty, standards, sanctions and the solidarity of the group.

My inquiry started with the practice of law and medicine and in this book I do not move beyond those domains. The medical and legal professions are prominent in the public arena, subject to the public gaze, exclusive and excluding the unqualified from belonging and participating in their practice. They are exemplary communities of interest. The common view holds that such professions are require solidarity, that they repudiate the accusations of outsiders, and that they look after their own. This view has led to assertions that self-regulation and self-discipline, will not avail to ensure good practice. But my investigation into the disciplinary practices of self-regulation found quite differently. Professions protect the profession. Members who are seen to transgress may be initially treated with compassion, but are soon liable to be denounced, pilloried, and driven out—never again to belong to the society of registered practitioners.

The standards of a group are seen most clearly when these are transgressed. Discipline appears where it is imposed on transgressors. It can be exerted as subtle, firm pressure within. When that fails recourse may be had to external pressures—the complaints mechanisms, investigations, prosecutions, tribunals. I turned to public enactment of discipline to see how a profession may uphold identity, status and reputation, when all else fails. This led to selecting for close observation those cases involving high-profile practitioners accused of scandalous complaints. They were prominent in the daily news; the media selected my sample.

Then a serendipitous issue emerged: Some of these notable practitioners were positioned at the centre of a wider scandal in the profession. They might embody all that had gone wrong and their going might serve to put an end to the scandal. Were some practitioners being scapegoated for the good of the profession, or were they being sacrificed by some equally intense and cohesive group?

These questions sent me to inquire into scapegoating as a sociological process, one adopted by a group to maintain its integrity, good order and purity. The scapegoat could be sociologically investigated; it could be found inscribed in myth and history. There were many accounts in anthropologists' tales, in the stories and plays of classical antiquity, in actions taken up in more recent drama, and in the literary criticism which teases out the recurrences of an ancient stratagem to rid the world of evil or the semblance of evil.

But could scapegoating figure in the justice systems of a modern democracy? I searched for all I could read about scapegoating and the purposes it might serve today. Scapegoating, I soon found, is not a simple victimisation which can occur at any time—whenever someone is picked as a focus for derision or contempt. Scapegoats take a larger role and act to resolve the mass disaster which spawned them.

All manner of troubles can alarm people and call for urgent remedy to restore good order and security. In modern societies rational ways of dealing with social and moral crises, as well as natural and human disasters, have been developed. These are the legislative and regulatory systems governing our lives and our living conditions. But, ancient ways of dealing with social strife or moral disaster do not disappear. Memories of what once availed endure in a people's consciousness. When new ways are imposed over the old, the older forms may be submerged, but they do not disappear. Culture persists, its persistence ensured through the stories, myth or history, told and retold from one generation to the next. Today's societies are heir to a very rich literary and historical heritage drawn from many cultures.

In Australia, as elsewhere, social evils call for legal remedies. We are quick to declare, 'there ought to be a law about it'. Contemporary society places its trust in the formal, rational procedures of modern law, but these may not adequately serve the interests and values of a particular community. The imposition of law can falter and fail to restore the order and confidence required for a particular group's security. Or its balance can tip in the opposite direction and its authority become too draconian or wide-ranging, and so disrupt further the moral security and the comfortable certainties of the group. Such balance has been difficult to strike in many areas where the protection of law is held out, for example around domestic violence or the rights of children. Particular communities may come to believe that the due processes of law do not serve the purpose of restoring order with a minimum of further disturbance. Or some may be embarrassed by the workings of law which uncover problems or evils which they feel are better hidden from public view. These feelings can prompt a search for solutions outside the law or a manipulation of law to serve special interest groups.

In countries whose legal system derives from England a common law tradition has evolved with many safeguards to ensure procedural justice, an ideal of fair play where justice is dispensed without fear or favour of persons or institutions. Many other European countries and nations long associated with those European states have developed a civil law system. Both traditions, one based on an adversary system and the other on the inquisitorial, endorse highly valued concepts of justice, but have adopted quite different procedures to ensure justice. The ends can be the same but the ways of achieving them are different. But, despite the ideals, procedures can be subverted to serve divergent ends. Law can be used in the service of diverse purposes. Thus at the centre of modern society occur pre-modern forms of punishment aimed at retribution as the way to restitution.

My investigations led me to uncover cases where the law appears to have been used for unjust purposes. These were cases where it appeared one person had been chosen for exemplary punishment to carry away the guilt of many and deter others from wrongdoing. I raised these concerns in April 1994 when interviewing Justice Michael Kirby, then President of the Appeal Court, Supreme Court of New South Wales. His response encouraged me to continue: 'if you can show where and how these things can occur then your research will be of great value for the continuing reform of law in this country'.

The cases presented in this book all raise questions about the possible failure of law to provide justice and good order. Still more alarming is the fear that the courts may be used as a stage for rituals which support vested group interests, sustain group solidarity and subvert natural justice. Some such are cases of professional discipline brought before legislatively constituted professional tribunals and then, after the Tribunal findings are handed down, brought before the courts of the State and the Commonwealth. Many of the cases I followed reveal practitioners who were variously villainous, venal, weak, stupid, incompetent—in one manner or another a danger to society. Some of the cases, however, trouble me deeply. They concern practitioners of distinction who came to be seen as the centre of scandals, troubles, and bad practices which were felt to be widespread in their profession. Crucially implicated, often instrumental, in their investigation and arraignment before the authorities have been communities agitated about a scandal which swirls around them. Often, but not always, the community is the professional collegiate. The group searches out the evidence, heaps accountability for the evil on one or more of their number and drives them out. Is this scapegoating? How can it come about?

I read about and watched the part that professional tribunals play in ensuring the competence and probity of professional practice and its practitioners. Tribunal determinations became the final act of a lengthy process of complaint, investigation, allegation, examination and cross-examination, submission and argument. These legal procedures come into operation when the less formalised tactics of self-regulation fail to ensure conformity to professional norms of practice and conduct.

In the great majority of cases the law worked well. The legislatively authorised professional practitioners, laypersons and presiding judicial officers, who sat on the tribunals, were guided by principles of justice and equity and concerned to protect the public. Good sense and fairness prevailed against gross incompetence and just plain villainy. But some matters went seriously wrong and there was no way to right the damage. I have come to believe that there are structural defects which imperil the working of some tribunals. The makers of these bodies have tried to weld features of the inquisitorial procedures of civil law tradition onto a common law adversarial system. The join has not taken and some professional tribunals cannot always ensure the safe carriage of justice. The Medical Tribunal labours under such a defect. The Legal Services Tribunal is of a different construction and serves the community and the profession better.

This is a book of stories about people who became scapegoats and so could serve to rid their communities of the troubles and confusions which had arisen. Because these are the scapegoats' stories the reader will be likely to attend mainly to their trials and tribulations. I should first describe how we may understand the scapegoat and the practice of scapegoating which appears in many civilisations including our own.

CHAPTER 1

*S*capegoats

In times of trouble the people look for what has gone wrong, where to lay blame, how the ills which beset them might be taken away. When the people are strong, banded into tightly linked communities, they respond vigorously and relentlessly wherever threats to their existence or their wellbeing can be felt. The ways of combating evil are many, but some are played out repeatedly because of their power to restore the integrity, the confidence, the psychic health of the group with minimum cost to the group itself.

Scapegoats, known to us from myth and history, both ancient and modern, can serve such a critical function for their communities. The scapegoat, as archetype, collective representation, or symbol comes to us through literature and stories told again and again. The phenomenon has been exhaustively studied in Greek and Roman civilisation. We have, moreover, many accounts of scapegoating in other communities distant in time or space from our own. For those with a knowledge of Christianity, the figure is familiar in the story of Christ as scapegoat, the divine man, worthy and able to 'take away the sins of the world'. An understanding of the scapegoat has entered our consciousness as one way of dealing with the ills which beset us.

The ways of dealing with the exigencies of life become the material of myth—those stories which tell, for those who would listen, how things began, how new things were created, how danger was averted, how the enemy was driven away, how the community was saved. Myths serve to explain the manifold conditions of human existence and survival. Myth arises in the experience of a people dealing with the demands and conflicts of everyday life and seeking to understand what is done to them and what they must do to continue. The content of myth is richly coloured for the culture where it takes root, and varies remarkably through time and place. The forms are repeated endlessly as deeply satisfying answers to recurrent questions. A moment's thought can conjure up many myths of creation and continuity, fertility, salvation, resistance, war, peace, health, heroism, sacrifice, and utopia.

In western civilisation we begin early to learn of myths from other times. These come to us in children's stories, history lessons, science classes, television, literary readings, and the study of legends drawn from distant lands. Some have provided a name for a widely observed condition or circumstance, others are signalled by the name of the archetypal figure of the central actor: the Oedipus complex, the gaze of Medusa, a Bacchanalia, Nemesis, Nirvana, Cupid's arrow, a Dionysian man, a Caesar's wife of respectability, a Daniel or a Solomon in judgment, a Messiah. We are not limited to our own present mythologies, but have become heir to the interpretive tales of other peoples.

Nonetheless, as European heirs of the Enlightenment we claim for ourselves a rationality which refuses the explanations of other times distant in the mists of superstition. We like to point to evidence for what Weber termed the growing rationality of society, the demystification of our world where formal rationality should determine what is to be done and how it is to be controlled. I would argue, however, that the undercurrents which steer how we might act still run deep in social consciousness; that we do, indeed, reflect upon and teach our children how dangers were abated and enemies resisted so that communities might survive in the past. Those lessons settle into social and individual consciousness. And effective ways of ensuring the integrity and maintenance of the social group are never quite foregone.

Myths proliferate and nowhere more palpably than in the telling of the eternal conflict between good and evil. They arise in a people's experience, in the sensate, affective business of everyday life. Myths are formed in the telling and retelling of the story, the imagery of the tale coloured to appeal to the views of the people for whom it can explain of the inexplicable.

Like all of our beliefs myths are socially constructed and we hold on to them for as long as they work for us, for as long as they serve to explain what is happening to us and what we must do about it. The myths upheld and followed in a society are constitutive for the society: the individual is of no matter. Myths are stories about the survival of the social. Myths hold out meaning, they interpret the human condition whether rooted in religion, in science, in national identity, in all the forms of belief which constitute culture. Emile Durkheim argued persuasively that myth and ritual were the founding elements of religion, itself the progenitor of society; myth is about what people believe and ritual is how they act out those beliefs (1995). Holding a society together are shared beliefs and practices—what is widely termed culture. These constitute the bond between members, the identity of the group. Durkheim pushed this idea further to point out and explain the perceptible differences in the way social groups are held together in a common identity. (Many sociologists have engaged with these issues of social identity and social consciousness, but, in the interests of clarity, I will stick with Durkheim's account.)

My point in this excursion into the nature of the social is to emphasise the significance of solidarity for the survival of the group and to signal the strength with which a firmly integrated society will maintain its wellbeing and security. The power of the group can be prodigious, particularly when its preservation is at risk. Survival is the imperious justification. The morality of the group is prem- ised on its survival.

Society

Society, Durkheim maintained, lies in the relation between people bonded by their shared material conditions of existence and by common beliefs, values, expectations and sentiments. But, as the group grows larger and more intensely interactive (what Durkheim termed an increasing material and moral density), it loses the solidarity based on uniformity and on likeness. The increasing differ- entiation of people, their abilities and functions, however, sponsored a growing interdependence within the large group and this overtook the earlier 'mechanical solidarity', based on the similarity among members of the group. In the large industrialised societies of the early twentieth century, in the nation-state, me- chanical solidarity based on resemblance decreased as 'division of labour' increased and social solidarity came to depend much more on cooperation be- tween persons and institutions specialised in activities functional for the whole. The interdependence called for a reciprocity in working for the good of the whole. Durkheim contrasts *organic* solidarity with *mechanical* solidarity. Me- chanical solidarity occurs in small groups where people hold to the same sort of values and ways of thinking; their actions are fairly predictable. Organic solidar- ity presupposes a large society where people tolerate each others' differences and are linked by interdependence rather than uniformity of ideas and habits. The smaller community coalesces by virtue of its homogeneity, its shared iden- tity of value and belief, and operates like a finely tuned machine. The larger society of city, state or nation allows for heterogeneity of belief, value and function—individuals and groups held by virtue of their interdependence and, indeed, by difference.

Sociologists have been quick to locate the basis of differentiation in the way societies are held together. The method of linking together is what makes and marks out the group, gives it visibility, identity, excludes what does not belong and defines its boundaries. The character of those links, of social relations, is nonetheless quite diversified. It can be shown, and indeed was shown by Durkheim and others, that modern societies owe their integrity and visible identity, in large measure, to internal interdependence, that is to a social division of labour throughout. But the 'older' forces for integration continue in modern societies. While the group can tolerate considerable diversity, a sense of shared identity, of group consciousness, is definitive of its distinctive presence.

The larger society today is held together by its interdependence, an interdependence spanned and held by an overarching shared consciousness. This is not the tight consensus of smaller groups distinguished by homogeneity, but a consensus about what may be tolerated and what decencies must be observed. Within such societies, characterised by mutually recognised interdependence, smaller groups flourish, their consensus running along sectarian lines. Only in times of appalling threat to its survival does a society (as distinguished here from the smaller community), achieve the cohesion of purpose and interest. War is exemplar of such a binding force upon a heterogeneous society.

Despite the pervasiveness of public media constituting communication within the larger society, individuals derive their identity and sense of belonging from more intimate social settings, such as family, friends, work groups, and special-interest associations. These espouse a dogmatic scheme of values, ideas, expectations and practices. It was only later in his life (when writing the preface to the second edition of *Division of Labour in Society*) that Durkheim declared the significance of occupational groups in terms that shouted guilds and professions. Groups, characterised by mechanical solidarity, shared goals, values and beliefs, and endorsed standards of behaviour and action, are everywhere. All manner of social movements, political parties, trades unions, academic *collegia*, self-help groups, organised crime, street gangs and, of course, professions endorse a uniformity of value and goal rationality which suffuses the whole and generates a marvellous sense of wellbeing. A group will preserve at all costs this generic identity, purpose and being. Survival justifies everything.

These exclusive, cohesive groups are bonded in adherence to shared beliefs, practices and ways of thinking which guide what each person might do as typical of their group identity. Such groups exclude the uninitiated, determine those who may belong and create an environment in which its members think and act in ways conforming to group interest. The ideology of the group informs all within, but its power is only known in the unlikely condition of individual resistance. Within the larger heterogeneous society, which is linked by its very interdependence and suffused with a broadly tolerant acceptance of an abstracted identity, there dwell smaller, homogeneous groups, which are tightly integrated by virtue of shared understandings and experience, recognition of common material interests and moral commitment to the good of the group. Consider social groups you may know of or have known: cliques of school friends, gangs of street kids, political parties, resident action groups, trade unions, self-help groups, feminist action, convents and monasteries, professional associations and societies. The list is endless. What is definitive is the close identity of the members with the whole such that much of their identity is drawn from that whole. The group's continuity and wellbeing assumes a remarkable significance and is to be protected before all else.

Durkheim elaborated on the moral being of the group in a later essay, *Professional Ethics and Civic Morals*, an exemplar of the moral suzerainty within a closed, cohesive, comprehensive community. The moral authority of such a group is tightly linked into its solidarity. The greater its strength and coherence, based on prolonged and frequent interaction of its members, the more comprehensively and pervasively does it command the loyalty and commitment of those members. A group's ethical system is primarily directed to its own wellbeing, not that of the society at large. Concern for the society outside the group's boundaries may be a constitutive element in that moral authority, but first the group must survive.

Many events can disrupt the social; many conditions can diminish the integrity and cohesion of the group. The common enemies of humanity, such as famine, pestilence, contagion, war, internecine strife, all have their counterparts threatening the specificity of the group. External threats are to be repulsed and evils coming from within are to be expurgated. The response of the group to apprehension of threat to itself or to the integrity of its pervasive ideology is determined largely by what will be effective with minimum cost to the group. The morality of the group is bound into its survival. Its continuance is primary to its constitution which, in turn, lies in the purposes it serves—the material and ideal interests and intentions of its members.

In large measure the hegemony of the group directs and controls the activities of the members in so far as these activities identify them with the group. Groups develop many ways of securing the adherence and enthusiasm of members. These include criteria for selection, rites of incorporation, instilling group expectations and standards, and sanctions imposed on transgressions. These are the disciplinary practices that bind the individual into the group—the ways of informing, controlling and integrating one into the life of the whole. The moral duty of the individual lies in conformity to the ideals and support of the objectives of the group. Among the most patent exemplars of the mechanical solidarity which Durkheim expounds is the association of professionals, the professional collegiate. Here the forces for group cohesion and integrity have developed powerfully; the *esprit de corps* among professional practitioners is signalled and displayed continually in the interaction within as well as in all activity directed to those outside the assumed territory. Whatever might threaten from outside is vigorously resisted and what might corrupt within is to be cut out. Maintenance of that identity, that public face and reputation, can become its paramount good. The significance of these forces for identifying a group of colleagues as a profession, or a specific discipline within a profession is pointed out in Chapter 2.

There are rules, implicit and explicit, to define the boundaries of right conduct. There are penalties to deter and punish transgressions. Legislation and regulation are enforced against the guilty individual. But, such legitimated procedures avail only when the infringement may be observed and the culprit identified. A seemingly intractable problem arises when the source of the trouble is unknown, the evil is generated by many, or the malefactor is known and of such authority and influence as to be beyond the imposition of deterrence and sanctions. The limits of law may be reached.

At these times a scapegoat can be chosen, accused of perpetrating the evil and, laden with the collective guilt, driven out of the community. The troubles which beset the many can be carried away by the one chosen to bear the wrongs of many. This ancient stratagem has been used repeatedly to signal a sort of psychic relief for the community beset with trouble not readily resolved. Although such a device offends modern notions of justice, it should be seen as a bid to preserve valued ideals and standards, as a community's self-preservation. Scapegoating is still practised and can be best understood in the context of a community upholding its identity and surviving.

Scapegoating

Scapegoats in myth and history are at the centre of a crisis which generates disorder and conflict. They are seized as cynosures for blame. The evils seen to affect the group are heaped on them. Sacrificing the scapegoat, its destruction or banishment, dissipates the trouble disturbing the people so order and stability can be re-established.

The scapegoat as tragic figure has repeatedly taken central stage in European literature. Euripides took up the issue, particularly in *The Bacchae*. The Lydian stranger, who leads the women of Thebes in strange and joyous dancing, is caught by Pentheus' servants, yet 'of his own free will he surrendered ... he even smiled and consented to be arrested and bound' (trans. Hadas & McLean, 1960, p.289). When The Stranger is delivered from his chains, the women still dance and revel beyond control in the mountains. After an ironic turn in the drama The Stranger leads out the curious and contumelious Pentheus who, spying on the revelling women, is discovered and killed—by his mother. Then the hunting and destruction of Pentheus ends the wild disorder; the women of Thebes return to their 'fair-towered town' and sensible rationality. Pentheus is dead and Agave, his mother, goes into exile. Is one or both the scapegoat?

The theme of the scapegoat recurs endlessly through tales familiar to us from the Classics and so many of those works revered in the study of European literature, until, as Vickery, echoing Rayner Heppenstall, observes 'it began to seem to me that all the key characters in fiction were scapegoats in one sense or another' (1974, p.267). Renowned anthropologist, Sir James Frazer, in his wondrous collection of tales, wrote of the scapegoat in the first version of his classic account of magic and religion in many cultures almost 100 years ago. Some remarkable studies of scapegoating by other authors followed and reached a fine culmination in Girard's *The Scapegoat*, which draws much from Frazer's accounts of the practice of scapegoating in myth and history and across many cultures.

One volume of Frazer's collection of tales, entitled *The Golden Bough: A Study in Magic and Religion*, is devoted to stories of the scapegoat drawn from the myth and legend (1933, part VI). Writing from the perspective of the community, not the lonely individual, Frazer explains the phenomenon of ritual expulsion of evil in terms of the relief which the group believed this act might give them. The community troubled by evil seeks to rid itself of the ills which distress and overburden its resources. Frazer takes the endless recurrence of evil for granted, and as an anthropologist assumes the wellbeing of the group as paramount. He sees scapegoating and all forms of ritual expulsion of evil in the light of the people's belief in the effects which their actions should secure. His analysis of the process into its essential components is instructive.

To understand the apparent acceptability of scapegoating primacy should be given to the community and its efforts to rid itself of the ills which distress it. The vagaries of nature, flood, drought, pestilence, storm, tempest and volcanic eruption, and the infirmities of the body, disease, accident and disability, are a part of life. Communities deal with these by all means available. When the repertoire of material, rational intervention is exhausted, the group, intent on repelling difficulty, on surviving and faring well, turns to whatever may have availed before. Communities simply act, on occasion or regular basis, to rid themselves of what afflicts them. The scapegoat serves as a receptacle, symbolically and materially, to carry evil far away from the group. Frazer details numerous accounts of scapegoating in many civilisations where human scapegoats are selected, readied and ritually driven away carrying the evils their banishment is set to remove (1933, part VI).

The scapegoat is not simply a victim for the ritual of sacrifice; its part is more active, it must be banished, it must take away the ills of the people. And so defiled and loaded with evil, the scapegoat cannot return. The human scapegoats, in Frazer's examples, are chosen and then may cooperate in their own preparation for the sacrifice. Often the scapegoat is feted and indulged to make ready for the predetermined fate. A humble person may be treated like a king and so become a fit and worthy victim. In some cultures the scapegoat may indeed be a king, a person of noble rank, or one endowed, in the eyes of the group, with divinity. 'The civilized Greeks of Asia and Athens habitually sacrificed men whom they regarded as incarnate gods' (Frazer, 1933, pp.273–4).

In ancient Greece the person to be offered as scapegoat was fed on the finest food for a year, then dressed elegantly and led through the city so that evils might be symbolically heaped on the head before the chosen victim is expelled. The ritual was played out in times of great calamity and came to be a practice adopted on a regular basis; the festival of Thargelia, at harvest time, culminated with the procession, sacrifice and expulsion of the scapegoat. Often associated with the driving out was a beating with branches, or sometimes a stoning, which Frazer interprets as a rite of purification to beat off all malignancy.

For the Romans the time for licence and carnival was the Saturnalia which fell in December as the world grew cold and the nights long. The mock king, chosen for his beauty to preside over Saturnalia, could do and have anything he wished. For thirty days the most delicious food, elaborate clothes, loveliest maidens were brought for his pleasure. If he were, and he usually was, simply a common man when chosen, the privileges were to befit him for his higher destiny—for the good of the people.

Frazer sets out his voluminous collection of the customs of scapegoating in a seemingly serendipitous sequence where incidents from diverse times and cultures are strung together. His main concern is to trace 'the use of the Dying God as a scapegoat to free his worshippers from the troubles of all sorts with which life on earth is beset' (Frazer, 1933, p.v). The theme of scapegoating, often tied into the cyclical sacrifice of a king, or man made imperial for the purpose, is sounded repeatedly through the many accounts collected over a lifetime of scholarship.

The significant features in Frazer's analysis are: (1) the scapegoat to be a vehicle into which evil is loaded before it is driven away; (2) where a general clearance of evil occurs as a periodic ritual the time usually coincides with a change in the seasons, such as before 'the wet' in the tropics or the beginning or end of winter in temperate zones; (3) the ritual of scapegoating is typically preceded by a period of licence; and (4) the scapegoat is often endowed with divinity which Frazer links to the practice of killing the divine animal or human (e.g. a god-king) before infirmity or the ravages of old age set in.

Jane Harrison, writing in 1903, examined the role of the *pharmakos* (human scapegoat) in Greek religion in *Prolegomena to the Study of Greek Religion*.[1] The book examines Greek ritual as a way to understand the religion of classical Greece. Harrison's inquiry is a more finely detailed one than Frazer's references which located the phenomenon in its global and historical context.

The *pharmakos*, as human scapegoat in the Athens of fifth century BC and earlier, is led out to take on all defilement of the city. *Pharmakoi* are for purification and the critical action is not their death but their expulsion. There is in this a close correspondence between the symbolism of the idea and the materiality of physical action. Purification, driving out of evil, is a matter of striking the vessel, of thrashing the bearer, which holds evil, a purging of all impurities and un-seemly matter. The calamity, which called for drastic action, such as famine or pestilence, was always of unknown origin. The attribution of blame is not clear-cut; the cause of evil is unknown or not to be spoken. But, although the source of disaster is unknown, the response can be clear and concrete. The ancient Greek texts describe how the *pharmakos* was chosen, beaten with specific plants (leeks, wild figs) as a mode of purification and remedy for the city; and ban-ished—driven out, or slaughtered, burnt and the ashes scattered to the winds and the sea (Harrison, 1960, pp.97–8). The ceremony, including the parading through the city, had transferred to the *pharmakos* all the ills of the city and so, imbued with evil, it could not be allowed to return. The expulsion was absolute.

The role of the *pharmakos* is not as victim for sacrifice, not as an offering to appease a god, but as an embodiment of the expulsion of evil as purification. The *pharmakos* was not an atonement but a riddance. 'The *pharmakos* is killed then, not because his death is a vicarious sacrifice, but because he is so infected and tabooed that his life is a practical impossibility' (Harrison, 1960, p.104). The infection is not from himself, but from the ills which have been heaped upon him; he is to bear away all that distresses the people.

The literal connotations of *pharmakos* lie, not with religion, but with magic. The Greek term translates as 'magic man'. His work is not of sacrifice but of *medicine*; he becomes materially a *physic* to purify, cleanse, and dispel conta-gion. This magic may seem irrational and be repugnant, but its efficacy was believed and belief in a medicine lends greater potency to the remedy. The per-son is in many ways incidental: the greater good legitimates the fate of the individual. Martyrs, religious or secular, bear witness to a greater good for their communities. We celebrate the same heroic fate in times of war: *Dulce et deco-rum est pro patria mori*. That lament by Wilfred Owen for soldiers slain in the First World War accords with the insistence by some scholars that the scape-goat volunteers (Bremmer, 1983, p.307). The myth held that the scapegoat came forward of his own accord. So in rituals which enacted the myth, where an animal was used, it must be tricked into shaking its head in agreement; a person who took on the role was lured by rewards of indulgence and distinction.

The distinction between myth and ritual is important. In historical or literary accounts of the periodic ritual, the one to be expelled may be a person of no importance, but one who must then be elevated into the important role by ritual accoutrements and enjoyment prior to banishment. For the purpose of the an-cient ceremony the one at the centre of the ritual purging must be made lovely and fit for the sacrifice of expulsion. The scapegoat of mythology is much more exalted—a person of great beauty or importance, but still rendered vulnerable by signs of liminality, of being on the margin of the community or caught in some transitional phase. The lame Oedipus, the Dionysian stranger in Thebes, the loveliest maiden, the old King, the child of the King, the son or daughter of the god, the prophet as chosen one—all have appeared as fitting scapegoats in mythology.

Although the rite was originally enacted when calamity befell, it became a feature of the festival of Thargelia as a rite of expulsion, of riddance, which nonetheless involved the loss of life to a human being (Harrison, 1960, p.109). In the regular periodic rituals the scapegoat could be tricked or lured into compliance. Various ruses were employed to prompt animal scapegoats into a gesture of acceptance: the goat, once water was poured on its head, would shake its head in a manner seen as acquiescence. Death was not inevitable for the animal or human scapegoats employed in these periodic rituals. Only expulsion was required for the purpose and could often be secured by stoning the chosen one. The scapegoat's fate was not a matter for regret. After chasing it away the community returned to everyday life without a backward glance. The scapegoat did not return and the community neither looked back nor took note of its fate. This completed the rite of purification and purgation (Bremmer, 1983, p.317).

The literature of classical Greece does not firmly delineate what must be the profile of the one chosen as *pharmakos*. Harrison (1960, p.97) quotes Aristophanes on the decline in quality of state officials in the new democracy: 'Any chance man that we come across / Not fit in old days for a *pharmakos*, / These we use'. The *pharmakos* may indeed have become an 'offscouring' of society, or a criminal set aside to fulfil a dual purpose, as both the expulsion of a *pharmakos* and the putting to death of an offender. But Harrison, like Frazer, notes that the *pharmakos* is consecrated for the purpose. The *pharmakos* is set aside, as it were made sacred in preparation for the part to be played. Harrison speculates that the definitive notion is taboo. Her main concern is, however, the social gist of the phenomenon, that is the presumption of the actuality (physical presence) of evil, the fearful expectation of its contagion, and the reliance on a physical means of expelling evil. The vessel with the capacity for filling with evil and for carrying it away was a human being. Later in the periodic routines of ritual a fitting and symbolic representation might serve instead. But *in extremis* magic required a human scapegoat for the purification. The difference between ritual celebrated in response to crisis and ritual performed according to a regular, routine cycle is important. Grave, immediate threat to a community calls out for a human sacrifice. The threat can only be dispelled through the special one selected to carry away the ills of the people. Later the rituals which re-enact the triumph over evil can use lesser beings to represent the all too human scapegoat who saves when the trouble is real.

The Scapegoat in Contemporary Literature

Myths have a continuing presence in civilisations where they are recalled to reverberate in the art and literature of later times. In traditional societies rituals and pageants present those ideas and values which celebrate and promote the identity and integrity of the group. To some extent the media is today the oracle and the teller of cautionary tales. As with myths, these can intimate what may be done, what will serve to hold onto stability and cast out troubles.

Particular myths and legends have entered twentieth century literature and become present for us, an idea cogently argued by John Vickery. In *The Literary Impact of The Golden Bough*, he recalls Frazer's remarkable accounts of myth and ritual in ancient religions and points to their reworking in the writing of some of this century's most famed writers: Yeats, T.S. Eliot, D.H. Lawrence, Joyce. Vickery searches for the sources of Frazer's manifest influence and points to his affinities with the scientific temperament of the times, his vigorous evangelicalism, his links with prevailing utilitarianism, his rationalism and faith in progress. Frazer was seen to bring to contemporary works on the evolution of mankind an enormous collection detailing the practice of magic and religion over millennia. His studies informed quite profoundly literary interpretations of human tragedy and dilemma and through that literature Frazer's own work gained a much wider audience. Frazer's *The Golden Bough* recorded primitive barbarism, but, as will be described later, the same barbarisms echo through contemporary renditions of present troubles. Writers educated in nineteenth century scientific thought, of which anthropology was a part, were equipped to use historical and mythical analogies to translate the horrors of that time. Scapegoating is a recurrent theme in late nineteenth and twentieth century literature.

The expulsion of the scapegoat, which some scholars believe had originally served both to stimulate the fertility of crops and animals and to purify the community before the season of renewal began, came increasingly to be for purification, for the expulsion of all evil influences. Frazer had demonstrated how the ceremony of the scapegoat was contiguous with beliefs and practices around the cyclic form of existence, where death, incarnation and birth follow ceaselessly. And, he claimed, in many cultures, the ritual served a further purpose: it signalled the immortality of the king (or kingship) through the death of the old, frail one and his reappearance in the person of the new king. Such a king does not await the debility and defeat of old age, but goes out to meet death—the community driving him towards the end.

The theme of the kingly scapegoat or the tragic hero, which recurs in the works of Yeats, is demonstrated most powerfully in *Parnell's Funeral* (cited in Vickery, 1973, p.227):

... a brighter star shoots down;
What shudders run through all that animal blood?
What is this sacrifice? Can someone there
Recall the Cretan barb that pierced the star?

Vickery's analysis of the story of Parnell, the Irish patriot who was hanged by the British authorities, shows him as a central figure of scapegoating. He is the noble scapegoat, outstanding leader of his people, a handsome and charming man of irresistible eloquence, seen to be at the centre of the political troubles. He can be singled out, marred by a fatal flaw, the vaunted adultery, which in the eyes of the Church and its people warranted his dismissal and persecution. Yeats layers images to evoke Parnell as intellectual and aesthete, vulnerable in his beauty, and a scapegoat killed and expelled by the crowd's attack on him. It is a relation between a man and his society—the society conjured up as Ireland's 'bare soul':

this bare soul, let all men judge that can
Whether it be an animal or a man.

Parnell's murderers are not simply animal or human, they are both and the slayers of the scapegoat hero.

Vickery extensively examines the character, Leopold Bloom, in James Joyce's *Ulysses*. Bloom is 'modern man as the scapegoat' (1937, p.381), not literally but in a functional and metaphoric manner. Bloom is different: a Jew in Catholic Dublin. He is made to wear the stereotypic labels, the snubs and insults pile around him to build towards his repudiation. As the time passes Bloom is abused and harassed, later apprehended, tried and sentenced for indecent sexual conduct and literary plagiarism. Then, for a while, ill fortunes recede only to recur in the meandering of his mind. At the end Bloom can be read as consciously accepting his scapegoat role and so becoming for the reader a figure of compassion not contempt, one capable of being accepted (Vickery, 1973, pp.381–408). In *Ulysses* scapegoating is a religious ritual whose power to alleviate the cultural tensions and anxieties current in a society lie in its projecting these distresses onto the victim which is to be driven out to destruction. The theme plays through the novel in Bloom's imaginings, delusions and dreaming—recurrences of guilt and sex and violence, carnival, reversals and victimisation—to end in death imagined.

In all such accounts, myth, legend, history, literary forms, even painting, the scapegoat can be one of three archetypes: the king or hero; the criminal or slave; or the fool. Examples include Yeats' Parnell, a hero among men. The scapegoat may be criminal as in Jesse in James Baldwin's *Going to Meet the Man* who becomes dehumanised in his callous insensitivity, or Bennet in Ellis' *American*

Psycho. The fool can become scapegoat: Yakov Bok of Bernard Malamud's *The Fixer*, Salvatore in Umberto Ecco's *The Name of the Rose*. Frazer believed that the riddance of evil afforded by the scapegoat merged in many places with the ritual slaying of the king before age or decrepitude weakened kingly rule. Apart from rituals perceived as meeting such a dual function are the customs which went to 'deifying' or otherwise distinguishing the one marked for scapegoating. The important feature of this long tradition of the scapegoat is the scapegoat's distinction: he is marked and set aside—sacred in all the sociological implications of that term.

Hero, criminal or fool, the scapegoat must be set apart and distinguished to make him equal to the role to be played. The one who takes on and carries away the ills which haunt the community must be equal to, and be seen to be equal to, the task. Communities choose a scapegoat worthy of themselves or make the chosen one take on a fitting worthiness. The scapegoat is to be marked, stigmatised, and eventually identified with the sources of calamity and evil fortune to be driven out.

Once alerted to the tragic theme of the scapegoat the reader can hear it sound through many tales. Vickery explains how his sensitivity to the presence of scapegoating prompted him to see it in all our dramatic and narrative literature (Vickery, 1976, p.267). In some literature and art the title announces the focus (Strindberg's *The Scapegoat*, David Boyd's painting *The Australian Scapegoat*) or otherwise points explicitly to the process enacted. The process is conjured in imagery associated with classical, pagan or Christian myth (consider the stories of D.H. Lawrence or the plays of Ibsen, notably *An Enemy of the People*).

Psychological explanations of the scapegoat phenomenon range widely from its use as a rational way of deflecting blame from those in authority (see Bonazzi, 1983) to an expressive response invoking notions of magical thinking where a precise set of actions can purge the evil. The scapegoat becomes a projection of the shadow (Jung), the despicable, the unbearable, the guilt of the psyche. The scapegoat is identified with the evil(s) and its driving out eliminates the guilt. This psychological description (here unduly simplified) suggests the durability, the necessity of the scapegoat and its recurrence through history. This sense of inevitability pervades much of current literature of scapegoating in distressed or dysfunctional families. While respecting psychoanalytical interpretations of the emotional need and the release afforded by the scapegoat to the (individual) psyche, my approach is from the other side of the social-individual relation.

Overall, the scapegoat's timeless purpose is to relieve the group of its guilt. This has implications at the level of the individual, for one person's psychic relief. But, does the scapegoat ritual succeed sociologically and anthropologically? The ritual may not, usually does not, rid the community of the feared evils which beset it, but it is efficacious if the community believes that it has a fresh

start in life, that it can 'go forward' purified and strong in its own integrity and
solidarity. Literary enactments of scapegoating and portrayals of the scapegoat
often tell of the failed ritual where the desired purging of guilt and reinvigoration
of community did not follow. Nor need the process succeed in contemporary
occurrences. Frazer's catalogue of events and practices show the functioning of
scapegoating in many societies, but he does not draw conclusions about the
necessity for that function. He simply implies that its continuance suggests that
people believed in its efficacy. The scapegoat driven out during the festival of
Thargelia was believed to carry away evil and so, believing in their own cleansing, the people felt vindicated and refreshed. Its contemporary utility remains to
be contemplated.

Scapegoating in History

In recent times Rene Girard's *The Scapegoat* stands as the most remarkable
study of the recurrence of scapegoating in myth and history. Girard prefaces his
analysis of Guillaume de Machaut's epic *The Judgement of the King of Navarre*
with a reminder of a necessary scepticism in documentary criticism which takes
note of a text's reception. Texts are not to be seen naively, but to be recognised
as interpretations and reinterpretations of events refracted through the views of
the narrator and the community where the stories are told.

Using de Machaut's account as exemplar Girard explains that de Machaut
recounts sights and events—the signs in the sky, the rain of stones, cities
destroyed by lightning, the Jews poisoning the rivers—as he understands them.
In his account de Machaut is trying to explain the public hysteria and the search
for a solution. Some of the events, like the tally of plague deaths, the fear of
disease and the massacre of the Jews, are real and supported in other accounts.
Girard then focuses on the reader and points to our own selectivity in interpretation. We take as real what is credible given our epistemologies. 'We are not
reading this text in a vacuum', but in the 'tight framework of historical knowledge
in which Guillaume's text can be placed' (Girard, 1986, p.5). Girard elaborates that
we can know the persecution took place because the story is told from the
viewpoint of the persecutors who believe their judgment of where guilt lay was
correct. The accusations may well be incredible to us, but the punishment meted
out with righteous violence is highly probable. Persecutors who describe their
persecutions are to be believed. Sadly persecutors rest securely on the right-
ness of the punishment. Texts which tell of collective violence are framed
subjectively and distorted to rationalise the judgments of the persecutors. Considering such texts from another time and place we have no difficulty in recognising
error and injustice, but the rightfulness of persecution in the context it occurred
is asserted by the inquisitors and their communities. An example widely ex-

pounded in feminist literature lies in the medieval witch trials by which the community, its members believed, could expunge the devil and his evil works (see, for a brief review Ehrenreich & English, 1976 or, in more detail Davis, 1975).

A major crisis has an equalising force; in the face of disaster distinctions of persons, rank and order are eroded. Those to blame can be in some manner implicated; they were not respectful of persons or distinctions. Girard's examples are the black male who rapes, or perhaps simply has sex with a white female; the queen accused of incest with her son; the foreigner who is ignorant of the nuances of language or custom. The proper order is overturned, all is out of place. In large measure the terror of plagues derives from the capriciousness, the horror of untimely death. When the young die first, as in this time of AIDS, the terror runs wild. In the face of disaster powerlessness, which looks in vain for causes, fastens on anything which might be invoked to dispel contagion or disorder. Social crisis can plunge culture into an eclipse where distinctions of person or act become invisible. There are many examples of such disorder and loss of distinction: in time of war where the young die early; in racial or ethnic 'cleansing' where whole villages, tribes or ethnic minorities are killed; in bushfires where the finest and the poorest houses are destroyed; in earthquakes where the wealthy and the indigent, the old and the young are crushed together. Then it seems that the margins are lost.

The concept of difference, specifically loss of difference and lack of respect for difference, is crucial in analyses of the stereotypes active in scapegoating. When calamity overwhelms a people, their culture drops its differentiation, their institutions lose distinction and people look to where they may lay blame. The choice of the one to bear the blame may be quite random, but there are factors which predispose that attribution. Minorities are vulnerable to blame. The scapegoat is in some ways marginal, different, apart from the group, or susceptible to being set aside. In times of crisis to be strange—the very poor or the very rich, the hero or the villain, the philosopher or the fool—is hazardous. Then the scapegoat can stand at the centre of persecution prey to those acts of violence, usually legal in form and prompted by extremes of a public opinion appalled by the crisis which breaks down social order.

Frazer concentrated on the ritual of scapegoating, whereas Girard turned to its mythic dimensions. Girard takes as exemplar the Oedipus myth played out in Sophocles' tragedy *Oedipus Rex* and indicates the key elements of the story, the four stereotypes of the scapegoating process. The tragedy is not just a literary text and psychoanalytic interpretation but a 'persecution text'. The people of Thebes are afflicted by plague. Oedipus stands accused of heinous crimes which do not respect the hallowed differences between persons. He was so ignorant of his relationship that he committed the crimes of parricide and incest. Oedipus is highly visible as king, and he is marked in a way that becomes a sign of his

vulnerability—Oedipus limps. In the end his destruction completes our catharsis.

Girard shows that myths exude the sacred, and histories also, are touched by
the sacred. In myth or actuality the persecutors, the mob, the distracted community, believe in the culpability of the victim, its scapegoat. Almost invariably
there is consensus in their judgment and a vicarious release in driving out the
one they have implicated in their troubles and made the bearer of evil. The
scapegoat is chosen, set apart, and, by taking away the disorder of crisis, restores order. This is the myth. Historical and contemporary renditions may not
be so signally successful. The 'guilty one' deflects the guilt of the people. The
physical impact of the disaster remains, but its social impact is eliminated.

Times of great crisis lead to a generalised loss of difference, of distinction,
and so undermine accustomed order. People look for the origin of their troubles
and find at its centre those whose offences eliminate difference. Marking the
disposition of the one to be blamed is a certain ignorance or elision of differences of power and status; the marginal one, the outsider is 'barbaric', unable to
tell or disrespectful of the difference. Such a marginal person, or persons, is
marked, picked on as victim, persecuted and fit to be laden with collective evils.
So burdened the scapegoat is violently subjected and driven out. The scapegoat bears the stigma which marks him for his cathartic destiny.

I have argued that the scapegoat must be worthy of his destiny or, once
chosen, be made worthy. Girard takes this further and imputes power to the
scapegoat. The receptacle for all blame is to be feared. As marginal, as strange,
the scapegoat is not known and, being unknown, may be capable of anything.
Here the imagination of the fearful community may conjure up imputations of the
unnatural which go beyond a mere immorality and serve to justify persecution.
The community is convinced of the guilt of its victim. To suggest that the one to
be banished is a scapegoat would be to deny the justice of what is done. It is just
this conviction of self righteousness which exempts the community from guilt.
They know not what they do.

The process does not end with sacrifice. The scapegoat is seized as a way of
resolving the crisis and restoring social relations disrupted by crisis. The scapegoat becomes the point of reconciliation as the one whose expulsion restores
order and saves the community. The scapegoat can never return, but as the
crisis subsides can be remembered as instrumental in the abatement of the troubles, especially the breakdown of social relations. The community sees itself as
without guilt, as victim of circumstances. The scapegoat becomes the active
agent, the catalyst, resolving all social ills. Such a recognition may occur long
after the event and is unlikely until memory raises the scapegoat to mythic
proportions as saviour. I would argue that this is a process for mythologies
not histories of the scapegoat. Myth transposes understandings into rituals—

scapegoat rituals are of reconciliation as in the classic rituals of Thargelia or Saturnalia.

Although we can recognise the scapegoat in myth or history, we do not recognise him in our midst; we would deny that we can scapegoat anyone however different, marginal, or distinguished. Court martials in other times have scapegoated officers for the failure of military systems or authorities. Those accused served as an example to cure a deeper, often systemic, malaise. Now they appear marked by their difference. In a remarkable series John Harris describes the trials of nine military men whose careers span two centuries—until the Second World War. They were accused, found guilty and expelled because a scapegoat was needed to amend the inadequacies or errors of the military body they served (Harris, 1988). Similar processes in the family when a child dies and grief must be assuaged. Again such a family is one observed and the writer, as counsellor, is not personally implicated in the process. It is too hard to see the scapegoating at the heart of one's own world. Family therapy takes account of such dynamics (Berman 1990; Pillari, 1991). Anti-Semitism or racism can likewise move into the procedures of scapegoating, but that is always an injustice perpetrated by others (see for example, Parsons, 1980). We can not see oursleves as persecutors.

Scapegoating in Professional Communities

This book presents scapegoats in our immediate history; almost all were found in just three years in the city of Sydney. In those few years other persecutions occurred in Australia and other countries. The stories told are of those whose misfortunes I followed.

Taking the daily newspapers as sampling framework I began to watch the procession of medical and legal practitioners brought before the public tribunals. Despite the complexities of the individual cases some on trial appeared to be villains and protection of the public required their deregistration. Some were foolish or ignorant and again the protection of the public was paramount. Some were victims of their own failings, mentally, psychologically or physically impaired. But others were different: highly reputed and valued practitioners, leaders in their field, esteemed by clients or patients. These were the cases that I followed and analysed.

In each case I have analysed an event to expose the multiple processes which constitute it. Scapegoating is a highly complex procedure, one which encounters deep fears of dissipation, disorder and internecine strife which threaten the very continuity of the group. To be effective the procedure must be in keeping with the culture of the people, should conform to prevailing values and mores and be highly visible. The ritual must be enacted in a right and fitting manner with due regard to law and good order. Rituals of purification and catharsis are public displays. To analyse the occurrence of scapegoating as an 'event' means to determine its processes. The scapegoating becomes a central component of exemplary punishment as deterrent and expiation. Foucault explains in 'Questions of Method' (1991, pp.76–8), 'This procedure of causal multiplication means analysing an event according to the multiple processes which constitute it'. This mode of inquiry starts with a description of an event, a trial, which occurs against the background of scandal. I then inquire into the multiplicity of phenomena associated with the trial and its outcome.

Scapegoating is a potentially effective disciplinary practice. At the one time it sanctions conduct by promulgating an exemplary punishment, it ritually expiates the evil feared to be widespread, and rids the group of the one implicated, marked with the evil. When scandal grown rampant threatens the identity and integrity of a closed and solidary community and that community is unable to deal with it, then scapegoating offers a way of clearing out and restoring order.

What makes this practice of scapegoating acceptable in the advanced democratic societies of late twentieth century capitalism? The hypothesis is that such practices possess 'up to a point their own regularities, logic, strategy, self-evidence and "reason" ' (Foucault, 1991, p.75). The seemingly irrational rites of another time and place can be translated into procedures which meet all the expedients of this moment, this place, this crisis. In ancient times the evils which the scapegoat could expel were famine and disease, failing fertility of flocks and people. Biblical myths tell of pestilence or sin. Today the threat may be substantively different, although the fear of disease still provokes the moral panic which slips easily into scapegoating. But, like the crises of long ago, the most fearful disasters are those portending the destruction of the community's integrity and identity—its sacred difference.

These cases occurred in the context of scandals which could destroy the good name of a profession. Professions hold fast to good reputation, to distinction, which yields their authority and influence. Failure to respect difference—from the mundane, the ordinary, the lay—threatens that prized distinction. In the disorder of crisis some could be marked by their ignorance, or their denial of difference inherent in status. To be marked was not a matter of innocence or guilt, but of being different from one's fellows and unaware of that difference.

Communities instigate scapegoating. The initiative lies with the group and is not sought by the one who is to become scapegoat. The community apprehends danger, feels a malaise or disorder which threatens its integrity and identity. We can find resort to scapegoating anywhere that people are bound closely together by common conditions and expectations welded into common interest and ideology. Such people draw much of their identity as persons from belonging to the group. The precipitant for recourse to a scapegoat is a severe and unmanageable crisis. Because they can find no solution, because they do not know what else to do, people turn on one of their own who must save all by taking on the communal guilt and bearing it away. To understand scapegoating it is necessary to look to the community which generates the awful sequence.

Notes

1. Harrison's book was revised for two further editions in her lifetime and reprinted several times.

CHAPTER 2

*P*rofessional *C*ommunities

Professions are tribes whose people are banded together by common interests and are given to specific ways of thinking and acting. They generate a sense of affinity and belonging among their members whose common interests and expectations result in shared values and norms. In such communities are found accustomed ways of acting, speaking and thinking. The expressions, 'we see things this way', 'we speak the same language', 'we see things differently here', indicate a shared consciousness and the distinction of being different from those outside the group. Scholars have found such close community in tribal societies where loyalty to the group and conformity with its practices is imperative. In large heterogeneous societies like ours such intensity of feeling and identity is rare at the national level. It does, however, come into play when the larger society is gravely threatened, such as in wartime. A strong sense of national identity can also be displayed during the ritualised conflicts of great sporting events such as the Olympic Games. Likewise one can identify it when Australia won the America's Cup in 1983. But, these events are short-lived and do not sustain our ongoing need for close fellowship and acceptance found initially in the family, in the friendships of school and in the groups into which we move in adulthood. People can find such fellowship in clubs, churches and other organisations devoted to consuming interests like sport, religion, politics, the arts. They can support a person throughout their lifetime or serve awhile until the next enthusiasm takes over. That inherent sense of acceptance, value, and commonality of purpose, of agreed values and habits, of belonging, is felt by many in the world of work as well as in 'life away from work', and has a strong bearing on psychic wellbeing. Its lack brings the loneliness of alienation and the pathology of anomie. There lies madness and mayhem; we cannot live for long by ourselves alone.

Professions, as such tightly integrated groups, foster communality among those selected and drawn into them. These particular enclaves create identity and generate exclusiveness of community and solidarity of shared values and purpose. Their work lies in carefully marked fields where only they, the certified ones, can operate. Over many years each of today's professions has developed its science, practised its art, and so generated renown in its special area. Its members are honoured for what they alone are allowed to know and perform. That good fame brings respect and trust. For professions reputation is one source of authority. From it flows a cultural authority which encompasses the concession of trust implicit in practitioners' licence to practise.

Professions have a long history usually tied to religious, tribal, and/or national origins. Vocation to the church and the calling to arms are often cited as the original professions. Both emphasised dedication to a higher cause and belonging to a special fraternity, or sorority. The church specifically committed its 'professed' to a life of learning and service. The ritual and language are significant. To enter religion was to take vows, to don a distinctive dress or habit, to follow a higher calling dedicated to the deity. Those origins are distant from the present, but the ideology of professions still reverberates with notions of commitment, altruism, learning, discipline and trustworthiness. Law and medicine, in particular, emphasise the vocational aspect, enacting rituals, adopting specific language and symbols, wearing the robes of their calling, taking the requisite vows or oaths on entry. This begins a 'deep and lifelong commitment' where 'it takes a rite of passage to get him in; another to read him out' (Hughes, 1963, p.657). I am not suggesting these intimations of glory to be the reality of professions, only that ideologies hold out ideals which beckon especially when lit by self-interest. The professions of law and medicine, which feature in this book, show clearly their ecclesiastical antecedents in their veneration of learning and expertise and their claims to the honoured grounds of integrity, trust and devotion to the gods they hold sacred. For medicine this is to ideas of healing, the aesculapian ideal inscribed in the Hippocratic Code. (The legends of ancient Greece are heavily inscribed on modern medicine.) For practitioners of the law the sacred inheres in Justice, most commonly symbolised as a blindfolded woman holding the scales in balance to represent impartiality and balancing the rights of one against those of the other. The ceremonies of entry to these professions— being called, entered on the rolls, registered—are solemnly enacted before the leaders of the profession and the public, to confer professional identity and proclaim the graduate's embodiment in the professional community.

While still bearing the imprint of their origins professions have changed and proliferated throughout this century. The generative progression of medicine through its tactical struggles with any who would resist or subvert its climb has been well told. Examples include Paul Starr's story of the rise of medicine in the United States in *Social Transformation of American Medicine*, and, for an account of medical sovereignty in Australia, Evan Willis' carefully researched

book *Medical Dominance*. Both writers concentrate in these books on the political strategies and approved practices that secured for that profession a
monopoly of knowledge and expertise. By dint of carefully measured collaboration with the State and reliant on the solidarity of their fellows medical practitioners
gained exclusive control over their field of clinical practice. Others, particularly
nurses, worked in that field but only under medical direction. That monopoly is
fiercely guarded by the profession and state regulation prevents incursion into
the body of practice by practitioners of other professions (or 'semi-professions'
to use the phrase coined by Etzioni in *The Semi-Professions and their Organizations*). Willis' historical case studies of the limitations placed on optometry, the
subordination of midwifery and the exclusion of chiropractic are persuasive of
his arguments tracing medical domination achieved over the past two hundred
years of Australian history. In contrast to these political histories of medical
sovereignty, Foucault's critical history contemplates the conditions which created modern medicine and focuses attention on the production of systems of
thought which now structure medical knowledge. In *The Birth of the Clinic*
Foucault puts knowledge at the centre of medical authority and influence. This
genealogy of medicine traces the emergence of a system of empirical knowledge
in the first half of the nineteenth century. The clinic, in this account, is the space
where a new system of thought based on a carefully regulated observation of
the pathologies manifest in the body of the patient was produced, 'where a
syntactical reorganization of disease in which the limits of the visible and invisible follow a new pattern' (Foucault, 1973, p.195). Foucault's argument for the
centrality of knowledge ordered into a specific discourse, which is owned by the
profession and legitimates the power of that profession, is significant for my
interpretation of the reaction of professional communities to threats to reputation and the order of things. The command of such knowledge and the legitimacy
accorded to the 'medical gaze' has authorised the practitioner to enter upon all
the zones of the body—to order physic, to pierce, to cut, to treat towards cure or
care. Important for the purposes of this book is the centrality of knowledge and
the reputation for knowledge and good intent on which that authority rests. In a
fashion that is much more accessible than Foucault's, Bryan Turner takes up the
Foucauldian method and demonstrates the strategic links which are intimated in
Medical Power and Social Knowledge (1987).

The story of the legal profession, the other profession to serve as context for
the processes described in later chapters, has also been told many times.
Rueschemeyer's work *Lawyers and their Society* (1973) comparing the legal
professions in Germany and the United States is a fine stimulus to thinking
about law, and his subsequent major work *Power and the Division of Labour*
locates professions as a powerful category in a world increasingly specialised
and knowledgeable. Like so many writers on professions, Rueschemeyer links

the authority of professions to a carefully maintained monopoly of knowledge and expert skill. Of particular relevance for students of the legal profession in Australia as well as the United Kingdom is Richard Abel's *The Legal Profession in England and Wales* and that has been followed by his and Philip Lewis' edited volumes which include essays by leading scholars writing on law in many countries (*Lawyers in Society*, 1988a, 1988b, 1989). The compendium edited by Burrage and Torsendahl in *Professions in Theory and History* (1990) and a major study of the Australian profession by Weisbrot in *Australian Lawyers* (1990) are essential reading for a student of the legal profession in Australia. For an overall view of the rise of several of the modern professions Larson's *The Rise of Professionalism* has become a classic in the Marxist tradition. Harold Perkin's absorbing interpretation of *The Rise of Professional Society* underlines further the contemporary authority of the disciplines and their claims to knowledge certified by the State.

In an attempt to understand the present standing of professions some sociologists, rather than explaining in terms of origins and the contingencies of history (the path followed by the writers mentioned in the preceding paragraph), have concentrated on defining and describing professions. They have drawn up a catalogue of characteristics apparent in those occupations commonly regarded as professions. This approach can be criticised but it does tell what professionals believed of themselves: that they held an esoteric knowledge and were skilled in its practical application, that their authority in this realm was respected by the public and that ethical codes governed their practice and behaviour. While practitioners are happy to believe and act on this rhetoric it tells nothing of the well springs of their power and privilege. This patently self-serving description tells about the ideology of a profession, but not about the sources of professional power and privilege which nourish reputation.

Knowledge and Control

Knowledge is crucial to professional identity and power. This specialist knowledge base is so valuable that practitioners seek to a maintain monopoly over it. A profession must control its field, must monitor access to that knowledge, hold in its surveillance the training of those who seek admission to the field, regulate the practice of those whom it certifies as competent and exclude any whose practice falls below the standards a profession holds out to the public (see Carr-Saunders & Wilson, 1933; Hughes, 1958; Becker et al., 1961; Jackson, 1970; Boreham et al., 1974). More recently sociologists have uncovered the multiple aspects of professional sovereignty and market closure generated by control of entry, training, accreditation, certification and regular renewal of licence to practise (see for example, Larson, 1977; Johnson, 1982; Willis, 1983; Rueschemeyer, 1986; Abel,

1988; Murphy, 1988; Derber et al., 1990; Daniel, 1990; MacDonald, 1995; Freidson, 1976, 1994, pp.199–216). These writers show with specific illustration from history and current practice, how professions assume and ensure monopoly of their field of knowledge and practice, and attain the reputation for skill and care in a society which consents to professional authority.

The control which a profession exerts over its knowledge base and field of practice has been secured with the help of powerful allies, most notably the modern state which extends its authority to validate the arrangements for registration presented by a professional body. Professions operate in fields of danger, at the centre of human affairs; their work gives access to 'guilty knowledge' (Hughes, 1977, p.288) and such secrets should only be open to those who can be trusted; work of this nature can have serious consequences to individual or a wider public if it is poorly done. The public has a strong interest in ensuring that these practitioners are competent and trustworthy in all respects. Such strategic power calls for a larger social control, that conceded in modern societies to the state. This relationship of state and profession has mediated the transformation of both (Johnson, 1982, p.191). The outcome for professions has been their securing remarkable control over their own work and standards of practice, but an autonomy highly dependent on state-enforced exclusionary licensing and regulation. From the state's side of the partnership its interest is to promote wellbeing and orderly conduct in the citizenry. The relation of state and profession is often conflict-ridden (Daniel, 1990), but it is a symbiotic partnership from which each side gains. In the case studies which follow professional bodies frequently turned to statutory bodies to clear out their troubles.

Disciplinary Practices

Linked to a profession's knowledge claims and licence to practise are the disciplinary exercises which reproduce that knowledge and skill. Selection, education and training, examination and registration are the first phases of lifelong disciplinary practices which create and confirm professional identity. Discipline conjures up many meanings, all, in one way or another, bear on the practice of a profession. Discipline connotes the field of knowledge, the inculcation of knowledge, the mental and moral training, identification and definition of standards, surveillance and sanctions imposed when standards are transgressed. Disciplinary practices constitute a form of surveillance, exercise and examination to subject the individual to the power of the norm, to standardisation (Foucault, 1984a, 1984b). Professionals in training must engage with and submit to discipline in order to make it their own. Professions have taken over discipline to command knowledge and expertise. But there is no reprieve from its continuing practice; discipline recurs endlessly and, like the skill of a gymnast, is lost when not practised. Medical science can be seen as a paradigm case of the ascent of power tied to scientific knowledge and the disciplinary normalisation (standard setting and monitoring) of the learned college (Foucault, 1984c, pp.162–6).

The limits to the power implicit in command of professional knowledge are set by a circumscribed certification. In courts the discipline of law prevails, in laboratories the discourse of the specific science is authoritative, in hospitals the clinician is final arbiter. A professional has authority and practical autonomy in their domain, not beyond it. The professional who strays into the field of a different profession becomes a mere layperson. The authority conferred by discipline holds only in its field of practice. Courts and tribunals make a space for the expert, but that space and the licence to speak is limited to the expert's specialist capacity. This can be discomforting for the specialist called to give expert evidence and required to limit that opinion to the issues raised by the lawyer or judge.

Knowledge and the power it generates must be governed, otherwise the potency of esoteric, practical knowledge imposed on human affairs threatens unbearably. The governance of a profession lies primarily in disciplinary practices, which deliver specific knowledge and skills as well as trained control over the exercise of that power for beneficent purposes. But fear of ungovernable power remains. The worry that disciplines shape practice only to serve the self-interest of profession and individual practitioners is not readily dismissed. Scientific knowledge in its application is powerful, but its potential is ambivalent and as readily turned to evil as good. This threat can never be comfortably banished.

The discipline of professions begins with examination for entry—only high achievers may enter. The offer of a place in a professional faculty is a significant prize. Then professional education can readily assume connotations of the sacred, especially in our times so often described in terms of the ascent of knowledge and identified as the age of information, professions, post-industrialism and post-modernism. The cults of knowledge flourish in universities where only the cognoscenti, the cultivated, are fit to guide or uncover social destinies (cf. Bell; Konrad & Szelenyi, 1979; Gouldner, 1979; Rueschemeyer, 1986; Perkin, 1989). All education is a form of ritual, notably in the faculties where elite education builds a bond among the acolytes in a sacred realm (Collins, 1990). The aspiring professionals participate so intensively that they come to identify themselves with the subject of the curriculum, that scheme which ties together bits of knowledge, connects up the bits of experience and invests the whole with meaning. The sense of being apart, special, initiated into following a calling, continues beyond university.

The disciplinary practices, enforced in university and maintained by learned society and college, are ostensibly directed to the expansion of knowledge and refinement of techniques, but they quite materially and unequivocally secure the knowledge base as citadel and exclude unschooled contenders for professional status. Only those, who have been selected, have submitted to the discipline of schooling and have succeeded through the examinations, are permitted to practise (Becker et al., 1961; Larson, 1979; Collins, 1979; Murphy, 1988). Through these practices the authority of a profession is sustained, its reputation for expertise and integrity justified and thus the grounds for trust in a professional system are exposed and trust itself is vindicated. Discipline has been taken into the trainee's soul. Surveillance can fall away. Self-discipline impels the certified practitioner to obey the code, to perform at best independently of surveillance. That is the hope implicit in a profession's self-regulation and the condition for its reputation.

The authority of professions is secured by a variety of strategies that monopolise knowledge and expertise and, in collaboration with the state, exclude the amateur whose knowledge is not certified, whose practices have not been disciplined in the regulatory, approved manner. The process of training anticipates later professional authority and inculcates values about intellectual excellence, good teamwork, self-discipline and endurance of long hours of study and practice—as well as a regrettable arrogance which assumes elite status. The discipline continues through hard work and constant practice and, most esteemed of all, the development of intellectual acumen in dealing with each client's 'case'. These processes are highly valued in the collegiate, which is unmoved by the neophytes' complaints of arduous or oppressive conditions. These processes will initiate the novice into the community. Professionals in training must cultivate devotion to their 'vocation' and become committed to the disciplines of work. Perhaps an old master says it best:

> There is no stronger means of breeding traits than through the necessity of holding one's own in the circle of one's associates ... Continuous and unobtrusive ethical discipline (Weber, 1948, p.329).

Professional reputation celebrates a tradition of arduous and difficult training and acclaims devotion to the discipline. The ideal is the engendering and sustaining of excellence. Yet, between the ideal and the reality falls the shadow of everyday inadequacy.

Limits to Authority

The extent and the limits of such authority are obvious. The authority of expertise, founded on discipline, is limited to the field chosen, the one secured by dint of education, training, exercise, examination and certification. Those disciplines permit claims to a moral authority and one which is, for professions, legislatively defined. The twin bases of an exclusive authority, cultural and social, make professions a significant force in contemporary society. Legislation and regulation ensure exclusive rights to practice and impose certified standards and so provide social authority. But, this legitimization is conferred on a cultural authority already derived from accepted claims to knowledge and reputation, a twin authority examined by Starr in his history of medical practice in the US. Foucault analysed the power exerted in the sovereignty of law and that implicit in the disciplines of science and, although both may coexist, he stipulated that legislative sovereignty diminishes as the disciplines extend and proliferate. I disagree with that proposition which sees the waning of one source of power in concert with the waxing of a new force for domination. For my purposes at this juncture, the important point is that a profession takes up the potential to dominate its field from both the force of law and the persuasion of discipline. Starr, in a fashion reminiscent of Foucault, identifies social and cultural authority as twin sources of professional power. The former is created by statute and the latter conceded to the highly gifted, to knowledge, to expertise. The latter is conceded by a public impressed by expert knowledge. Cultural authority is grounded in ideals, values and meanings which support relations of trust between practitioner and client. The social authority of a profession is defined in statute.

A modern society depends on the services of professionals and this, in part, motivates the concession of authority and calls for its regulation. Additionally the practitioner must be of good repute if they are to be trusted with authority and allowed to enter areas fraught with danger for the client. Professionals work in a cosmopolitan world of science and learning, in a realm of abstractions and collegial connections that equip them for, in public expectation, the working of wonders. This exaggerated regard is based on false premises which have been repeatedly uncovered; a most persuasive exposure was accomplished by Ivan Illich's in *Disabling Professions* (1977) and *Limits to Medicine* (1976) (see also Taylor, 1979). But such critiques only become relevant when they demolish professional reputation for trustworthiness among the public at large. The potential for such demolition is always there and it grows (Barber, 1983, 1990).

Reputation and Trust

Discipline can be understood as the focused energy which creates a profession. The way this creative force is shaped and the appearance it takes are matters of multiple cultural and historical contingencies. Profession is a species which grows everywhere but its varieties are myriad. Its public face in our world is one of awesome capability. But there is still a problem. Knowledge and its correlative power come into play in practice and in its application such knowledge is dangerous. Professionals work with 'guilty knowledge' (i.e. with secret confessions of clients' or patients' misdeeds and mistakes) through times of crisis and terror as well as in calmer periods to aid and abet the client's project. At specific times we call in professionals to protect us, save us, advance our cause, enhance our person and status. The possibilities for professional practice proliferate in a world where the consumer would be sovereign. Indeed, as Zymunt Bauman points out, the freedom to choose what we will buy is probably our only freedom (1990). Professions adapt readily to the climate of the marketplace. Because of the promise held out, the public presentation and reputation of profession must go beyond the image of knowledge, expertise, practised excellence and stand for moral concern and responsibility. The powerful must be good, or at least be seen as good if they are to hold on to power (Gouldner, 1971, pp.486–9). How firmly founded is this knowledge? How accomplished are the skills? And, of critical significance, can professions and individual practitioners be trusted to behave well? Reputation is all. Any slip into distrust diminishes reputation and the cultural authority it confers.

Professions rely heavily on reputation for responsibility and care as well as for expert knowledge and skill of a very high order. Reputation underpins the rational emotion of trust which brings clients to confide and entrust their affairs to the practitioner. A client's relation is with both the individual practitioner and the professional system, but the latter relation of trust is separately at risk. The practitioner mediates between client and professional system and gives access to the services held out by the whole system. To operate effectively a profession, as well as the individual practitioners, depend on the good standing and public confidence in the whole system. The client or patient may claim 'I can trust my lawyer [or doctor] but I don't trust the legal profession [or medicine in general]'. In the long term, however, the trust must be extended to the whole system of knowledge and practice or the client will withdraw and avoid any further practitioner–client relationship. So, the professional community has a strong interest in maintaining both society's general trust and the client's specific trust in a practitioner. An expert's trustworthiness may be upset by outsider perceptions of behaviour which is linked not to incompetence but to nonconformity with larger values and virtues. Given this sensitivity of trust it should not surprise that the rebel undergraduate is coaxed into the demeanour and image which conforms to the conventional presentation of the full professional before the time for graduation is reached. Professional reputation is fragile; the client's reliance is emotionally tense, albeit rationally governed; issues not relevant to the matter in hand may assume salience and subvert trust. Trust is a way of simplifying and continuing despite the insecurity of inadequate knowledge in risky circumstances; the 'leap of faith' implicit in trust may be rational and necessary, but, in its instability, small, seemingly irrelevant things can upset it.

Trust is imperative for the working of the relation between client and practitioner, but, because of the significance of reputation in all this, trust is also at the crux of relations among the practitioners. Reputation, the goodwill of a profession, is the *sine qua non* of professional practice. Without it there are no clients, no patrons, no customers. Professions guard reputation zealously and only accept into their citadel those who can be trusted to hold it high. Trust is not limited to situations of alienating fear and complexity but belongs in the tight relations of groups held together by a shared identity and ideology. To assume a professional identity after years spent in initiation into the constellation of ideals and values, beliefs and theories, skills and practices is to invest awesome trust in one's fellows. If the group is disgraced everyone loses. Before such trust is extended, the new entrant has been tested through all the processes invented in universities and by a period of probation, of internship, pupillage or clerkship. The graduate after the requisite probationary time enters an elite band confident in its superiority. *Esprit de corps* permeates the internal dynamics of the group and generates a sense of trusting collegiality. That trust among the elite does not extend any further; nor does the measure of trust within a profession stretch to those outside. Professionals insist that each must have confidence in the probity and candour of their fellows. To be found to have intentionally deceived another lawyer gives grounds for exclusion from the profession; likewise to openly criticise another physician is an offence described as such in the medical code of ethics.

Ethics

Although much attention has been paid to professional education and to the monopoly of knowledge, of cultural capital, secured therein, less note has been taken of the disciplinary practices constantly imposed on the practical work of professions. These are the collegial customs, codes and sanctions imposed within a profession on its members, by its members, for the benefit of the whole. These are the professional ethics and regulations, the exclusions and sanctions, which govern the group in its relations within and with the world at large. Beyond knowledge and expertise, instilled through university training and continuing education and practice, lie issues of responsibility. Professional ethics, it should be recognised, are invariably directed to the good of the profession and are rooted in its solidarity. The morality of a group resides in its consciousness of and care for itself—this is not oriented to the individual but to the group's welfare. 'A system of morals is always the affair of the group and can only operate if this group protects firmly its authority' (Durkheim, 1957, p.6). Shared interests and values establish predictable expectations extended through the whole group. If one falls, all are in jeopardy. Scandal is hazardous for the whole of a profession.

Analysis of a profession's ethical code reveals that it functions primarily to promote fair and courteous relations within, to minimise conflict and, at the same time, to reassure the public about its sense of responsibility to society (Maley, 1974). In large measure ethics buttress group interests. These become ambiguous and at variance with one another when groups diversify (Brint, 1994, pp.5–19). In another study I have shown how cleavages in the medical profession opened markedly during a prolonged conflict where the interests of different sections diverged significantly (Daniel, 1990). These cleavages had evolved from disciplinary distinctions, demarcations of areas of practice, differences in employment status and the relations of practitioners to the great teaching hospitals, as well as through deeply divisive ideological and political disputes. There remained a close identification with the profession of medicine, but material interests split that solidarity and yielded smaller specialist conclaves each with its own expectations, privileges and conditions of practice (Daniel, 1990, pp.86–92). What became patent was the primary cohesion and unity of purpose of specialist groups of all kinds. Here might be found the mechanical solidarity described in Chapter 1. Under the aegis of the specialist colleges medical specialists have built tightly integrated professional societies which project the interests, standards and expectations common to that group. Within the specialty a commonality of purpose and an ethos of comradeship promote consensus about the norms which govern the activity of the group. Such collegiate spirit often emanates from the hospital. In the course of an interview about sanctions governing professional life it was explained:

> ... you should not underestimate how hospitals figure in this; doctors work together in dangerous situations, must cooperate and must trust each other. You never know who you will rely on next so a solidarity develops between all of you. This happens in training and for most specialists this tie to the hospital continues. Even in general practice, which is more individual, we rely on each other. We have to (Daniel, 1990, p.84).

Similarly deep divisions in the legal profession, most apparent in the divided profession of barristers and solicitors in the United Kingdom and several states in the United States, Canada and Australia, have been extended to various disciplinary specialties and to character and location of the professional firm. I would surmise that specialist solidarity, and indeed professional solidarity, is more evident in medicine than in law. A telling statistic lies in the bringing of complaints against lawyers: in one year (1995–96) 10 per cent of complaints against barristers were instigated by other lawyers—barristers or solicitors (*Annual Report of the Legal Services Commissioner of New South Wales*, p.19). The report does not provide data on the source of the complaints, but personal observation suggests that the same is true for both arms of the profession. The very nature of adversary legal practice militates against a closeness in the union of practitioners. Nonetheless, legal practitioners all revere the same ideals, insist on integrity, probity and procedural fairness, and owe allegiance to the Court, a sort of secular church. As Tribunal decisions show, those who ignore such values are punished with admonition, financial penalty or removal from practice. To lose one's good name in law, or medicine, is to lose one's livelihood.

This view of professions as closed communities trusted to operate in hazardous or crucial areas of human experience opens out to an understanding of the power of professional norms and group concern for its all too valuable reputation. The survival of the group is paramount. Professional ethics tend the interests, cohesion and distinction of the whole. In a period of crisis, of alarm and confusion, the weight of group strength can push it too far, beyond a larger ethic of fair play and justice to one as well as all.

There are strong forces and varied sanctions operating within a profession to ensure conformity. These have been described as procedures of socialisation and peer pressure, informal rebukes, loss of referrals and 'quiet words'. A fascinating exemplar of these approaches appears in the institution of 'The Three Wise Men' within the English medical profession. These senior consultants constitute a quasi-formal mechanism of self-regulation by serving as an informal investigative committee which calls in the nonconforming or errant doctor for 'a quiet word' directed to straightening out any deviance from established professional and clinical standards. Marilynn Rosenthal's extensive research and thoughtful analysis in *The Incompetent Doctor: Behind Closed Doors* provides an excellent view of this and a range of other procedures used in the self regulation of medicine in England. The particulars vary but similar internal disciplinary practices operate in Australia.

Laws Protecting the Public

Beyond the sanctions of the collegiate lies the encircling protection of the law. The trusted integrity of professional practice can be buttressed by law whose courts can assuage the failures of trust with economic remedy for the negligence or misbehaviour of practitioners (Lieberman, 1981, p.134). The appeal to law occurs when trust fails. When professional standards are flouted aggrieved persons can address their complaints in formal terms to professional associations, regulatory bodies or the courts. This recourse to law signals that trust in practitioner, and often in profession, has gone. At this point legal regulation and surveillance overtake professional practice. Professions may and do use the mechanisms of law to buttress self-regulation, but such public exposure of probable incompetence or misconduct endangers reputation and trust. Law provides for both passive compliance and active cooperation. Legal processes can show grounds for mistrust and serve as a substitute for trust. But such systems afford no basis for trust, a calculating emotion that looks to the intrinsic character of profession as grounds for cooperation and compliance. In the public regard that character is signalled in reputation, in the case of professions, a reputation for discipline to be sustained throughout a professional career. If disciplinary practices slacken or if presumed good intentions and careful conduct are lacking, then discipline is seen to fail and trust is lost. What might then serve in its stead?

The law now governing professions is directed to protection of the community. Professions, aware of such responsibility, rely on self-regulation as integral to the trust needed in effective professional relationship, whether of lawyer--client or doctor–patient. Encircling professional practice stands the legal structure of statute and regulation posed as guarantee of protection should trust falter or professional self-discipline fail. Parliaments have enacted legislation to establish organisations to receive, investigate and pursue complaints about health services and legal services. These bureaucracies are usually government funded and are required to work closely with the relevant professional bodies. The professions through their statutory registration bodies fund the independent tribunals which hear cases of complaints which the mandatory investigation finds of sufficient seriousness to warrant disciplinary action of ascending penalty up to and including deregistration. Within the professional association conduct committees may review complaints of a less serious nature and determine appropriate action; this only occurs after the complaints have been investigated and assessed as being of less gravity. The government bureaucracies work closely with the relevant professional bodies, as required by law.

The heavy reliance of professions on the regulatory powers of the state has been a significant factor in the assertion of professional authority and the securing of professional monopoly in critical areas of learning and practice. The state has granted those monopolies and maintained them through statutory arrangements for certification and registration which exclude the amateur and the unschooled, which reject as invalid the claims of other competitors. Collaboration with the state continues in professions' regulation of the standards which validate their authority. Professionals prefer self-regulation to be achieved by peer review and collegial pressure and the force of their own associations. But, when these are inadequate (and they patently can be) the force of law can be invoked to sanction the incompetent, the negligent, or the reprehensible. This is where the strong links between professional registration boards and governments count; where the law is brought in to handle the conflict and provide remedy or punishment.

Complaints about Practitioners

Every year more than one thousand complaints are brought against medical practitioners and legal practitioners in New South Wales. After complaints have been investigated they may be dismissed, assessed as being sufficiently serious to lead to possible finding of unprofessional conduct or, more seriously, professional misconduct. Matters of less seriousness can be sent to a professional subcommittee, usually termed professional conduct committee. Such a committee acts in a confidential manner to review evidence of the complaint and either dismiss or find complaint(s) proven and in the latter case order a reprimand or one of several sanctions short of suspension or deregistration. Should investigations and review of the complaint(s) suggest the likelihood of a finding of professional misconduct, and hence the imposition of heavy penalty, the matter is brought before a professional tribunal. These tribunals hold statutory powers and are presided over by a judge or, in the case of the legal profession, a lawyer invested with quasi-judicial power.

Complaints against medical or legal practitioners may be brought to the attention of the statutory authority of the profession—Medical Board, Council of Law Society or Council of Bar Association respectively—or to a complaints commission set up under the legislation in each Australian State. These latter statutory bureaucracies have only been established in recent years in New South Wales and other Australian states. The external regulation of law and medicine differs in significant respects.

Until recently complaints against lawyers (solicitors or barristers) were brought to the attention of the relevant professional body which investigated, determined the gravity of the complaint and, if satisfied that there was a case to answer, referred the matter to the Professional Standards Committee or Legal Services Tribunal. The Tribunal consists of four persons: a layperson and three senior lawyers (solicitors or barristers as appropriate) one of whom presided as the nominee of the Chief Judge of the Supreme Court, the highest court in the state. In 1993 a statutory body was established by the New South Wales Parliament. The Legal Services Commission was empowered to receive all complaints, including those made to the professional body which must be referred to the Commission. The Commission may investigate, review and generally oversee the outcome of all complaints. The Commission reports that, in practice, it investigates a minority (less than 20 per cent) of complaints. The majority are investigated by officers of the professional body's conduct division and the cost of this is borne by the profession. In effect the processes of receiving, investigating, adjudicating and determining the orders to be imposed still lie with the lawyers' professional associations, but the Legal Services Commission is informed and involved and may undertake its own investigations.

The first point of reference to assess gravity of complaints, dismiss or assess and determine sanctions for less grave matters of complaint is the professional conduct committee appointed by Bar Council or Council of the Law Society. These committees consist of six or seven legal practitioners and one layperson to each committee which meet separately and jointly as one large Professional Conduct Committee. Serious complaints which may warrant heavier sanctions are sent to The Legal Services Tribunal.

The Legal Services Tribunal follows the rules of the Supreme Court, including rules of evidence and due process. The proceedings are carried out on an adversarial basis with the professional body (Law Society or Bar Council) bringing the action against the practitioner subject of the complaint(s). The proceedings have the status of a Supreme Court hearing, except that the Tribunal is limited in the extent of penalties which may be imposed. Its sanctions extend through reprimand, conditions imposed on practice, suspension, cancellation of practising certificate (removal from roll of practitioners of from the Bar) and a range of financial penalties. Practitioners may appeal the Tribunal's findings or orders, such appeals being heard by the appellate division of the Supreme Court. The appeal may be on points of law or issues of fact and the new hearing may be *de novo*, unless the appellant agrees that the hearing can be limited to specific issues.

For the medical profession a different system operates. A complaint about the service or conduct of a medical practitioner may go to either the Health Care Complaints Commission or the Medical Registration Board and each informs the other of all matters; the Commission, however, carries out the investigation. This New South Wales statutory body replaced the Health Complaints Unit, a division of the Health Department, in 1994. The enabling statute defined and widened the powers of the earlier Unit and the Director of that Unit continued as Commissioner. The Commission investigates and, when it finds reasonable grounds for a complaint, allows the Medical Board to bring matters likely to be less serious to its Professional Standards Committee. Additionally the Medical Board has a further facility to deal with practitioners where evidence points to impairment by reason of physical or mental illness, or addiction to alcohol and/or drugs. Complaints likely to lead to a finding of professional misconduct must be brought to the Medical Tribunal.

The Medical Tribunal is constituted of a District Court judge, a layperson and two medical practitioners. In the event of a tied decision the presiding judge exercises a casting vote. Proceedings against a medical practitioner are heard by two medical peers, a layperson and a judge, but, as has happened, the judge and the layperson may overturn the medical practitioners' judgment. This contrasts the outcome on a Legal Services Tribunal where, if there is dissent, the practitioner's legal peers retain balance of power. Furthermore the Medical Tribunal, like most administrative tribunals, (but unlike the Legal Services Tribunal), is not bound by rules of evidence, can inquire into events, call for further evidence and freely address questions to witnesses. It presides over and involves itself in a proactive hearing which resembles the inquisitorial model of civil law countries. A medical practitioner may appeal the Tribunal's determination or orders but only on points of law or about the orders imposed. No appeal against the facts as decided may be made. Appeals are heard by the Suprême Court.

Courts of justice in Australia follow the common law system developed in England and followed in North America, but tribunals in this country are different. Only the Legal Services Tribunal follows the rules developed through common law. There are reasons advanced for the differential treatment of the two professions; these relate to the particular duty of lawyers to the Courts they serve and the requirement that the Court (or its agent Tribunal) deal with them according to the rules of the Court. Effectively lawyers through their professional bodies have maintained control over the regulation of the profession. Medical practitioners have not. Nor have they been able to ensure that disciplinary procedures are conducted according to the traditional processes which developed to ensure natural justice in common law countries. The Medical Tribunal's freedom to ignore the rules of evidence may put natural justice at risk.

The Professional Communities in this Study

In the chapters which follow a number of significant cases of professional misconduct are scrutinised to discern the forces which combined to discredit the professional. These case studies involving doctors and lawyers brought before professional tribunals were chosen to show how communities of interest can protect themselves against disorders and disasters which threaten their reputation, even their survival. Care is taken to identify the community which sees itself at risk. These are usually professional groups, although the actual community may be merely a disciplinary group within a profession. For example, the speciality of psychiatry is a specific community which holds to its medical status but defines its own distinction. People do belong to more than one community and they can also work across two or more different fields. In these cases banishment from one area may not be fatal because the profession reigning in the other sphere may support such colleagues and shepherd them back to its fold. The story of Harry Whelehan and the Party in government in the Irish Parliament illustrates this saving grace. In at least one of the cases presented several communities of interest were disturbed by troubles and affronted by scandals. Dr William McBride was marked by several interest groups as centre of their troubles.

The stories presented in the following chapters rely heavily on the public record available from the judgments of tribunal and court; written submissions prepared for litigation; transcripts of the presentation of evidence; and media reports and commentaries. In the more recent cases I, or one of two research assistants, attended the Tribunal and Court hearing and took notes as the events unfolded. Watching the everyday drama yielded a deep understanding of the emotional trauma endured by complainant and practitioner alike. Adjournments during the day made possible conversations with some of the principal actors, their advocates and supporters. In this book the focus is on celebrated practitioners who stood out from the crowd and, in their turn, raised particular questions.

In all but one case I have spoken at length or corresponded with the central actor about their experience of investigation, arraignment, hearing and the aftermath of the decision. I have been privileged by the candour with which they recalled and in may ways relived those years. After the interviews I submitted my written account and interpretation to the participant whose corrections of fact were incorporated in the final draft of the chapter.

The one person not interviewed was lawyer Carol Ann Foreman. My research assistant or myself attended the weeks of the Tribunal and the days of the Supreme Court hearing of the Law Society's appeal against the Tribunal's orders. We watched this tall, elegant, proud woman who listened day after day to the complex particulars she was to answer. Subsequently she left her practice in the city and her home address. I tried to establish contact through her solicitors, but to no avail.

Each chapter explores the state of the profession and its public image immediately before and at the time the complaints were made. Each case history outlines the development of the central character's career and place in the profession at the point when complaints were made. It then traces the proceedings of investigation, prosecution and defence. It analyses the narrative to discern the purposes which these process might serve.

CHAPTER 3

*S*candals in *P*sychiatry

In the past two decades the increasing number of complaints about doctors has alarmed the medical profession, a global trend reflected in Australia. Social observers have echoed the views of writers like Bernard Barber who pointed to the erosion of trust in the relationship between doctors and patients, and between the profession and the society as a reason (see Barber, 1983, 1990; Giddens, 1990). Certainly negligence claims against medical practitioners have increased in Australia, although not to the extent of North American experience outlined by Lieberman (1983) who describes an endemic proclivity for litigation increasingly concerned with professional negligence. During the past decade some increase in civil actions against practitioners can be noted in Australia. This upward trend in actions for negligence and related torts (adverse outcomes where someone can be held responsible) has prompted steep rises in the cost of professional insurance premiums for lawyers and doctors. A still sharper increase has occurred in complaints brought against both medical and legal practitioners, although only a very small proportion of these are carried through the processes of investigation to prosecution before a professional tribunal. Nonetheless, the upward trend in complaints is reflected in a rise in those successfully prosecuted by the complaints handling bodies. This activism on behalf of clients has been enhanced by recent New South Wales legislation which established commissions vested with wide powers of investigation and prosecution of complaints against medical practitioners and lawyers respectively.

A Healthcare Complaints Unit was set up within the Health Department of New South Wales in January 1984. Ten years later the Unit was succeeded by the Healthcare Complaints Commission. As the original Complaints Unit became better known and investigated an increasing number of complaints, the number of practitioners brought before the Medical Tribunal increased. In the four years from 1984 to 1987 the number of healthcare complaints increased five-fold with the majority concerning medical practitioners. Complaints brought in this way

43

do not usually allege damages of a quantifiable, usually financial, nature. Those actions are typically brought in the civil courts and are directed to securing a remedy for the damage suffered. It is common for lawyers handling such matters to act on a contingency basis where they will be paid if they secure a financial award for the plaintiff.

An analysis of matters brought before the Medical Tribunal since 1984 shows some interesting shifts in the character of complaints. The earlier high incidence of 'Medibank fraud' (defrauding the government insurance authority) was over-taken by matters relating to practitioners' drug abuse or the overprescription of drugs for known addicts. For some years these complaints were most likely to be found proven and to result in severe penalties, usually deregistration or moni-toring conditions imposed on practice. By 1990, however, the Tribunal was dealing with an increasing frequency of complaints concerning the sexual misconduct of practitioners. (The complaint of sexual misconduct includes a range of impermis-sible behaviours from overtures or gestures with a sexual connotation through to sexual assault.) The taboo forbidding any sexual congress between patient and doctor is explicit in the Hippocratic code governing medical practice and held to be implicit in modern codes of medical ethics. In very recent years these codes have been revised to ensure sexual conduct between doctor and patient is explicitly forbidden. The Tribunal found only one case of sexual misconduct involving a medical practitioner proved per year in the years 1960, 1971, 1983, 1986, 1987, 1988 and 1989. In 1990 complaints of sexual misconduct were proved against three practitioners, and in 1991 another three practitioners were deregistered on these grounds. The high incidence of such complaints has con-tinued until this day with almost half of complaints brought before the Tribunal in this category.

Although complaints of sexual misconduct as well as medical fraud and drug addiction feature in the records of Medical Tribunals, the majority of complaints concern inadequacy of treatment, lack of care in diagnosis, poor communication and rudeness. Some of these complaints are found to be without foundation and are dismissed, some addressed by conciliation, and some result in advice and counselling. In the four years from 1992 to 1995, eighteen medical practitioners appeared for the first time before the Tribunal in New South Wales. Half were facing complaints of sexual misconduct involving patients. (In addition a small number of cases were applications for reregistration after being suspended some years earlier and a very few were appeals against the Tribunal's finding to the Supreme Court.) Not surprisingly these particular cases attract strong media attention and public curiosity.

Scandals and Crises in Psychiatry

By the end of the 1980s Australian psychiatry was in crisis. Psychiatry was riven by conflict and controversy, and whispers of scandal had grown into loud alarms. The news media were running stories about the fate of patients admitted to psychiatric hospitals. Complaints about deep-sleep therapy (DST) and other practices associated with the Chelmsford Private Psychiatric Hospital were growing; some patients had died during treatment and others had committed suicide soon afterwards. Deep-sleep therapy, a promising physiological intervention which might have broken the cycles of depression or neurosis troubling patients, could destroy both patients and the profession.

There had long been concern about conditions in psychiatric hospitals, both private and especially public. The Richmond Report some years earlier had urged that many long-term patients would fare better in the community so long as adequate clinical, nursing and domestic services were provided. The move to 'deinstitutionalisation' began and patients were returned to their families, to hostels, and to wherever they might find adequate shelter. Without sufficient community services, however, this became a highly visible problem, one which eventually disturbed the public conscience.

Then damaging stories about psychiatric hospitals emerged. Evils were being uncovered at Chelmsford Private Psychiatric Hospital. Evidence about incompetence and carelessness had first been heard during an inquest into the death of a patient at Chelmsford in May 1967. As the years passed more stories accumulated. Calls in the New South Wales Parliament for a public inquiry were repeated and eventually prompted the announcement in May 1988 of a Royal Commission with its terms of reference narrowed to focus on the deaths and injuries consequent of deep-sleep therapy at Chelmsford. The extent of negligence and disorder was uncovered. In addition to the negligent use of deep-sleep therapy, electroconvulsive therapy (ECT) and very large doses of drugs had been administered to patients without their informed consent. Subsequently the Royal Commission was to find that the scandals at Chelmsford were known to the medical profession, especially the psychiatric profession. No action was taken on their part. The Royal Australian and New Zealand College of Psychiatry (RANZCP) had not taken any action nor made any formal inquiries, and the Complaints Unit of the New South Wales Health Department had failed to act.

The Royal Commission into deep-sleep therapy, soon known as the Chelmsford Commission, exposed the psychiatric profession's inability or reluctance to maintain discipline and regulate itself. Although the scandal of Chelmsford had been widely known, neither the NSW Government's Health Department nor the profession of psychiatry had intervened. Only the press had signalled repeatedly the damage which was being done to patients admitted to the hospital. The

Sydney Morning Herald had first raised alarm with a report of the inquest into the death of a patient after undergoing DST. The stories continued in the print media and later on television.

Dr Harry Bailey, the psychiatrist who introduced DST, committed suicide shortly before the Chelmsford Commission began. Later the three other psychiatrists involved in DST were found by the Chelmsford Commission to be negligent, dishonest, and unscrupulous in treating patients without their informed consent. (Subsequent civil and criminal actions, brought many years later, against these practitioners were to fail because of excessive delay in bringing prosecutions; this issue is taken up in Chapter 7.) From its opening weeks in October 1988 and through the next two years, the Chelmsford Commission investigated a catalogue of stories of death and damage caused by psychiatric intervention at the hospital. The Commission released its report on 20 December 1990. Deborah Lupton's 1993 article in the *Australian and New Zealand Journal of Psychiatry*, 'Back to Bedlam?', recalls the horror tales which flooded newspapers for the next month, then abated, only to surface intermittently in later years when patients brought further claims of negligence.

At this time other disturbing stories were uncovered. Dr Bailey had been reputed to have had sexual intercourse with patients; a practice apparently being undertaken by other psychiatrists, some of whom claimed such sexual interludes were therapeutic. Professional literature overseas, particularly in the US, had already raised the alarm to this practice. A plethora of journal articles and books examined the extent and the potential dangers of sex between doctor and patient. These ranged from cautious general discussions of ethics, such as *Ethics and Psychiatry* (Dwyer, 1988), to the more explicit collection *Sexual Exploitation in Professional Relationships* (Gabbard, 1989). If 10 per cent of male therapists (psychiatrists and psychologists) reported incidents of sexual intimacy with patients why should Australian psychiatrists be any different? Practitioners were divided about the harm, harmlessness or possible benefit of sexual intimacy. The condemnation of sexual involvement with patients spoke of exploitation, abuse and incest. Mainstream medicine, always suspicious of psychiatry, sought to distance itself.

Disputing Discourses

Beyond the resurgent alarm over the plight of the mentally ill, the public was becoming increasingly aware of bitter internal divisions within psychiatry. All therapies were being contended by one sector or another; the critical discourse fragmenting the profession.

Psychiatry, like all medical disciplines, derived originally from philosophy. But, unlike much of clinical medicine, contemporary psychiatry comes immediately from two different philosophical traditions—from psychology as a social science and from the natural science of biology. More specifically, its emergence was fostered by a learned fascination with the working of the mind inside the human body. Conflicts and controversies attended the emergence of psychiatry as a clinical discipline. Freud and his disciples disputed modes of diagnosis and therapy and so generated the progenitors of the many modalities of psychiatry which now flourish.[1]

The division between psychological and pharmacological therapies is readily recognised given their different intellectual lineage. Psychiatrists, by virtue of their medical monopoly in prescribing pharmaceutical remedies, can use a wide range of medications and extend their treatment to include 'physical' interventions such as ECT and psychosurgery. Debates about the utility of pharmacological remedies have raged intermittently for decades and were recently heightened by the publication of Breggin's *Toxic Psychiatry* which invited equally critical replies. Pharmaceutical prescription remains the domain of medicine and is firmly tied into what was once termed the medical model, which privileges the biological over the psychological and cultural bases of disease and illness. Psychiatrists vary considerably in the extent to which they prescribe therapeutic drugs, or more draconic interventions. Psychologists are more restricted in their approach to therapy in that they cannot prescribe medication and cannot undertake surgery. Practitioners in both disciplines, however, espouse a baffling diversity of sub-disciplines and become practitioners of one clinical art or other.

Among practitioners and researchers who give some place to psychological intervention in mental illness other deep lines of division have opened up. Currently the dominant schools in psychotherapy can be distinguished as behaviourist or dynamic. The former applies principles of cause and effect to human behaviour, and focuses on changing behaviour patterns as the way of dealing with an underlying pathology which causes dysfunctional or inappropriate behaviour. Dynamic psychotherapy emphasises the interaction between therapist and patient, and seeks to uncover the patient's difficulties from all the complexity of originating conditions. Therapist and patient work through difficulties and problems to realise the patient's therapeutic goals. The process recognises the continuing flux in patient response and the dynamism of a therapeutic relationship, such that therapist interacts perceptively and flexibly with the goal of facilitating the patient's achievement of therapeutic health goals.

Behavioural therapies have advanced beyond the earlier stimulus–response styles of conditioning, such as aversion therapy. Cognitive behaviour therapies retain the positivist assumptions of science and seek to reduce complexity by concentrating on what can be observed and, preferably, measured. In this model the relation between therapist and patient tends to be along traditional clinical lines where the doctor is knowledgeable and directive. Cognitive behaviourism is recognised as an important development beyond earlier simplistic assumptions about the causes of human behaviour, its deviance and aberration, and the implicit model has attracted a strong following.

Cognitive behaviourists make strong claims for the efficacy of their treatments and cite articles detailing the measurement of its success (see, for example, Andrews, 1991, pp.845–8). Practitioners of dynamic psychotherapy do not disagree with those claims for specific neuroses but tend to point to the long-term efficacy of their interactive practice in resolving depression, personality disorder, family dysfunction and some forms of schizophrenia.

Dynamic psychotherapy distinguishes itself from cognitive behaviour therapies by an emphasis on the dynamic relation between patient and therapist who together work at bringing disruptive and dysfunctional attitudes into present contemplation, so that the origins of distressing problems may be known and dealt with. Dynamic psychotherapy usually achieves its ends over a lengthy period. Some practitioners anticipate good interim results within six months and recommend that it should yield the full extent of benefit within two years. There is however strong disagreement with this view, particularly from the Australian Society of Psychotherapy. Processes of transference and counter-transference are involved and become the way the patient transfers past disabling attitudes onto the therapist, prior to resolving the issues.

Cognitive behaviour therapy uses repeated stimuli and exercises to modify behaviour and attitudes which have disabling potential. The practitioner assumes the traditional clinical role of directing the patient. Authority relations are patent. Dynamic psychotherapy assumes a sensitive interaction where the therapist reads the signs and helps the patient recognise the dynamics which set the pattern for present difficulties. For some conditions the relationship with the patient is one of equals working out problems together; for others the model is of a parental authority intent on optimum development for the child. In general terms 'the talking therapy', as all forms of psychotherapy were often dubbed by both detractors and advocates in the 1980s, is based on empathy and understanding between therapist and patient. And therein, claim its detractors, lies the problem. The therapist does not keep the requisite distance, does not maintain the boundaries, may become a friend, even an intimate friend.

These public disputes may promote intellectual stimulation and instigate research, and its funding, to settle such matters, but they do not enhance the reputation and hence the trust reposed in psychiatry by its clientele.

Psychiatry in the Faculties

The formal institutions of psychiatry are of recent origin in Australia. In 1959 Professor William Trethowan of Manchester University came to New South

Wales to set up training in psychiatry at Sydney University. Two years later Professor David Madison was appointed to the foundation chair in psychiatry at the University of Sydney. In 1963 the first Professor of Psychiatry, Dr Lesley Kiloh, was appointed to the University of New South Wales. Subsequently David Madison became Dean of Medicine at the University of Sydney and then moved to the University of Newcastle to establish a Faculty of Medicine. He appointed Dr Beverley Raphael, another outstanding female practitioner, as the first Professor of Psychiatry in the new Medical Faculty. Prior to the establishment of these institutions the few medical practitioners with academic training in psychiatry had gained their qualifications overseas, usually in the UK or the US.

Meantime a number of practising psychiatrists affiliated in the Association of Psychiatry had promoted the establishment of the Royal Australian and New Zealand College of Psychiatry in Australia. The College assumed responsibility for the training and examination of medical practitioners seeking specialist qualifications in psychiatry. The activities of the College have extended into supervision of standards of practice and conduct; eventually in 1993 it was to develop a code of ethics specific to this medical specialty in Australia.

Disorder in the Profession

As the Chelmsford Commission completed it hearings in 1990, the profession felt the dismay of the scandal of Chelmsford Hospital which brought disrepute to the physiological interventions of psychosurgery, ECT, and especially, deep-sleep therapy. As well there were those distressing allegations of sex with patients associated with charismatic figure of Dr Bailey, whose suicide had delivered him from further disgrace. The psychiatric profession turned their attention to the rumours of sexual abuse and exploitation. Many in the collegial establishment were ready to believe that the location of this misconduct lay in the psychotherapy paradigm. People in the mental health system, both in administration and in the domains of clinical practice, were fearful of further scandal and were keen to turn attention away from the spectacular breakdown of good clinical practice in one of the leading psychiatric clinics. They heard the noise about sexual depredation as a trumpet call to a field where censure would reassure all who had been alarmed that the mental health community was incapable of imposing self-discipline and putting its own house in order.

Complaints about sexual misconduct had first become public in 1985–86. The earliest investigation revealed the guilty and punished with rebukes and some loss of practising rights. Soon more draconian action became commonplace and deregistration was the usual determination. An analysis of the Complaints Unit's annual reports from 1989 to 1993/94 revealed that it had received 159 such complaints about doctors in the six years from 1989 to 1993/94 (Health Care Complaints

Unit *Annual Report 1993/4*, p.28). Although most could not be substantiated, 23 complaints in that same period were finalised before the Tribunal and almost all resulted in the doctor's deregistration. Newspaper headlines at this time were about doctors, most often psychiatrists: 'Sex Case Psychiatrist Struck Off' (*Sydney Morning Herald*, 8 Feb. 1989); 'More Cases Against Doctors' (*Sydney Morning Herald*, 2 Aug. 1991).

To the notoriety of Chelmsford were being added increasing charges of sexual encounters of psychiatrists with their patients. Within the medical profession rumours about the sexual activities of colleagues in psychiatry now circulated: 'they're all doing it'. There had been little research into this problem in the Australian context, except for one small study by Medlicott published in the *Australian and New Zealand Journal of Psychiatry* in 1968. In the US, however, the issue had been vigorously pursued; Gabbard's (1989) compendium of such studies is probably the best known to Australian practitioners, but it was preceded by many earlier inquiries (see Galletly, 1993, for an excellent review). To the stories of sexual encounters circulated in medical circles were added talk of some psychiatrists' belief that sexual intimacy could enter into the therapy. These beliefs were not aired publicly in Australia, but had been uncovered in US surveys (Kardener et al., 1973; Gartrell et al., 1989).

Mainstream medicine, always suspicious of psychiatry, its multiplicity of paradigms, varieties of treatment and uncertainty of clinical outcomes, worried about referral of patients or averted its gaze. Clearly something had to be done to restore good order and professional reputation.

Then came a grave accusation against a high profile psychiatrist.

The First One: Dr Winifred Childs

In 1988 a woman terminated what appeared to have been successful therapy with a psychiatrist. Some few months later, towards the end of that year, she consulted another psychiatrist and, in the course of that therapy, had told of her anger and disappointment at being used and rejected by the former psychiatrist, Dr Winifred Childs. In February 1989 this psychiatrist, with the permission of her patient, contacted the Complaints Unit. The patient, S, was invited to the Complaints Unit and urged to make an official complaint. This done, the investigation of the allegations began.

Complaints brought to the attention of the Complaints Unit can be somewhat distracted and inchoate as a layperson puts together a comprehensive account of the lack of competence or bad behaviour of a health practitioner. The key features which relate to law and regulation are drawn out of this account and the complainant usually requires help in formulating a complaint. This assistance is part of the Unit's everyday activity. The elements of the complaint are put in order and an investigation commences. At that time statute governing these matters did not require that the practitioner be informed at this stage. Thus Childs was not told of the complaint, but learnt from a colleague some time later that she was being investigated.

After graduating in medicine in 1959, Childs worked as a general practitioner for some years and then took up a training and research fellowship in psychiatry in the newly formed Department of Psychiatry at the University of Sydney, to which David Madison had been appointed as founding professor. In 1967 Childs became a member, and later a fellow, of the Royal Australian and New Zealand College of Psychiatry. One year later she commenced private practice as a psychiatrist. She undertook further postgraduate clinical training in psychoanalysis through the Australian Society of Psychoanalysis. Shortly after completing the five-year course she was appointed to various training and supervision posts and served in executive positions on the Australian Society of Psychoanalysis, including that of chairperson of the Society's National Coordinating Education Committee. Then came further teaching and supervisory appointments at the University of Sydney and the University of New South Wales and consultancy appointments to Prince of Wales and Prince Henry Hospitals. Childs welcomed the opportunity to teach and train others in her profession, and by the late 1980s held teaching positions at three of the great teaching hospitals in Sydney, Westmead, Prince of Wales and Prince Henry, and was heavily committed to teaching the Masters of Psychotherapy and the Masters of Adolescent Psychotherapy in the Department of Psychiatry at the University of New South Wales.

Over the years further study and experience prompted her to move from psychoanalysis to a style of psychotherapy of a more humanistic and dynamic nature. She had become critical of the great power assumed by the psychoanalyst and the dependency built up by a patient during psychoanalysis. This dependency was constituent of patient–analyst relations which frequently continued for many years of treatment. Childs claimed that her style of therapy, 'humanistic, psycho-dynamic, supportive therapy' (humanistic psychotherapy), an eclectic approach which draws on a number of modalities, developed a working alliance intent on understanding the patient's psychological problems and overcoming or solving them through an egalitarian psychotherapeutic relationship; 'It is not a power relationship, it is where I and the patient have an equal commitment to the work at hand' (Childs, pers. comm., 28 Oct. 1995).

Winifred Childs had married young, while a student in Medical School, and had borne and reared two children with her husband, Bruce Childs, whose political career had culminated in his election to the Senate of the Commonwealth Parliament. Senator Bruce Childs was, and remains, a powerful man on the left-wing of the Australian Labor Party. By 1980 Childs, a woman of strong socialist principles and practice, was at the height of a distinguished medical career. She enjoyed a fine reputation as a teacher and supervisor, was widely recognised as an excellent psychiatrist and a highly skilled psychotherapist. She was open to new ideas and understandings in her discipline and was ready to try cautious adaptations in her practice. But, at the time her good fame was growing, troubling events were accumulating in her profession. And Childs herself entered a troubled phase of her own personal life in the mid 1980s.

Her thirty-year marriage to Senator Bruce Childs was encountering serious problems and there were some months of separation in 1985. The couple moved back together in the latter half of 1985, but the reunion did not last long and they separated at the beginning of 1986. Later that year Childs was hit by a car and after a period of hospitalisation was immobilised at home for many months. A rift between Childs and the Sydney Institute of Psychoanalysis (to become later the Psychoanalytic Society) had developed in 1984 and widened considerably over the next three years until, in October 1987, the Institute expelled her from all administrative and training positions.[2] After returning from a period of study in California she had started to develop a more eclectic form of psychotherapy and became critical of many aspects of analytical therapies. This critical evaluation was then a strong feature of her university teaching; students, she maintained, should look critically at all therapies and be ready to continually monitor their effectiveness. Her outspoken criticism provoked antagonism, particularly her criticism of the frequency of psychoanalytic sessions over a prolonged period. Childs disparaged the practice of seeing people too frequently, i.e. four or five times a week, over several years. Consequently her own mode of practice made much more modest claims on the patient and the public purse.

By late 1987 Childs had become significantly personally isolated and politically alienated from the dominant divisions of her profession.

A woman of strong personality, keen intelligence and frank speech, Childs had moved to a different style of practice in a profession bedeviled by the conceptual fashions and fads which have beset mental health therapies. As a woman of the left she had maintained radical socialist views from her student days, her university teaching attracted a strong student following that valued her supervision. She worried about the clinical and cost effectiveness of current therapies: those which relied heavily on pharmaceutical intervention, on behavioural conditioning and psychoanalysis. She openly criticised aspects of current psychiatric practice and urged scepticism on her students. She advocated humanistic psychotherapy which took patients into partnership to resolve their own case, and repudiated the power relationship between patient and practitioner which dominated psychiatry. Childs challenged psychiatric hegemony and so was seen as a danger to the profession as it then constituted itself. She was not alone in her rejection of prevailing practices, other psychiatrists, ranging from senior colleagues to psychiatrists whose training Childs had supervised, came forward and supported her form of psychotherapy. They were, however, a minority, many of whom were not of the same persuasion as the psychiatry profession dominant in university and teaching hospitals.

The Investigation

Alerted to the complaint made by S, the Director of the Complaints Unit, Ms Merrilyn Walton, contacted the Unit's senior consultant on mental health care, Dr John Ellard. Dr Ellard, a leader in his profession, a longtime chief censor (examiner) and Chairman of Clinical Standards Committee concerned with ethical matters of the RANZCP, advised Walton to send him complaints in writing, whereupon he would convene a meeting of the National Standards Committee of the RANZCP. Childs was not advised of this meeting to hear the allegations about her conduct. The complaint was then referred to the Medical Tribunal.

The first statutory declaration provided by the complainant to the Complaints Unit reflected a confused and disturbed writer. This statutory declaration was subsequently replaced three times. The fourth statutory declaration submitted was used as the basis for the complaints regarding Childs.

The Complaint Unit's investigation had included visits to other medical practitioners specialising in psychiatry, and sought to build on previous allegations by outlining these and asking the practitioner what they could add to the picture. One of my informants characterised the visitation and questioning at his rooms as 'investigation by slander'. He felt that he was meant to be shocked by their allegations and so prompted to fill in the jigsaw with what gossip he had heard about the practitioner.

A colleague of Childs at the Prince of Wales Hospital phoned her on 9 April to tell her that an investigation was under way. The next day she phoned her insurance company, the Medical Defence Union. Childs then wrote to her College, the RANZCP, and asked if she were under investigation; she received no reply. She also phoned a senior academic colleague whose postgraduate students she had supervised and was told 'I am sorry. I cannot speak to you'. The Complaints Unit informed her by a letter, sent on 24 April, that complaints about her were being investigated. The next day Professor Gordon Parker, the Head of Psychiatry at the University of New South Wales where Childs held a teaching appointment, called her to his office. The investigators from the Complaints Unit had called on several senior academics at the university. Professor Parker relayed the additional allegations which had been raised—of her sleeping with students, shopping with patients, medifraud—and told her to take sick leave. After rejecting this advice Childs was told, 'we [the University of New South Wales] will investigate from Prince of Wales Hospital in parallel with the Complaints Unit'. Childs consulted her lawyers and was advised to take a leave of absence. Professor Parker agreed to this and gave her ten minutes to farewell the group of postgraduate trainees whom she was supervising. She had been teaching in the School of Psychiatry at the university for eleven years, and had been a co-founder of the Adolescent Services Unit in 1978.

Childs does not know how many investigators were involved or how much of the investigative team's time was given to her matter—the Complaints Unit does not keep time sheets on individual cases. In October 1989 the Medical Tribunal commenced its hearing. The period of time of waiting for the Tribunal to begin, Childs says, was the worst. She read and thought, and looked for models whose resilience and inner strength might guide her. A sense of peace entered her soul during this period and she began moving towards Christianity, later becoming a Catholic.

She was, however, unprepared for the ordeals of the Tribunal hearing. She was shocked as the expert witnesses called by her counsel were ridiculed and mocked. The sarcasm and remarks of the Presiding Judge distressed her, especially when he referred to her as 'Mother Hubbard'. Throughout the hearing the presiding member of the Tribunal referred to her as Mrs Childs, as if the matter was already determined. She was appalled to read a day's transcript and find it censored of untoward remarks made by her judge and her accusers; the transcript does not tell all of what occasioned this distress and misgiving. (The presiding member of tribunal and court sittings may edit the record to accord with corrected memory.) The hearing continued for seventeen days over five months.

Tribunal Hearing

The complaints brought to the attention of the Tribunal hinged on her relations with the complainant, S, and, later in the hearing, her two-year personal relationship with a fellow psychiatrist and former patient, W. (The substance of this latter complaint arose from evidence brought to the attention of the Tribunal after commencement of the hearing.)

The Complaints Unit, as nominal complainant, was represented by a senior barrister (a Queen's Counsel (QC)) and a junior barrister. Childs was equally strong in her representation by a QC and a junior barrister chosen by her medical insurance company, the Medical Defence Union. At a later interview she told me that this choice of representation came to worry her when she discovered that her counsel was an acting judge in the District Court as well as a private practitioner. She worried lest his appearance before the Tribunal, presided over by a District Court judge, might constitute a conflict of interest. (In effect, she believes, he was acting as counsel before a judge of the court in which he periodically held an acting judicial position.) She did not raise her worries at the time.

Providing the particulars of all aspects of conduct which may bear on professional misconduct is common legal practice. In this case, as in many others, there was a long list of particulars grouped under the headings of misconduct with a patient (two occurrences) and breach of confidentiality. Counsel for the nominal complainant, i.e. the Complaints Unit, categorised these, as follows, as severally amounting to professional misconduct:

1. The practitioner's attendance with the patient, S, at group sessions of Transactional Analysis; at such meetings discussing, in presence of the patient, her own problems including those arising from her relationship with W; sometimes taking coffee with the patient after such sessions; travelling by car with the patient to and from such sessions.
2. Inviting the patient to attend a weekly public event, 'Politics in the Pub' at the Harold Park Hotel, and dining afterwards with a group of persons, which included the patient, at a restaurant nearby in Glebe.
3. Leaving the patient unattended at the practitioner's rooms on two occasions while she took up appointments to inspect houses for sale and on one occasion going with the patient to view a house for sale.
4. Inviting the patient, a short period after therapeutic sessions had been terminated, to visit the practitioner's home, and there drinking wine and smoking marijuana with the patient, and expressing her love for and wish to make love with the patient.
5. The practitioner informing the patient that she rejected the advice of her own therapist that practitioner and patient only meet when a chaperone was present.
6. Engaging in sexual activity with the patient after consuming wine and marijuana and, on the next morning, expressing a preference for more vigorous lovemaking, a preference taken by the patient as a rejection.
7. Disclosing to the patient, S, confidential information about four other patients of the practitioner.
8. Engaging in a personal relationship with an ex-patient, a fellow psychiatrist, W, whose therapy with the practitioner had ceased shortly before commencement of the intimate relationship, which can be described as a de facto husband and wife relationship lasting two years.

A layperson can be puzzled by the way a catalogue of misdemeanours are cited in legal proceedings without any indication of the gradation such that the trivial stands on equal terms with grave and serious charges.

In response Childs accepted the first two matters as largely correct (adding minor amendments) and argued that attending such events with the patient and several other friends did not detract from the benefits the patient derived from therapy and were, indeed, part of the planned movement towards termination of therapy. As to the third matter Childs explained that the patient had waited for a few minutes while she looked at a property, and that the patient had expressed an interest in giving her opinion of a house on another occasion. Childs contested the evidence giving rise to complaints about activity of a sexual nature (points 4, 5 and 6) and gave a different account of these 'interludes' which did not reflect adversely on herself. From Childs' evidence it appeared that the patient, S, not herself, had expressed an interest in sexual activity and subsequently made advances which were gently put aside. There was no corroborating evidence to support either version of events. The Tribunal, however, accepted the complainant's version and rejected that of the practitioner—a common practice where practitioner and complainant proffer conflicting accounts. The Tribunal takes the view that the patient has nothing to gain by lying; the practitioner, on the other hand, faces the possibility of considerable loss and is more likely to be motivated to lie. There is a presumption of the *bona fides* of one party and not the other—an assumption not accepted in a common law court. In this case the patient's emotional and psychological state was not considered. The Tribunal noted the possibility that S's 'feelings against the respondent might be so strong as to lead her to make unwarranted and untruthful allegations against her', but decided her 'to be a witness of truth' (Medical Tribunal of New South Wales of April 1990. *Re Dr Winifred Childs and the Medical Practitioners Act 1938.* Reasons for Determination at 81). Childs, like other practitioners brought before the Tribunal, was shocked to find the scales tipped against her. She does not accept the reasons advanced in the judgment for preferring the evidence of her accuser where it conflicts with her own or with that of the medical practitioner witnesses called by her lawyers.

On the four matters of breach of confidentiality (point 7) Childs maintained that in three of the four instances described she had not disclosed the identity of any patient, and of the fourth instance she had not discussed the case at all. In defence she explained that it was common psychiatric practice to debrief and discuss worrying cases with another person of integrity and competence, and that S, as a specialist nurse and a mature-age social work student, was a suitable person for such debriefing sessions. Furthermore S had personal experience which could give further insight into the problems of another patient. She stated that she had discussed the features of the case without identifying the patient.

Childs' response to these allegations highlighted the different view she took of the doctor–patient relationship. As mentioned earlier, her approach to therapy, humanistic psychotherapy, involved the formation of an alliance between therapist and patient to realise the patient's goals of good mental health, autonomy and effective adult function. This modality includes the deliberate planned use of a friendly relationship as an agent of support to facilitate reaching a defined therapeutic goal. In practical terms her approach meant that friendship and trust with a patient could develop. For mainstream psychotherapy this approach meant a breakdown of established doctor–patient boundaries, an ignorance of 'allowed' limits. Childs was to be admonished as a person who did not observe and respect the difference in status between people, especially patient and practitioner.

The last and eighth complaint, brought forward during the hearing, referred to Childs two-year de facto relationship with a senior psychiatrist, W. W was subpoenaed to tender a statement and be examined about his relationship with Childs. W had been Childs' patient in psychotherapy for nine years. The condition for which he was being treated had improved considerably and therapy was concluded in December 1985. His marriage had deteriorated and he and his wife had separated. W was strongly attracted to Childs, and the two made an appointment with the Medical Defence Union to consult about the ethics of an intimate relation after therapy had been finished. Childs recalled that the advice given by the officers of the MDU noted that there was no inequality between the two, both were psychiatrists of standing, and that the therapeutic relation had ceased and, hence, an intimate relationship would raise no professional problems. Within a short time Childs and W entered an intimate relationship and lived together for two years. After some months after ending therapy with Childs, W had sought treatment from one and, then, another psychotherapist; both treatments ineffectual. Two years later, at the time that his relationship with Childs was disintegrating, he commenced therapy with a third psychiatrist and was continuing with that treatment at the time of the Tribunal (October, 1989).

Childs agreed that the particulars regarding W were correct.

The nominal complainant (the Director of the Complaints Unit) put before the Tribunal expert opinion based on the submission of complaints as set out in affidavit and statements by S. The veracity of the complaints was not for questioning, rather the medical experts were asked their opinion of the seriousness of these complaints in a medical/psychiatric treatment context. The Tribunal reserved determination of the truth of the allegations to itself.

When the Complaints Unit had first sought the advice of Dr Ellard, he, as Chairman of the Clinical Standards Committee at RANZCP, had called a special meeting of that committee. He discussed the complaints against Childs with three committee members and heard no significant deviation in opinion from the one which he tendered by report. Childs was not informed of these deliberations and only viewed the first (later rejected) statutory declaration signed by S. On the basis of these discussions Ellard claimed:

> the matters set out would attract the strong disapproval of Dr Childs' peers [and] ... are sufficiently serious for them to be referred to an appropriate statutory body with a wide range of powers (at 31).

Nor, it was claimed did perusal of a second statutory declaration change this opinion. These firm deliberations suggest that the profession was beginning to atone for its inaction on the psychiatric practices of the Chelmsford Private Psychiatric Hospital.

The Tribunal relied heavily on the opinion of Dr Ellard who, as adviser to the Complaints Unit and the most senior specialist in psychiatry called by the complainant to give evidence, assisted the Tribunal over several days. In the course of hearing evidence, especially that of Childs and of Dr Ellard, a significant clash of epistemology and practice in psychiatric therapy became apparent. Dr Ellard rejected as improper both the forming of a personal friendship with a patient or an intimate relationship with a patient after the conclusion of a lengthy period of therapy. Nor could he accept the possibility of equality in the relation between therapist and patient, adding that in ordinary medical conditions where there is pain or illness the patient 'feels a debt and some dependence on the doctor' (at 34). With regard to questions of confidentiality Dr Ellard stated that a practitioner might 'sound off' to a colleague about a hard session with a patient, and that such a colleague would 'normally be another psychiatrist or someone of that sort' (at 33). He did not agree that a suitable person might be a nurse or social worker.

The applicant called several more specialists to give their opinion of Childs' conduct, (under the presumption that the allegations were correct). In turn the respondent called expert psychiatrists to review the complaints and attest to her good professional and moral character.

The first specialist called by the Complaints Unit to give evidence, Dr Spelman, a practising psychiatrist and a member of the Clinical Standards Committee, agreed with Dr Ellard's interpretation of the ethical issues. He added that a psychiatrist must maintain her or his distance emotionally from the patient during and after the course of therapy, and that it is undesirable to have any social interaction between patient and therapist. This view was corroborated by the psychiatrist to whom the complainant, S, had been referred by Childs. The psychiatrist, Dr Banning, did not think that a patient–therapist relationship was ever an equal one: 'once a patient always a patient' (at 39). Similarly, Dr Joan Symington, a member of the New South Wales Institute for Psychoanalysis called by the Complaints Unit, deplored any personal relationship with a patient; she disapproved strongly of all aspects of Childs' relationship including the modality termed humanistic psychotherapy. She would not accept that there could be a post-therapy friendship.

Evidence elicited by examination and cross-examination of Childs and the complainant, S, conflicted at several points. Where S had spoken of Childs' proposing sexual contact on the occasion she visited Childs' home in June 1988, Childs maintained that S had been insistent about sexual contact and was angry and petulant when the overture was rejected. Childs had recounted this incident to her own therapist, Ms Catherine Munro, and Ms Munro corroborated her statement. The second occasion, when according to S there had been sexual contact, was also recalled in different terms by Childs. Ms Munro recalled for the Tribunal her conversation with Childs on 18 April 1989 when Childs spoke of the incident as a 'brief contact and touching and caressing of hair' (at 44). This interlude, Childs had told Ms Munro, had been at the insistence of S and that she, Childs, had consented unwillingly and then withdrawn after that brief encounter. This evidence corroborated the therapist's notes of conversations with Childs, subpoenaed for the Complaints Unit.

S's therapy, which had commenced in 1985, had been interrupted when Childs was hospitalised following a car accident in the latter months of 1986. Her therapy had continued during 1987 and moved into a termination phase during the first half of 1988. Childs explained to the Tribunal that in this last phase any residual dependency on the therapist and any mystification of the therapy in the mind of the patient should be dissolved and the patient encouraged to expand his or her social network. By late May 1988 the patient, S, and therapist, Childs, agreed that therapy should cease, the goals having been accomplished. The last appointment was on 1 June 1988. Childs defended her social activities with S and her attendance with her at Transactional Analysis sessions as part of this process. Similarly she defended her friendship with S as a supportive relation of equals.

Childs denied the claims that she had at any time expressed love for S or any wish to make love to her. Her account of the night when it was claimed she had made love to S differed radically from that of S; some affectionate playing with hair and face and stroking of breast initiated by S had been broken off when Childs felt ill and retired to bed. She had smoked a marijuana cigarette with S and blamed the interlude, and her feelings of nausea, on the marijuana, which she had then used for only the second time with untoward and unwanted effects.

In further evidence Childs defended the presumed breaches in confidentiality. 'Debriefing' she explained as expressing feelings and discussing one's difficulties with patients, a useful adjunct to therapeutic work and necessary when carrying out emotionally charged psychotherapy of patients. In the latter part of 1988, after termination of S's therapy, she recalled discussing problems associated with three patients, two of whom were the patients of psychiatrists she was supervising. She had not identified patients by surname and had emphasised that the discussion was confidential and S agreed to this proviso.

Discrepancies appeared between statements made by complainant S and a psychiatrist whom S had visited in the time proximate to the alleged sexual intimacy interludes. S had consulted Dr Helen Borman in her rooms and told of her distress: that she wanted to have a sexual relationship with the respondent (Childs), but the respondent was not interested and only wanted friendship. In other particulars (e.g. the occurrence or not of particular social occasions) Dr Borman further disagreed with S's account. The Tribunal stated that the psychiatrist, Dr Borman, reinforced Childs' evidence and conflicted with that of the complainant, S, but, nonetheless, preferred S's account on the grounds that Dr Borman was under great stress at the time of her consultations with S. (Her husband had been gravely ill at the time she was treating S and he had died subsequently.)

In response to the last complaint regarding Childs relationship with W, the officers of the Medical Defence Union claimed that they could not recall exactly the advice given to Childs and W, and that there were no records available of the advice given at the appointment. Expert evidence was called by Childs' lawyers. In response to questions four psychiatrists assessed the development of social relations between patient and therapist in the termination phase of treatment. They stated that mature people after conclusion of therapy could rationally make decisions about entering personal or sexual relationships. A conflict within the profession about the propriety of friendship with patients and, after termination of therapy, of sexual relationship between doctor and former patient became apparent.

At the conclusion of hearing evidence the Tribunal reserved its decision. Then came the months of waiting for its findings.

The Finding of the Tribunal

The Tribunal's decision, handed down on 9 April of the following year, was damning of Childs, whose evidence was brushed aside where it conflicted with the complainant's and whose approach to the practice of psychotherapy was condemned. The Tribunal viewed the complainant, S, is 'a witness of truth' (at 81). Where her evidence conflicted with the respondent, Childs, or with other psychiatrist and therapist witnesses (Dr Borman, Ms Munro), the Tribunal chose to believe the complainant.

In regard to the complaint about Childs' relationship with W, the Tribunal determined that W had not been an autonomous person when he sought and entered into a sexual relationship and that advice purported to have been given by the officers of the Medical Defence Union, to allow considerable time after termination of doctor–patient relationship, had been ignored.

The findings of fact were critical to the outcome and from these there was no appeal. The Tribunal determined that the complaints were factually correct and constituted professional misconduct on all matters, as particularised by the Complainants Unit.

The Tribunal summarised the issues before it. With regard to any relationship of the psychiatrist with S and W, the Tribunal raised the following questions:

(a) Is it professional misconduct to have a personal relationship with a patient or ex-patient?
(b) Is it professional misconduct to have such a relationship with S?
(c) Did sexual conduct with S amount to professional misconduct?
(d) Was it professional misconduct not to have proper regard for the psychological wellbeing of S by reason of lack of adequate skill, judgment or care?

With regard to issues of confidentiality the Tribunal directed itself to consider:

(a) the duty of medical practitioner/psychotherapist to maintain patient confidentiality;
(b) the circumstances when it may be proper to communicate personal information about patients to another person; and
(c) whether the psychiatrist's statements about patients to S amounted to professional misconduct.

The Tribunal accepted the evidence of four specialist psychiatrist witnesses for the complainant that 'it is not open to medical practitioners to discuss confidential information concerning patients with any person the practitioner may trust' (at 96). This absolute statement had been qualified a few pages later, but it was held that the complaint of breach of confidentiality had been sustained.

The five psychiatrists called by the respondent's lawyers to attest to her integrity and the quality and propriety of her clinical and moral practice, were rejected as unreliable. The Tribunal described these expert witnesses as either friends or associates of the respondent or as not being capable of 'truly independent expert evidence ... they probably misconceived their function' (at 100). The Tribunal viewed them as 'unqualified to give expert evidence ... standing on the fringe of psychiatry', and stated that they were biased by friendship with Childs and were convinced that Childs was being persecuted (at 102).

Psychiatrists called by each side held opposing views of the propriety of a psychiatrist having a sexual relationship with an ex-patient. One group, of whom Dr Ellard is the most senior in the profession, held to the firm line that it is improper to enter a sexual relationship with an ex-patient, although Dr Ellard equivocated on the point that after sufficient elapse of time such a relationship with a fully recovered, non-dependent patient might be permissible. The psychiatrists called by Childs' lawyers (of whom Associate Professor Neil McConaghy was the most senior), stated that a sexual relationship with a former patient is permissible so long as the psychiatrist believed the person was not dependent and not likely to be damaged by the relationship. The Tribunal rejected the expert opinion of this latter group.

The Tribunal concluded that 'psychiatrists of good standing and repute would

strongly disapprove of the respondent's conduct' (at 102) in altering the relationship with a patient to one of friendship of varying intimacy evident in the
close sociability of the relationship of Childs with S during 1988. Despite the
claimed different nature of therapy adopted by Childs and her associates, the
Tribunal stated, 'this group is obliged to adhere to the conduct of the profession
as a whole' (at 105). The respondent had thus jeopardised the treatment of S by
showing:

> gross disregard for her welfare ... exposed the patient to a significant risk of
> deterioration of her psychiatric stability ... exploitation of the respondent's
> therapeutic relationship with S (at 106).

The judgment concluded that the particulars of this matter justify separate
findings of professional misconduct.

Moving on to the next category of complaints, alleged breaches of confidentiality, the Tribunal decided there was no bona fide purpose in the disclosure of
information concerning patients to S and that, for several reasons, S was not an
appropriate person to receive such information.

On the third set of complaints the Tribunal determined that the respondent's
entering into a personal and sexual relationship with W, a practising psychiatrist
who had been in therapy for so long, was grave professional misconduct. At this
point in its deliberations the Tribunal adjourned.

At the meeting with her lawyers that evening, the Medical Defence Union,
which had assured Childs of their commitment to insure against all costs, declared it was not liable for a punitive outcome which required its client to pay the
other party's legal costs. Childs held to the liability of the insurer for all the risks
against which it insured. She wept in shock at the betrayal and was dismissed
from counsel's chambers and waited in the lobby. After the lawyers' meeting, her
solicitor approached Childs and spoke with concern about liability which could
take all of her assets. Subsequently the Medical Defence Union was to decide
that the terms of the practitioner's insurance covered the legal costs incurred by
the doctor and, if the Tribunal so ordered, those of the other side. Childs at-
tributes the insurance company's revised view of its liability to strategic lobbying
as a response to her case by colleagues in New Zealand as well as Australia.
(The company insures the majority of medical practitioners in both countries.)

Later that month, on the 20 April 1990, the Tribunal sat to hear any submissions that might affect its orders regarding the practitioner's future practice, the
findings of professional misconduct on several counts having been determined.
Two senior colleagues came forward and agreed to supervise Childs' practice
and thus support her continued registration. Dr Kyneur spoke of her good character, and of his belief that Childs had recognised that her conduct had fallen

short of the standard required. Childs however did not agree to declare her guilt and express such contrition for the Tribunal. During an adjournment, friends with political expertise had urged her to recant, to be contrite, but to no avail. Childs did not, and does not, accept that she was guilty of misconduct, and insists that S's allegations were untrue. The Tribunal looked for contrition but Childs was adamant—she was not guilty as charged and expressions of contrition would be false and demeaning. Years later Childs explained to me (pers. comm., 5 Oct. 1995):

> I had told the truth throughout; at the end all I had was my word; I couldn't give them that. To have responded to pressure and given a false confession would have lost my integrity and then history is lost.

Letters of commendation and character references from psychiatrists, medical practitioners, patients and persons of high repute in the community were received by Childs and her lawyers, and submitted to the Tribunal to ameliorate the severity of orders. The listing of forty-three referees included professors of sociology, politics, economics, psychology and psychiatry, a former President of the Australian Psychoanalytic Society, Ministers of the former Commonwealth Labor Government, Ministers of the New South Wales Labor Government, the Minister of Health in the New Zealand Government, a Supreme Court judge, twenty-six medical practitioners (most specialists in psychiatry), and several distinguished former patients. All strongly supported her professional ethics and personal integrity. Two of Childs' referees were leading academics in psychiatry. No references, however, came from the current establishment in psychiatry (that is, persons holding positions of authority or influence in the universities, colleges or institutes of the discipline). The Tribunal took little account of these letters of commendation and diminished the value of most stating that they showed 'insufficient recognition of the seriousness of the respondent's conduct' (at 111). Similarly the Tribunal had two weeks earlier put aside the evidence given under examination and cross-examination by five specialist psychiatrists called by Childs' lawyers. It had largely agreed with the challenge, mounted by counsel for the Complainant, to their 'objectivity, standing and credit'; this challenge was recapitulated in the Reasons for Decision (at 100–4).

At the resumed hearing the offer of two senior psychiatrists, Dr Kyneur and Professor Katz, to supervise Childs' practice was rejected. Childs was herself a senior psychiatrist and hence, the Tribunal deemed, such an offer was not feasible. More weightily the Tribunal observed that the practitioner had not shown that she accepted the finding of misconduct, nor had she shown contrition. Thus she could not be permitted to continue practice under any conditions.

Two weeks later, on the 8 May 1990, the Tribunal delivered its orders before a packed gallery: Childs must be deregistered and pay the costs of the applicant.

That evening Childs walked with three women friends, each leaders in their respective fields, through the city and down to Lady Macquarie's Chair, a point overlooking Sydney Harbour. The four women kicked off their shoes, lit cigarettes and declared 'It's over. Life goes on'. Six years later Childs recalled 'the relief and joy of leaving the surreal world of male-dominated law and returning to the real world of nature and enduring friendship' (pers. comm., 14 Oct. 1995).

At its British headquarters the Medical Defence Union agreed to pay the legal costs involved. There were important points of law to be clarified by the courts. Perhaps weighing into that decision was the added recognition that other doctors, seeing Childs abandoned, may decide to transfer insurance away from this medical defence organisation. The company agreed to see the case through to an appeal.

Childs decided to appeal against the decision of the Tribunal.

The Appeal to the Supreme Court

Appeals from the Medical Tribunal cannot involve issues of fact; an appeal can only be made on points of law or an objection to the orders. The advice of her lawyers was that an appeal might be mounted on the grounds that misconduct leading to deregistration as prescribed in the Act could arise only in the practice of medicine, that is at the time that therapy was being provided. Three judges of the Court of Appeal sat for two hours on 17 September 1990 to receive relevant submissions. Two months later, on 13 November, they delivered their judgment. For Childs it was an anticlimax. Believing she had done nothing wrong, she had been determined to fight on, to appeal the Tribunal's decision. But the legal niceties of grounds for appeal did not go to the core of her grievance, that the Tribunal had erred in rejecting much of her evidence and misconstruing her moral and professional philosophy. Her words lay mutilated in the judgment.

The Supreme Court judgment criticised the Tribunal's failure to link particular acts or omissions to specific professional defect amounting to professional misconduct. Nonetheless all submissions brought by Childs' lawyers failed.

The first issue turned on there being temporal boundaries implicit in the phrase, 'in the practice of medicine'. The Court rejected the proposal that this circumscribed the period during which conduct prescribed as 'professional misconduct' could occur. Conduct, which shows defects in adequate medical knowledge, experience, skill, judgment or care, can occur at any time. On the second submission, the Tribunal's rejection of the evidence of Childs' expert witnesses and hence the view of an alternative school of clinical practice, the Court found that regardless of the nature of her therapy or technique it must conform to the accepted ethical standards of the profession. Childs' definition of the term 'debriefing' was accepted, but disclosure of a patient's identity had been 'rightly rejected by the Tribunal' (*Childs v. Walton* (1990) CA 40252 at 12). The fourth objection rested on denial of natural justice, implicit in the complaints unit incorporation of a complaint regarding W, was not allowed. The *Medical Practice Act 1938*, s. 5.32, (NSW), read with sch. 4, cl. 5(2) of that Act, provides that further complaints may be added after a hearing has begun.

The Supreme Court's final submission reviewed the Tribunals orders that her name be removed from the Medical Register and that she pay the costs of the Complaints Unit. The impressive testimonials submitted by medical practitioners, patients and persons in prominent roles were reviewed. The Court set itself to consider all aspects of 'the serious example of misconduct which caused detriment to those whom it exploited' and was most concerned that Childs had not, at the conclusion of the hearing and before the orders were made, come forward to express contrition. 'Contrition, if accepted as honest, may indicate that no occasion for protection [of the public] exists' (Samuels J at 19).

From Childs' perspective the appeal had been useless. Her expulsion was complete. Today Childs believes that were she to reapply for medical registration she would be rejected. The scapegoat cannot return.

Review

Winifred Childs' case raised many issues and questions about the doctor–patient, or rather the psychiatrist–patient relationship. Such questions include: Must power be conceded to the psychiatrist, or, as Childs and others of like mind maintain, is a partnership of equals intent on therapeutic goals possible? Is friendship between psychiatrist and patient permitted? What relationship, if any, is permitted when therapy has ended? How long before, if ever, a psychiatrist and former patient may begin a personal relationship? Are patients of psychiatric services or psychotherapy inevitably dependent persons dominated, to a greater or less extent by their therapist?

This case also highlighted some issues and questions regarding the law, in particular, features of the inquisitorial nature of tribunals which sit uneasily with the adversary system of common law jurisprudence. To what extent should the rules of evidence prevail? And especially pertinent, are those rules governing admissibility of hearsay evidence suspended in tribunals? The answer to this is that hearsay is admissible as evidence before most tribunals, before the Medical Tribunal, but not the Legal Profession Tribunal. How far does the burden of proof lie with the applicant and/or the complainant? The uncompromising punishment inherent in deregistration and loss of reputation is relevant in this case as in criminal trials. In this aspect tribunals are also different from courts, all that is required is 'reasonable satisfaction' or 'comfortable satisfaction' that the matters are demonstrated—something just a little more persuasive than 'balance of probabilities' in cases with severe implications. In the Medical Tribunal the expectation is that the patient who complains has little or no cause to mislead, but the practitioner has every cause to do so. Hence the probability lies with the doctor having done what is alleged.

The issue of greatest concern for this sociological analysis is the function that the deregistered psychiatrist serves in resolving a crisis in her profession. In regard to Childs' case: Was the catharsis of this sacrifice and this purging needed? Why was Childs the chosen one? Was she sufficient to the task of carrying away the 'evil' which beset psychiatry in Australia at that time? Can she return to her professional community? And finally, did the legal rituals of ritual punishment and expulsion work?

Others of Childs' persuasion were to follow. Many were her colleagues and former students whose practice of psychotherapy differed from that of the majority of the profession, and like Childs' therapy dismissed the significance of boundaries and disregarded the distinctions of status between therapist and patient. Her banishment did not avail. Further purges were to be found necessary.

Unlike the other major medical specialties, psychiatry has in recent years been riven by disputes and plagued by scandals, regularly exposed in the media and given currency in the gossip of those 'in the know'. The profession did not even have its own code of ethics as directive for behaviour. The Chelmsford Commission served to merely uncover what some had known and everyone had suspected. The profession had not acted, perhaps was unable to act, to set its world to rights. Patients had died needlessly, more were damaged, and many, it was whispered, were exploited. All in all it was an evil state of affairs. In the meantime the dissension over therapies raged and every enclave assailed the credibility and efficacy of the others. Demoralisation and disorder prevailed throughout the profession.

Helpless in the face of disaster psychiatry looked for where to lay blame and how good order might be restored. It failed to act to halt the scandals of Chelmsford—Parliament had ordered a Royal Commission to clean out those stygian stables. The sexual exploitation of patients, said to be rife, might be quashed by an exemplary case. So, it was inevitable that when the possibility of such a case came to the attention of the psychiatric establishment, to the RANZCP itself, it should be seized eagerly. There had been cases of sexual abuse and exploitation in earlier years, but they had been dealt with unobtrusively by reprimand, imposition of conditions on practice (usually the presence of a chaperone), and only once by deregistration. The practitioners involved were not important people: little was heard of their problems. But, now the times called for draconian action.

The complaint which now came forward implicated a female psychiatrist, prominent in a male profession and, at that time, one of only two female academic teachers in that discipline in Sydney. She later commented, 'I held three teaching positions, was influential with a strong student following and I was independent'. She practised psychotherapy, one of several contested modalities, but one with a strong following. As she stated to me in a meeting, 'I was the last link with an earlier period in academic psychiatry, with Maddison at Sydney University and Kiloh at University of New South Wales' (pers. comm., 14 Oct. 1995). Several years before the first complaint was raised, she had moved out of the mainstream of psychotherapy, of which she was openly critical. She drew eclectically from several school of practice to create humanistic psychotherapy, which stressed a more egalitarian, active partnership between therapist and patient. She was getting good results and was teaching about her style of practice in the universities. However, Dr Winifred Childs had become marginalised in the dangerously shifting fields of psychiatric practice. This marginalisation was replicated in her social milieu when her long marriage to a Senator disintegrated and her strong sockalist stance was perceived to lack the buttress of a leading man of the left. Then, when the first complaint was raised, she found colleagues, women and men, moving away from her: 'It seemed I had a contagion'. In retrospect she recognises the danger of her position. But who would have guessed her fate at that time?

The scapegoat of legend, vulnerable in its marginality, had to be worthy of the task. Where the disorder was great an insignificant victim will not avail to dispel the troubles. Such victims being useful only for annual ritual, and even then the victim was to be adorned and feted, and made special. Psychiatry was beset with troubles and a minor player would not do. Childs was highly successful, acclaimed by patients and former patients, popular with students and respected, if not liked, by colleagues in her university and college, as well as her profession. She was at the centre of debates about the direction psychotherapy should be taking.

Her very involvement in the intellectual arguments of her profession implicated her at the core of the disorder. She was steeped in the dissension. It took little more to plunge her into the midst of the scandal of sexual exploitation. The accusation of a disappointed and disturbed friend, formerly her patient, could do that.

Her therapies, moreover, were new, even creative and disrespectful of the difference between doctor and patient. Recall Girard's focus on the concept of difference, specifically loss of difference and lack of respect for difference, which is seen at the heart of disorder. In times of calamity the distinctions of people and institutions are swept away, and Childs' rejection of the distinction of power and status between doctor and patient could be seen as impious and disgraceful by her tribe.

The crowd turns out to repel the scapegoat. Epithets and calumnies can be heaped on it. The popular hero of Yeats' *Parnell's Funeral* was thus reviled at his trial and sent to his hanging. Childs was accused of disgraceful things beyond the particulars which eventuated at the Tribunal: she had committed fraud (the financial evidence dismissed the charge of medifraud); had slept with students (no evidence could be found); had determined to fornicate with several therapists (no evidence likewise found). Enough was found to condemn her. Much was made of the 'Doctor's Lesbian Encounter' (*Sydney Morning Herald*, 10 April 1990, p.3). Questions about the credibility of the complainant were not permitted.

The ritual of hearings, complaint and evidence, of specialist opinion and denunciation of offences, and of interrogation took many months. The Tribunal retired to return on an ordained date to deliver its decision. Much later the judicial hearing of the Supreme Court was restricted to deliberation on matters arcane to the one whose exile was now determined. The inquisitorial process achieved all. In the annual rituals of distant cultures various devices prevail on the animal scapegoat to shake its head in agreement with its fate. But in history human scapegoats are active, they reject and fight back. Childs did not agree and so found the calls for her contrition, her acquiescence, contemptible. She walked with courage. At this moment she confronts and refuses the myth.

Childs has not leapt into oblivion, but accepts with a sense of liberation her continued exile from the established profession of psychiatry. She cannot come back. Lest she doubt that, warnings are sounded: 'these psychiatrists who still practice as therapists will never be registered, can never come back into medicine' (*Sydney Morning Herald*, 5 April 1992, p.9). If the scapegoating is efficacious the evils will be borne away; to let the scapegoat return is to risk the return of disorder, the plague, the calamity, whatever required the expulsion in the first place.

The case against Childs decided, the psychiatry profession, in search of order and righteousness, found a suitable code of practice, largely borrowed from psychology and US laws governing psychiatry. The Code was promulgated by the RANZCP in 1992 (see Pargiter & Bloch, 1994 for a detailed exegesis of its derivation).

In the past five years Winifred Childs has built a busy psychotherapy practice which can be characterised as helping people through personal and institutional crises, teaching the means of coping with social adversities and human inadequacies, and instilling confidence and hope. She enjoys an excellent reputation as counsellor and friend. Childs remains active in politics and maintains her involvement with the intellectual movements. Excluded from her professional community she has found a new people.

Notes

1. *Phenomenology and the History of Psychiatry* (Beumont, 1992) provides a brief history of clinical psychiatry from its eighteenth century beginnings with the French physician Philippe Pinel, and reviews experiment and epistemology and the shifting status of psychiatry's conceptual models.
2. Looking back on Childs' practice the Chairman of the Institute, Dr Neville Symington, agreed that Childs' methods did not accord with those of his organisation and stated that the members were exasperated with her. In the context of a media interview he recalled that Childs' relationship with W had played a part in the Institute's decision to remove her from all official positions (*Good Weekend Magazine*, 8 Dec. 1990, p.67). This aspect had not been raised in 1987 when Childs was removed from the honorary positions held in the Institute, and this added rationale took her by surprise when she read of Symington's reservations.

CHAPTER 4

*T*he *C*ost of *J*ustice

In this chapter the scene shifts away from medicine and its specialties to the profession of law and its disciplinary practices. The central figure in this story is again a woman, of similar age and distinction to Winifred Childs, but of different style and temperament. Carol Anne Foreman was a woman of enviable repute for remarkable legal acumen and brilliant negotiating and advocacy skills on her clients' behalf (at one time she was regarded as Sydney's leading divorce lawyer and was a senior partner in one of the city's highly respected large law firms). But her aggressive expertise and tireless determination, which would be highly commended in a man, were seen as unbecoming in a woman lawyer practising in the Family Court. She was feared and respected and she resolutely resisted being set on the margins of the professions. During her twenty-five years in practice she had attained a fine reputation and continued to serve her profession well in lecturing and giving papers for the benefit of her peers and younger practitioners intent on family law practice. Foreman found herself the object of a complaint initially raised by a judge of the Family Court. The matters referred by Mr Justice Moss to the Attorneys-General (State and Commonwealth) and the Law Society of New South Wales arose out of evidence presented when a young woman brought an action to retrieve part of exorbitant fees charged for bitter divorce litigation.

Complaints about lawyers' fees recur endlessly through other places, other times and become legend in stories found in fiction and learned treatise. Shakespeare, Adam Smith, Charles Dickens and J.M. Keynes tell cautionary tales about the ruinous cost of buying the lawyer's defence. The public has always been concerned about the high cost of going to law. Stories of lawyers' excessive financial demands on their clients have long dogged the legal profession. But every so often this common body of complaint inflates disturbingly.

In recent years worries about the high cost of law (some say the high cost of justice) has excited public attention in the media including legal journals. Perhaps greater public expectations about access to law, inadequately met by legal aid schemes, highlighted the issue. Citizens have come to regard legal rights and remedies as essential services in a modern democratic state.

Public Opinion and the Cost of Law

In 1989 the Chief Justice of the High Court of Australia, Sir Anthony Mason, addressed the 26th Australian Legal Convention on the magnitude of legal costs. His speech was largely devoted to concern about government decisions to view court fees as an additional source of revenue. His widely publicised views also highlighted the overall cost of going to law. At that time a number of government inquiries into 'the cost of justice' were running at both State and Commonwealth level, and Law Reform Commissions in Victoria and New South Wales had accepted a reference from the Attorney-General to investigate legal costs including practitioners' fees. Law journals were also confronting these problems (see, for example, the 1989 issue of the *Law Institute Journal* devoted to the cost of justice). Certainly such articles tended to focus on the fees to file a matter for Court, costly delays and inefficiencies in the Court process, and the desirability or not of contingency fees. These costs impinged on the client but did not contribute to professional incomes, and the profession could blame the bureaucracies of the court system. Nonetheless, influential members of the profession were aware of public dissatisfaction. Earlier research had cited the two main reasons for public distrust and dissatisfaction with the legal profession as stemming from the excessive cost of legal services and the lack of communication between solicitor and client (Gandolfo, 1989, p.954).

By the late 1980s the media were concentrating attention on the problem, and their reports of the high cost of law put lawyers' fees on the public agenda. During that same decade the legal services business had prospered. Stimulated by buoyant economic conditions and significant extension onto global commercial law networks, the big city firms had grown prodigiously and acquired grand offices exquisitely furnished. Salaries and profit share enjoyed by partners in the big city firms were thought to be equally grand. Mergers, takeovers, receiverships and titanic struggles in the corporate world served to inflate legal fees and justified the ostentatious consumption reflected in the city firm's domain. In part it was the financial and commercial excesses of the 1980s which pushed up legal fees, as rapid structural changes, including tax minimisation, takeovers and mergers, were orchestrated from the law offices. Huge fees became commonplace and tax deductible. Law firms reflected success and status in the opulence of their premises, and in the lifestyles of their senior partners. Stories about excessive legal fees proliferated, the media criticised them, and judges condemned their behaviour in the courts.

The controversy was pushed along by a spate of protests about legal fees appearing in the newspapers early in 1991. *The Bulletin* took up the cry under the headline, 'People v Lawyers v Money' (Warneminde, 11 June 1991, p.28); the article citing the salaries and fees typical of the largest law firms, QCs and senior barristers. The article quoted a judge of the Queensland Supreme Court condemning lawyers' adherence to the 'Rolls Royce' model of practice rather than inexpensive operations to secure a quick result for their clients. And, with a significance to be seen later, the Chief Judge of the Commonwealth Family Law Court, Justice Nicholson, accused 'rapacious' lawyers of gross overcharging and of 'blatant rip-offs' (*Sydney Morning Herald*, 7 Dec. 1991, p.35). The Family Court was one of the places where the cost of law patently impinged on 'poor people' and the innocent.

The New South Wales Government of the day declared itself opposed to proposals to increase conveyancing fees and promised a review that would 'take the axe to legal costs' (*Sydney Morning Herald*, 22 July 1991, p.1). Its position oscillated during the following weeks and eventually some rises to the statutory charges were permitted by Parliament. The weight of conveyancing fees falls rather heavily on home-buyers, but this is the cheaper and more predictable end of legal services, the province of small, hard-pressed firms in city, suburbs and country towns. By November 1991 the focus shifted from the cost of law hurting 'middle Australia' to highlight the cut in subsidised legal services to low income-earners and Social Services recipients. The focus of such stories was on the high cost of law to the average citizen and the taxpayer. But the top end of the profession was not entirely ignored.

In August 1991 the *Sydney Morning Herald* ran a four-part feature on substantial court delays, high legal fees and costly restrictive practices entitled, 'Winners and Losers in the High Cost of Justice' (13 Aug. 1991, p.6). The concern of senior members of the State Governments and the Commonwealth Government was cited. One month later, the South Australian Attorney-General told the annual Australian Legal Convention that the fees charged by large commercial firms and senior counsel are 'symptomatic of the general malaise in Australian society' (*Sydney Morning Herald*, 10 Sept. 1991, p.2). Newspaper reports were peppered with comments garnered from speeches and commentary by members of the judiciary rebuking the legal profession for excessive fees, criticising the lack of independent scrutiny of legal bills, and pointing to the emotional trauma of going to law. In October of the same year, a *Sydney Morning Herald* editorial lamented 'The High Cost of Lawyers' (17 Oct. 1991, p.10), and called for the involvement of non-lawyers in royal commissions and similar committees of inquiry.

In 1991 a Commonwealth Senate inquiry into the cost of justice was asking questions, gathering evidence and not finding solutions. The New South Wales Attorney-General characterised the problem as the inaccessibility of legal services to all but the very wealthy and the very poor—those whose poverty entitles them to legal aid.

It was widely believed that the highest fees were exacted by the big city firms whose client were typically able to pay and did pay without unseemly protest. The newspaper stories did not point specifically to such firms, but the implications were patent. In writing a carefully researched feature article 'Matrimoney: Our Million Dollar Divorce Law Debacle' for the *Sydney Morning Herald* in December 1991, Valerie Lawson outlined several cases of apparent overcharging by 'a city lawyer' or member of 'a city law firm', but was properly cautious in identifying only solicitors already struck off or admonished by the Courts for such conduct (p.35, 38).

Complaints against lawyers taken to law society, legal ombudsman and other complaints handling bodies have always been numerous, and a small but constant number have been concerned about overcharging. Figures from the Law Society of New South Wales for the five years up to 1992 show such complaints running at about 100 per year against the State's 10,000 strong legal profession. Despite the high status of their profession lawyers have never enjoyed a good press. But the continuing publicity given to the issue of excessive fees and overcharging in 1990 and 1991 was unusually fierce. It fed the widespread belief that the excesses of 'greedy' lawyers were undermining access to justice by ordinary people buying a house, seeking a divorce, settling property, or dealing with the minor exigencies and crises of everyday life.

Judicial Criticism of the Cost of Law

Although lawyers were generally untroubled by public criticism of their fee structures, they could not so easily push aside censure from the Bench. By statute and long tradition, both solicitors and barristers are officers of the Courts of Law. They are enrolled as solicitors of the Court or called to the Bar of the Court after examination of their probity and competence, gained through stringent education and training in the law. The judges, presiding in the Court, are the ultimate disciplinarians of the profession. Self-regulation of the profession through peer pressure, and the sanctions of the law societies and bar councils is a proud and protected privilege, but behind and above this stands the judiciary. Several times in the course of interviewing judges about the discipline of the profession I was reminded of judicial surveillance and authority in the Court and in all matters related to the practice of law. That authority is symbolically invoked when law graduates appear before the Chief Judge of the Supreme Court to be called to take their place as barrister or solicitor of the Court. In statutory terms it is the Chief Justice, or his/her nominee, who presides over the Legal Profession Tribunal which hears serious complaints about the conduct of lawyers.[1]

Judicial concern was mounting. Some judges were outspoken, and have continued to be outspoken, about the unconscionably high cost of legal services. Judges whom I subsequently interviewed raised the problem, and some pointed to the excessive fixed costs of keeping up appearances, as well as maintaining the necessary infrastructure of a high-powered firm operating in the international commercial market. Moving into global markets has heavy cost implications. After reflecting on such costs one judge linked these to the extravagance of premises which take in magnificent views from several floors of a building at the high-price end of town. He continued by deprecating the time-charging practices which impelled partners and salaried solicitors to insist on a regimen of recording 'billable hours'. When I observed that monthly productivity targets imposed the heaviest stress on the most junior solicitors he dismissed my observation and insisted 'it's always been demanding work' (pers. comm., 17 Aug. 1993). Fees relate to work done; the real problem is that 'the firms, the senior partners link charges to time spent rather than performance or productivity'.

Judicial criticism of grossly inflated fees and apparent overcharging had to be taken very seriously by the profession. But how were the excesses to be curbed?

On 24 October 1991, after a four-day hearing, the Family Court ordered a significant reduction in the bills levied for the services of Foreman. Stories and commentary in the news media had already roused latent community anxieties about legal costs. Mindful of the profession's image and respectful of judicial admonition, the Law Society monitored these concerns. It is unlikely that any of this disturbed the large law firms intent on securing the work of corporate clients and success in the world market for legal services. Those at the centre of a scandal are often the last to know.

In a feature article about the troubles besetting Family Law procedures, journalist Valerie Lawson cited the fees in the Foreman case and quoted the Chief Judge of the Family Law Court, Justice Alistair Nicholson, as saying, 'Costs seem to be getting out of all proportion. A fee of $500,000—I find that appalling' (*Sydney Morning Herald*, 7 Dec. 1991, p.35).

The Status of the Profession and the Top Law Firms

The big city firms are seen as the top end of a prestigious profession. Richard Abel has commented on the Heinz & Laumann depiction of Chicago lawyers in the 1960s as being separated into two hemispheres quite different in status, clientele and style, as well as field of practice. Writing twenty years later Abel observed that this polarization had intensified to such an extent that a sharp distinction was now apparent between the 'elite' lawyers in the largest metropolitan firms and 'ordinary' lawyers representing small business and middle-class individuals (Abel, 1988, pp.228–32). David Weisbrot observed a similar, if less pronounced, division in the Australian legal profession where partners in major city firms, along with QCs, form the elite of the profession (Weisbrot, 1988, p.253).

Studies in many common law countries, including the United States, the United Kingdom and Australia, show that recruitment to a large metropolitan firm is based on the quality of academic credentials and the persuasiveness of the 'right' connections. Such connections, through family, school and associates, do count in Australia, but meritocratic criteria are more significant. The elite firms recruit on the bases of certified merit and an assumed intellectual rigour, as well as work ethic commitment. Law graduates who secure a place in these firms are typically the highest achievers who anticipate that the long hours and dedication to legal work and to the firm will bring the reward of high salaries and an eventual offer of partnership. These expectations are valid. Starting salaries for all law graduates are comparatively low in Australia, but the salary slope is steep and gratifying for those placed in the biggest firms. The most productive often secure a non-equity partnership after a decade or so of employment as a senior associate. Places in large city firms are eagerly sought by law graduates, and those marked by their university as brightest and best often score such a prize.

Organisational culture is strong. Solicitors, the partners as well as the salaried, work long hours in an intensely competitive world. The rhetoric endorses the importance of teamwork alongside a recognition of the excellence which specialisation can bring. The law in such firms, has always been a discipline to be practised with expertise and commitment. But economic change can shift priorities in any organisation. More intense competition in a tumultuous commercial environment has prompted revision of traditional management practices and continuous monitoring of fee structures and associated profitability. In the past large firms to ensure their productivity employed managers with expertise in accountancy rather than law, and these senior staff were responsible to the managing partner. The role of managing partner has now become more demanding and authoritative as the firm's goals are scrutinised. Signalling the immediate future, *Australian Business Monthly* (January 1992) profiled managing partners of leading national law firms. Illustrating the text of the article were photographs of tall handsome lawyers posed against backdrops of fine buildings and elegantly computerised offices. In response to the difficulties of a recession and the opportunities available in the international market for legal services, the major law firms were to grow larger and adopt best management practices and sophisticated accounting procedures. The skilful leadership of managing partners had become highly significant. With scholarly and practical acumen, Phillip King's widely respected text, *Professional Practice Management* (1995) tells the same story—that of the growing significance of the managing partner's authority in the successful law firm.

A Case of Overcharging?

On the 5 November 1991, a front page newspaper article proclaimed, 'Top Lawyer Quits after Row over Fee' (*Sydney Morning Herald*). Within this article the
newspaper linked the departure of the senior partner, Foreman, to excessively
high fees. Five years earlier, in 1986, she had been 'headhunted' and drawn away
from another large firm to run the family law division of Clayton Utz. Now she
appeared to have been forced out of that firm, although the newspaper could
only quote one of its senior partners as saying that Foreman's departure was 'by
mutual agreement'. The managing partner observed, 'family law fits more into a
boutique business. It's not a matter of income. It's a matter of strategic planning'
(*Sydney Morning Herald*, 5 Nov. 1991, p.1).

This story emerged from a review of the action taken some weeks earlier by a
client of Foreman. The client, who disputed her bill, had taken the matter to the
Family Court of Australia. This legal saga had commenced two years earlier
when the client, a young woman of a wealthy family, had begun an acrimonious
divorce action. She was grievously distressed by the violent marital breakdown
and had sought a substantial property settlement. While still contemplating her
options the young woman had engaged the services of Foreman, in one of the
largest law firms in the country, Clayton Utz.

At her first meeting with her lawyer the client had sought advice about possible divorce action. Two months later, after a violent domestic incident, the young
woman determined to proceed with a divorce. Her lawyer, Foreman, was widely
regarded as 'the best' and was famed for her skill in negotiating successful
outcomes for her largely female clientele. (Rather crudely it was claimed in Sydney's legal circles, 'if you want your husband's balls for breakfast, get Foreman'.)
Whether or not such fame creates a benevolent image, her prowess in divorce
matters and her skill in all issues before the Family Court of Australia were
becoming legendary. Foreman addressed legal conventions, lectured at semi-
nars and contributed generously of her expertise to her profession's continuing
legal education programs. But she was not popular with many of the legal fraternity. She was said to be aggressive, impatient and imperious. Certainly she
possessed an incisive intelligence and a capacity to work long hours—a combination prerequisite for success in the world of big city law firms. And as a lawyer
engaged to advocate her client's cause and interests in adversarial court settings, she was reputed to be a formidable opponent.

Foreman represented the young woman in her divorce action and secured a
settlement to the satisfaction of the client. The bill for these services, however,
was not deemed satisfactory by the client. There is argument about the size of
the bill, with one newspaper reporting it as 'more than $500,000' (*Sydney Morn-
ing Herald*, 7 Dec. 1991, p.35). The story sparked public disquiet: How could a

divorce cost so much?

Foreman had headed a team of lawyers who had worked for months on the case. Litigation had taken a total of 57 days in the Family Court and the commercial division of the Supreme Court. Several benefits (a house, a car, and alimony of $1000 a week) were negotiated, along with a cash settlement of $579,000. The legal costs, said to be $500,000, took almost all of that. Six months later, in February 1991, the client consulted another divorce lawyer and commenced proceedings against Foreman's firm over the fees charged.

In October 1991, after four days of hearing in the Family Court, the matter of excessive fees appeared to be settled and the client was refunded the difference between the fees charged and an itemised account calculated on the family law scale as routinely recommended by the Law Society. Approximately $80,000 of the half-million dollar account was returned to the client. This was the matter brought before Justice Moss and, although the law firm had conceded and settled, the Judge was sufficiently concerned to refer aspects of the matter further. The Law Society appears to have delayed for some time before responding, but it had already received a complaint from Foreman's own firm. (According to an article in *Justinian*, a satirical journal circulated mainly within the legal profession, the Law Society was, at that point, only investigating the alleged overcharging aspects of the Foreman case (July 1992, p.5).)

Much of the client's argument with the lawyer and the firm over the fees hinged on the existence of a costs agreement. Such an agreement, which would authorise specified rates for legal services considerably in excess of the schedule recommended by the Law Society, was commonplace for clients of very large firms. If a fees agreement had not been made, a client could approach the Court to review the account and, the appropriate calculations made, determine a reasonable charge in accordance with the schedule. In contradiction of the firm's assertions Foreman's client denied the existence of a signed costs agreement, and much time was spent on examining the authenticity of a copy of the said original agreement as distinct from one of a later date produced by the client's father. After prolonged argument the firm agreed to repay some of the fees paid. Because it had conceded the argument it could not rely on the disputed costs agreement; the copy, not the original, now in the firm's files was not acceptable to the Court. Nonetheless the firm insisted that a signed costs agreement existed.

Justice Moss of the Family Court was uneasy about various aspects of the case. There was the issue of overcharging. There was the possible collaboration in this divorce case of two solicitors, Foreman and another; this other solicitor had become a close friend of the wife, had formerly been the couple's solicitor, and knew the details of the husband's financial situation. Some little time later the Judge heard submissions about the conduct of the two solicitors to determine whether one had a conflict of interest (he assisted the wife's case although he had previously been the husband's lawyer) and whether Foreman had used information provided by that solicitor in the Family Law case which precipitated the fees dispute. A further issue, represented in the press as his central concern, was the existence or not of a costs agreement and hence the question of whether or not Foreman's charges were fair and reasonable. Justice Moss reviewed all submissions to determine whether there had been overcharging, whether the other solicitor had improperly provided confidential documents to Foreman, and whether Foreman had improperly applied such professionally privileged material to the case. After considering the submissions and arguments put before him, Justice Moss did not make any findings of professional misconduct against either solicitor. He observed that the original accounts had been subject to an assessment at the direction of the Court and had been reduced according to set scales.

This might have been the end of the matter with the Court intervening to ensure reasonableness in rendering an account for legal services. But concerns about the high cost of law had sharpened and Foreman's troubles continued. Also there was said to be a complaint, its nature unspecified, brought to the attention of the Law Society by Clayton Utz.

Excessive Legal Fees: Professional Misconduct?

The complaint taken up in the public domain was that of exorbitant fees. Newspapers continued to feature articles on the high price of justice. In the face of implied criticism the Law Society argued in favour of reduced fees for 'Aborigines and other needy people' (*Sydney Morning Herald*, 9 Mar. 1992, p.2). The President of the Law Society, John Marsden, denied that solicitors were responsible for inflation of legal costs and called for the judiciary to change the system to minimise delays and unnecessary court appearances (*Sydney Morning Herald*, 4 April 1992). In Victoria the Law Society's National President focused on the need to remove restrictions, including advertising restrictions, to promote higher standards without higher cost. Despite media protest in New South Wales, a new scale of barristers' fees provided a substantial increase in the base or standard rate. The Premier of New South Wales, along with Marsden, joined in vehement criticism of the barrister fee increases and a week later the daily press editorialised against the high cost of lawyers briefed to appear in government inquiries. The question of high legal fees was on the public agenda, but the issues were complicated and confused. For the public what mattered was the exorbitant legal costs.

Signs of Foreman's unpopularity with her profession had appeared in *Justinian*. The July 1992 issue featured an article entitled, 'Carol Foreman's

Family Law Special: A Story to Keep!' (p.1). This article gave details of the fees dispute and the issues bought before Justice Moss of the Family Court. The account was faithful to the details of the Judge's determination and comment, but the impression given of Foreman was unflattering. One month earlier the Discipline Committee of the Law Society had directed the Conduct Division to begin its investigations into the alleged overcharging aspects of the case. The Law Society now had a significant case to investigate. The lawyer in question was now a sole practitioner, Foreman having resigned the partnership in Clayton Utz.

Twelve months from the date that the complaints against Foreman had been lodged with the Law Society, proceedings commenced before the Legal Profession Disciplinary Tribunal.[2]

Proceedings before the Legal Profession Disciplinary Tribunal

The complaints brought against Foreman by the Law Society were particularised as:

1. Misleading the Family Court by:
   (a) producing a document different from the original time sheet when subpoenaed to do so; and
   (b) swearing in a false affidavit that a document which she produced was a copy of a Costs Agreement dated 7 September 1989, when she knew that this was not so.
2. Abusing the process of the Family court by including in her Affidavit matters irrelevant to the costs proceedings, but intended to dissuade the Applicant from continuing her costs application against the firm.
3. Propounding false documents namely
   (a) a copy of the time sheet of 7 September 1989, reconstructed by the solicitor; and
   (b) a copy of a letter to the client (the costs agreement) dated 7 September 1989, reconstructed by the solicitor.
4. Gross overcharging: a sum 'grossly in excess of a sum for legal costs which would be charged by Solicitors of good repute and competency' (*Legal Profession Disciplinary Reports*, No.1, 1994, at 2);
5. Improperly receiving and using facts and documents (provided by the wife's friend, former solicitor to the couple).

On the 10th day of the hearing the Law Society added further complaints that the solicitor either gave false evidence, failed to conduct herself with complete honesty and candour in giving her evidence to the Tribunal, or sought to mislead the Tribunal. These complaints related to her replies when questioned before the Tribunal about an interview she had given to a journalist from the *Sydney Morning Herald*.

Media attention fastened on one issue: gross overcharging for a divorce and settlement action. On the Saturday before the case opened a profile of Foreman was headed 'Piranha or Pussycat?' (*Sydney Morning Herald*, 31 July 1993, p.39); the accompanying cartoon depicted Foreman with a wide-eyed face, her body representing both a fish and a cat, along with a dollar sign for a tail. (The piranha reference arose from her reputation as a deadly opponent in courtroom battles.) In the article journalist Lindsay Simpson speculated on how Foreman's reputation as a highly successful female lawyer might bear on her current difficulties. In an interview with Simpson, Foreman avoided questions directed to her fees and hourly rates. She acknowledged the several matters of complaint, but gross overcharging dominated the discussion. The story from the interview reported Foreman's antagonism towards her former firm, which 'wanted to close family law down because it was not making enough money' (*Sydney Morning Herald*, 31 July 1993, p.39). The firm, she admitted, had 'sacked' her, and she had set up her own practice where she was free to set her own rates.

Newspaper reports of the first day of the hearing listed the matters of complaint but focused on one. Banner headlines pronounced 'Lawyer Accused Over Gross Overcharging' (*Sydney Morning Herald*, 3 Aug. 1993, p.2). Then, as the hearing continued over the weeks, the news of each day's hearings included reviews of the story so far and listed first 'gross overcharging', the fourth complaint in the Tribunal's catalogue. This simple issue, the high legal costs, dominated public debate in the media.

The Tribunal was told of Foreman's highly successful career in family law which had brought her to senior partner status in two of the city's major law firms. She claimed to be doing 'the best quality work for the highest quality clients', and had contributed significantly to the profession by writing and lecturing, and her involvement in continuing legal education. References from distinguished people and clients attested to her outstanding reputation as a solicitor.

The Tribunal heard from the managing partner of Clayton Utz that in late 1990 (after the conclusion of the divorce case whose aftermath led to complaints) the recently appointed managing partner had decided that the Family Law division of the practice should be closed because it was not paying its way. As she later told the court, Foreman knew of concerns about the profitability of her division before this date. Then, at a five-minute meeting in December 1990, this managing partner appeared, as Foreman recalled in the Tribunal, to put her career on the line. At that meeting she was told that she and another partner expert in family law would be moved from their specialist field to go and work for a junior partner in the firm. In the Tribunal Foreman spoke of this action as being as if her whole professional existence was being cut away. She entered a traumatic phase of her life. Later before the Tribunal she was to acknowledge her reputation as an outstanding family law practitioner and state that she gained 'enormous satisfaction from the respect and esteem of my peers ... apart from my family I had no other central issue in my life'. If she was in doubt about the significance of that meeting a memo a month later to all partners shattered any complacency: no further family law matters were to be accepted by the firm and that division was to be closed down.

In some ways the problems of profitability in the family law division were sociological. The slow return on work in progress stemmed from clients' (particularly female clients') inability to pay fees until divorce and settlement proceedings were concluded. Hence the firm 'carried' the costs till the end. Very few, if any, of the big city firms take up the divorce actions of their clients. In response to these inquiries such firms are likely to redirect potential clients to more appropriate, specialist firms, or suggest a smaller firm whose costing structures allow it to pay attention to what, regardless of the financial assets at stake, can be emotionally distressing proceedings.

When the managing partner had formally advised Foreman and the other family law partner of his concerns a prolonged series of memo-exchange followed. In evidence before the Tribunal, Foreman stated, in regard to those first three months of 1991, 'I was humiliated and not allowed to take on any Family Law matter' unless it was first referred to the managing partner. She felt she was 'unfairly treated and rejected by the partnership'.

Foreman had been quick to object to the firm's decision to close the family law division. In response the firm called an extraordinary partners' meeting on 23 March 1991, and determined that the family law division would operate on a strict commercial basis for six months until 30 September 1991 when its financial performance would be assessed. Foreman, who had sought the reprieve, accepted the trial from March to September of that year. In evidence to the Tribunal she said stated of this trial, 'I became totally cost driven ... increased my hours of work enormously'. Computer print-outs of hours worked commonly showed 12.5 hours daily, not including work done at home. She told of mounting stress: 'I kept working harder and harder and billing more and more ... I became isolated, stopped going to partners' lunches, ate in my office'. She found herself becoming 'extremely antagonistic towards some partners, specially those checking up on me', and her health deteriorated (she lost weight, had insomnia, and felt extreme irritability). Her staff, too, were overworked. But by the appointed day earnings and billings had improved dramatically and the indicators showed good financial returns for work done. The division for that period was, according to all financial indicators, the best performer in the firm. Foreman recalled, at the Tribunal, that by the end of that period she was close to breakdown, was not practising as she should, and was no longer 'caring and compassionate but just a cost collector'. She spoke calmly before the Tribunal:

> I had outperformed every single partner in the whole firm ... I couldn't have gone on because I was literally killing myself just to prove they were wrong.

The Gravest Offence

In July of the previous year, Foreman had revised her own papers to record the corroborated recollection that she had handed the fees agreement to her client in that divorce action. Her revision of her own records was not a problem; these were her records and were not altered to disadvantage the client. These matters eventually bore on the events on a Sunday in October 1991 when, in response to the client's claims of gross overcharging, Foreman rewrote documents to be produced to the Court. This became the crux of the Law Society's complaint, and was the inexcusable failing which undid a remarkable career.

Foreman told the Tribunal that on Sunday, 20 October 1991 she had been in the office and, among documents prepared for submission to the Family Court in relation to the dispute over costs, she had seen her original time sheet. She noted with alarm that it was not as she had revised for her own records, nor produced in discovery for the Court. She then created a reconstructed time sheet to conform with her revised copy. Subsequently she could not recall what, if anything, she had done with the original. She remembered feelings of panic and nausea, but not of what she had done with the original. Consequently she admitted to the Tribunal that she must have altered the documents. The trial of her division had just been completed and the figures were to be released the next day. This was not a time for anything to go wrong with matters in which she was involved.

The next day the reconstructed time sheet was produced to the Court as if it were the original. Because the costs dispute in which the reconstructed document was produced to the Court eventually settled, this deceit did not affect the outcome. The deceit, however, was discovered by the other partners of the firm, and on the following Sunday (27 October 1991) they confronted her with misleading the Court and demanded her resignation. Foreman claimed that the fee structure and management policy of the firm had driven her to 'practice in the manner that was not compassionate, not caring and being totally cost driven, was impossible, ... that policy forced me into my terrible error' (*Legal Profession Disciplinary Reports*, No.1, 1994, at 6). That she had felt embattled and stressed to the point of breakdown was not disputed. This may have counted in mitigation of the eventual penalty, but the Tribunal proceeded to decision: 'the solicitor persevered in a deceitful course of action to protect her career, her position in the firm and inevitably the firm's position in the costs proceedings brought by the client'. She was guilty of professional misconduct.

Related to this issue was the Law Society's complaint that Foreman had propounded a document which she knew to be reconstructed. With respect to this complaint the Tribunal acknowledged Foreman's apprehension of a 'pressure of a real, but not disabling nature' at the time of concocting the time sheet. But, to fabricate such a document and produce it to the Court as valid was further professional misconduct.

The Tribunal then turned to examine the complaint that there had been no costs agreement with the client in 1989 and that Foreman, as her solicitor, knew this. A finding on this matter would go to the matter of overcharging. The client's recollection of events given at two different times conflicted. Staff of the law firm recalled sighting the costs agreement which was misdirected, returned and lost again. The solicitor, the Tribunal reasoned, had no part in creating any costs agreement and was not aware of any such concoction.

The Tribunal examined the next complaint, that the solicitor had abused the process of the Family Court by producing an affidavit largely irrelevant to the issues for another unacceptable purpose. It was suggested that she wrote the affidavit to implicate another solicitor, a dear friend of the client, and so dissuade the client from proceeding. But the affidavit had been written on the advice of her barrister to show that the involvement of the other solicitor gave the client access to and the benefit of independent legal advice if she had wished to take it. Without a requirement for examination or cross-examination of any witnesses involved, the Tribunal dismissed this complaint: 'This complaint was misconceived ... failed to show any breach of duty by Miss Foreman' (at 13).

The most publicised complaint, that of gross overcharging, was not the subject of extensive examination of available evidence. The evidence and the earlier decision of the Family Court persuaded both sides. The issue came down to a determination about whether or not there was an agreement to accept charges at such a level or waive the client's concern about cost. Hence the complaint of gross overcharging was dependent upon whether or not a costs agreement existed. In view of evidence brought before the Family Court, and subsequently before the Tribunal, it was held that there was probably such an agreement, but either way the fees charged were not solely Foreman's responsibility. It became apparent, in evidence put before the Tribunal, that the charges made were those of the firm and were calculated by its accounts department. But, it was claimed, some personal responsibility lay with Foreman. As a senior partner she could not avoid all responsibility for the fees imposed on her client by the firm. But being satisfied that a costs agreement existed this complaint against the solicitor was dismissed. In making submissions counsel for the Law Society did not address this complaint. In its decision the Tribunal accepted that the complaint had been answered to its satisfaction, but stated nevertheless 'these issues should be flagged for the benefit of the profession' (at 2).

Then came the supplementary complaints that Foreman had either given false evidence, misled the Tribunal, or had not been candid and honest with the Tribunal regarding her recall of an interview with a journalist from the *Sydney Morning Herald*. The published text and, it soon appeared, the tape of the interview was made available to the Tribunal. Much of the questioning hinged on whether or not she had stated to the journalist that she was singled out because she was 'a high-profile woman', and the context in which this response emerged. Before the Tribunal Foreman had stated that she had not said such a thing. She further explained her denial referred to the whole sentence not just the phrase. In its determination the Tribunal stated it was troubled by the solicitor being 'inappropriately pedantic and evasive'. At no stage of the proceedings did Foreman or her counsel suggest that her troubles in the firm were the product of the manifest tendencies to exclude women from the senior ranks of the legal profession. Foreman had asked no quarter as a woman, although her exclusion from the fraternal elite in her own firm could be readily discerned as the evidence of her conflict with her partners unfolded.

The Tribunal pursued further the issue of what Foreman had said in the newspaper interview. The newspaper cited her as saying that there was one element of the complaint which she would admit to. When questioned during cross-examination about such an admission Foreman had denied it. Subsequently she was to claim that she had started to answer the journalist's question about alteration of documents when senior solicitor Mr Kim Garling, who had accompanied her to the interview, interrupted and answered for her. However, it was not clear from the newspaper's tape recording how that part of the interview flowed. Garling was not called to give evidence. The Tribunal was dissatisfied concluding that Foreman had not given false evidence or sought to mislead the Tribunal, but 'she had failed to conduct herself with complete honesty and candour' (at 14). That lack, they concluded, constituted professional misconduct.

Character references from leading members of the legal and accounting professions, as well as clients, attested to Foreman's outstanding reputation as a practitioner and person of the highest integrity. One QC, who examined the grounds of complaint and Foreman's admissions of altering a document, stated that he believed this was a serious error of judgment, in consequence of partnership pressures to which she was exposed at the relevant time, but it was completely out of character and not likely to occur in the future. His reflection on all aspects led to his conviction that such conduct would be so at variance with expectations of Foreman in the future that 'she would not thereby be established to lack the fitness and propriety required of a solicitor' (at 15).[3]

The Tribunal, like other professional disciplinary bodies, accords priority to the function of protecting the public against practices that fall below the requisite standard of competence, integrity and responsibility. The Tribunal reached a finding of professional misconduct on three counts which devolved from Foreman's producing a false document to the Family Court and, in one part of her evidence, failing to speak with complete candour and honesty to the Tribunal. Furthermore it held that any display by her of contrition was minimal. But it balanced against these findings her previous character and her reputation for honesty and integrity attested by the character references from her peers.

The Tribunal formally recorded its strong disapproval of the solicitor's professional misconduct and imposed a heavy fine—the $20,000 imposed is towards the upper end of monetary penalties available to it.

Implications of the Case So Far

People have always been critical of the cost of professional services, particularly legal services. At the time of Foreman's case, however, public interest in legal rights and remedies, including debates about a national Bill of Rights, had turned attention to 'the high cost of justice', particularly to escalating legal fees. To a much more significant extent the legal profession was itself sensitive to these debates, and that sensitivity was heightened by judicial disapproval. The time was ripe for someone to serve as an example to all.

Some years earlier the Law Society had investigated complaints about a solicitor's gross overcharging and had brought these to the attention of the Legal Profession Disciplinary Tribunal. The case ran for almost two years. In April 1991 the Tribunal found that his grossly excessive fees amounted to professional misconduct. The solicitor's name was removed from the Roll of Solicitors— he was deregistered. The solicitor, Vegelhyi, appealed the decision.[4] But Vegelhyi was not a big city solicitor, and his fate attracted little public attention.

When the newsletter *Justinian* ran a cover story on Foreman's fees and the end of her partnership with Clayton Utz, anxiety about excessive fees spread. This article was published fourteen months after Vegelhyi had been deregistered. Foreman's reputation as one of the best, perhaps the leading, divorce lawyer in the city ensured that a case involving her would serve as a lightning rod at the centre of the storm: the scandal of gross overcharging could be dissipated by one exemplary strike.

Clayton Utz submitted a complaint (or complaints), against Foreman to the Law Society. The nature of this initial complaint(s) was unknown, but by the time the Law Society came to investigate gross overcharging, it had become one of several complaints. It was only the allegation of gross overcharging, however, that seized the popular imagination of the community. Divorce had become a common trauma and here was a case of a young woman being grossly overcharged by a leading lawyer; this is how the media represented the client's plight.

The Law Society, as is proper for a professional association, was mindful of the profession's reputation, and they were aware that the high cost of law was diminishing this. The concern of the judges about access to justice and lawyers' fees generally was probably a greater stimulus to action. People have always baulked at the cost of legal services but the present judicial criticism weighed more heavily. The wider community was concerned, but the sense of alarm centred in the profession and impinged on its confidence about self-regulation, particularly its maintenance of control of its own field and its practitioners. The Society took time to thoroughly investigate Foreman's practice.

When the complaints concerning Foreman came before the Tribunal, a newspaper headlined the situation as, 'Lawyer accused of Gross Overcharging' (*Sydney Morning Herald*, 3 Aug. 1993). Foreman, however, was not found guilty of gross overcharging. Much was made of proceedings in the Family Court when the client had disputed her bill. Eventually that matter had been settled, a somewhat lesser amount agreed and approximately $80,000 of the earlier $500,000 charged was returned to the client. I listened to the evidence of witnesses called before the Tribunal and it appeared that accounts were charged by the firm. Foreman had kept a running record itemised on her time sheets of all activities undertaken on behalf of the client. Her hourly rate, as well as that of all partners and employed solicitors, was set as agreed by the partners of the firm. The time sheets were sent regularly to the accounts department which prepared accounts to be sent at regular intervals to the clients. If there had been gross overcharging it was the firm, not the individual lawyer, who was responsible. Foreman could not be laden with this guilt—the Tribunal dismissed this complaint.

Three complaints, however, were upheld: (1) she had misled and intended to mislead the Family Court by failing to produce the original time sheet and producing another document which differed materially from the original; (2) she had propounded a false document (the reconstructed time sheet) to the Court; and (3) in relation to the interview she had given to the *Sydney Morning Herald* reporter, she had failed to conduct herself with complete honesty and candour in giving evidence the Tribunal. On all three counts the Tribunal found her guilty of professional misconduct. Strong character evidence and her own prior reputation persuaded the Tribunal that it should not remove Foreman from practice as a solicitor:

> The disciplinary and protective obligations of the Tribunal will be fully met
> by the imposition of a fine serious enough not only to mark the Tribunal's
> strong disapproval of the Solicitor's conduct but also appropriate to the
> circumstances of the case (at 17).

Foreman had avoided the worst penalty, that of removal from the Roll of
Solicitors. She had not been driven out, nor had she taken on the shame of gross
overcharging which had seemed near to slipping on to the firm which had ejected
her. Matters to her discredit had been uncovered before the Tribunal and her
'escape' was deplored in many sectors of her profession. She had misled the
Court and the extenuating circumstances of her partners' severe and prolonged
pressure to discontinue her division, her field of expertise, was dismissed as part
of the stress inevitable in the practice of law. If she had been marked, she was
now maimed.

The Law Society appealed the determination claiming that the Tribunal had
erred in settling a fine of $20,000 rather than removing her name from the Roll of
Solicitors. Shortly after this appeal was lodged, Foreman cross-appealed and
took issue with the finding of unprofessional conduct arising from one supplementary complaint (complaint (3) above), and with the order that she pay the
Law Society's costs in the Tribunal.

The Appeal to the Supreme Court

Appeals against determinations and orders made by the Legal Profession Disciplinary Tribunal may be a hearing de novo, that is a hearing of all matters of fact
and a determination on the basis of the relevant law. The Law Society's appeal
sought Foreman's deregistration; they did not appeal against findings on matters in which Foreman was exonerated. In particular the Law Society did not
appeal the issue of gross overcharging. It had become apparent in the Tribunal
that Foreman had merely recorded her time to be charged at the firm's agreed
hourly rate, as had other members of the firm, whether partners, employed solicitors or paralegals. All accounts were signed by the partners, as well as Foreman.
Some comments in the Appeal judgment were directed to excessive fees, but the
burden of gross overcharging had slipped from the solicitor and it was not in
contemplation that it might fall on the firm or elsewhere.

Foreman told the Tribunal that she first altered her copy of time sheets to
represent what happened during her first interview with her client in September
1989. This alteration was done some time later when collating her records for
management and long before the client's objections to her account were brought
before the Family Court. But on the day before this time sheet and other documents were required by the Court she had noted that the firm's earlier photocopy

of the original now differed from own amended photocopy, and she altered the document which the firm had readied for production to the Court. She knew she had altered her copy of the original many months earlier (so that her record complied with her recollection of events). She was later to describe her actions as 'completely shameful and dreadful'. During the trial to assess the division's profitability she had worked ceaselessly and performed at the highest level. Her physical and emotional energies were totally depleted by the ordeal.

Confronted with what she had done she had been forced to resign her partnership and had since established her own firm specialising in Family Court matters. Clayton Utz brought a complaint to the Law Society; the date of this action is not on record, but ten months after she had left the firm, in August 1992, the Law Society filed a formal complaint(s) against Foreman. A year later the Tribunal had reached its decision.

The three judges of the Appeal Court upheld the finding of professional misconduct in respect of misleading the Family Court. All took a very serious view of Foreman's conduct. They did reject the Tribunal's finding that she had failed to act with honesty and candour in giving evidence before it of her interview with the *Sydney Morning Herald* reporter. There was a measure of agreement that Foreman was most unlikely to commit such an offence again. The decisions of the Tribunal, and subsequently of the Court of Appeal, reflect the protection of the public not punishment. But, it was argued, a solicitor should be able to be trusted 'to the ends of the earth' and failing this should be expelled from practice. Mahoney J noted that in such a decision three factors should be considered: fitness to practice, deterrent, and reputation of the profession. The reputation of the profession is of foremost importance, the plight of the practitioner secondary.

On 6 May 1994 the hearing concluded. Three months later the Court handed down its finding of professional misconduct. The majority ordered that Foreman should be removed from the Roll of Solicitors.

The Presiding Judge, Justice Kirby, favoured a different and novel penalty. His judgment accepted the enormity of the pressure on the solicitor and the manifest unlikelihood that she would ever offend again: 'it is sad that one default will result in her removal from the profession in which she has practised successfully for many years'. Kirby proposed that her practising certificate be cancelled, that she secure employment as a solicitor in a community legal body offering legal advice to disadvantaged persons (such as the Legal Aid Commission or the Aboriginal Legal Service), and after four years consider reapplying for a full practising certificate. She had, however, deceived the Court, and Kirby P found her conduct as reprehensible as did Mahoney J and Giles J, despite factors in mitigation—the pressure she was under, the trust and regard in which she was held by her referees, and her assurance that she would not do such a thing again.

Mahoney J and Giles J ordered that she be struck off the Roll of Solicitors, and so it was decided.

A newspaper headlined the outcome, 'Struck off: The Piranha in a Power Suit' (*Sydney Morning Herald*, 6 Aug. 1994, p.1).

Much of the judgment of both Kirby P and Mahoney J was devoted to the issue of excessive legal fees. This matter had not been raised by the Law Society in the evidence called or in submissions, but the Bench was not of a mind to ignore it. During the hearing and in judgment attention was given to the pressure for profitability. It had to be recognised that in 'this cost-driven age of meeting budgets and targets solicitors choose to and do practise in that environment'. The important issue was the fiduciary obligations of a lawyer. These took into account 'the power of the solicitor to engage and so charge for other staff on a time basis; and the conflict of duty and interest which may arise under a costs agreement for costs on a time basis' (Mahoney J, *The Council of the Law Society of New South Wales v. Foreman* (1994) CA40607/93 at 22). Mahoney J did not revert to the complaint of gross overcharging on Foreman's part, but pointed to the budgetary pressures placed on her conflicting with her fiduciary obligations and the consequent toll on her energy.

Although the issue of gross overcharging had not been addressed by the Law Society's appeal against the Tribunal's orders regarding Foreman, the Judges of the Appeal Court took this up in their decision. Kirby P found it 'virtually incredible that legal costs in a dispute between a married couple over matrimonial property could run up legal costs in the figures mentioned here' and, added to others, close to 'half a million dollars' (at 21). He pondered whether the Court should order an investigation, 'it appears astonishing and prima facie appalling' (at 21). The Court, he stated, can and should request the Law Society to investigate this matter further, concluding:[5]

> Time charges have a distinct potential to result in overcharging ... I depart from this case with a real sense of disquiet that what may arguably be the most serious issue revealed by it may not have been fully considered in a way protective of the true standards of the legal profession and the legitimate expectations of the community ... the judges should not put on blinkers when a fundamental problem is disclosed. As it is, in my view, by this phenomenon in this case (at 22).

The Law Society, which did not proceed further against the solicitor, has done nothing in relation to the firm, Clayton Utz.

Foreman sought to appeal to the High Court, but the appeal was not allowed.

The Ongoing Problem of Grossly Inflated Fees

The judiciary continued in their concern about excessive legal fees which acted to limit ordinary individuals' access to law. There are few cases where the complaint of gross overcharging is central to matters brought before the Legal Profession Disciplinary Tribunal. Some time before the Foreman hearings, Veghelyi's case had brought such an opportunity for public repudiation of grossly excessive fees. In 1989 complaints about solicitor Anthony Veghelyi had been raised by over forty of his clients. The Law Society had investigated the complaints and found that the majority were about gross overcharging, although some suggestions of misappropriation or misapplication were also raised. The Tribunal hearing had continued intermittently over twenty-two days during 1989. Before a decision was announced a member of the Tribunal had died suddenly. With a new member appointed the Tribunal reconvened the following year to take further evidence and hear submissions by counsel for the solicitor and the Law Society.

In April 1991, at the end of the prolonged and intermittent proceedings, the Tribunal found against the solicitor on many issues. These included eleven matters of gross overcharging, eight of appropriating moneys to himself for professional costs without the client's authority, and three of misconduct at common law. The pattern of professional misconduct was confirmed by the multiplicity of cases where gross overcharging or misapplication of client's money occurred. A significant aspect of the decision was that among the adverse findings, gross overcharging was found where fees ($215,810) for a Family Law matter had been charged in 1986. The matter was unusually difficult and complex: the client was extremely demanding and required the solicitor's utmost time and attention without particular regard to cost. The Tribunal accepted these submissions, but found the fees charged were too much and charged with gross overcharging amounting to professional misconduct. Veghelyi appealed the decision. Attention in the daily press had been minimal.

In February 1995, almost four years after the Tribunal's decision, the Appeal came before the Court of Appeal of the Supreme Court of New South Wales. Their decision agreed with the findings of the Tribunal on all but two matters and held that the solicitor should remain deregistered. No account of the outcome was found in the Sydney press.

The Court, however, took the opportunity to clarify important issues about the conduct of legal practitioner disciplinary hearings. Three of Mahoney J's dicta are instructive for the purpose of this study[6]. The third of his dicta addressed his concern about inflated legal fees: 'Gross overcharging may of itself constitute professional misconduct' (*Vegelyi v. Law Society of New South Wales*, CA 40237/91 at 7). This had not been judicial opinion in the nineteenth century but it was clearly so in the twentieth century. Earlier views notwithstanding the Courts have traditionally exercised control over excessive fees and unnecessary demands made by solicitors. Clients are often vulnerable to their solicitors and in making decisions ordinarily place trust in their solicitors. Lawyers are in a position of advantage by virtue of their knowledge and familiarity with their professional work and trust is placed in them. This view is followed in both the United Kingdom and the United States where a lawyer's fees should be reasonable, and violation of that rule constitutes professional misconduct. Many factors bear on what is fair and reasonable. Such determinations do take account of what other solicitors are charging for such work, and might include an analysis of the solicitor's practice, the resources available and its location geographically and in the professions' hierarchy.

Foreman: Was She a Scapegoat?

From 1990 media reports on the high cost of justice sharpened public anxiety about escalating legal fees. Lawyers and their professional association, the Law Society of New South Wales, became more sensitive to public concern when the judges took up the issue and used any opportunity to voice their alarm about what was becoming a scandal. The Courts too were also being criticised about purported inefficiency and delay, but the focus was on lawyers' fees. Excessive charges are difficult to control and the fees of the largest firms fees are often the most. A successful prosecution against a high profile lawyer could have a deterrent effect and could reassure the public that the Law Society was acting to control gross overcharging.

Veghelyi's case might have been exemplary, but it did not capture public attention. Veghelyi had practised in a country town and in outer suburban Sydney; he was not a notable figure and the complaints against him, with the possible exception of one divorce case, related to unremarkable compensation and minor commercial matters. The order for his removal from the Roll of Solicitors was not noted in the daily newspapers. Many lawyers are the subject of complaints brought to the Legal Profession Disciplinary Tribunal but only the very well known, the big city lawyers, feature in the daily press. This contrasts with the scrutiny of medical practitioners who are brought before the Medial Tribunal and possibly evidences the activism of Health Complaints bodies.

There seemed to be no ready cure for the malaise diagnosed by the judges. The illness was endemic at the elite end of the profession whose ostentatious style and profitability was fed by the fees met by litigious corporations and rich clients. These firms claim to be the 'best' and few individuals can afford their services. The cure for habits of gross overcharging would require rigorous practices of austerity. These were not in prospect.

The profession made claims about self-regulation and the Law Society was the body responsible for its invigilation. How was it to demonstrate its care for the integrity and responsibility of the profession?

Then Carol Anne Foreman was caught in the spotlight. She became a successful solicitor and for many years was the wife of a leading solicitor and a former Lord Mayor of Sydney. After their separation her career had developed even more strongly. Foreman was a distinguished practitioner regarded by many as the best divorce lawyer in town. At a time when few women were achieving senior partnership, she had won that status with one large city law practice and had then been 'headhunted' to join another of the top firms. Family law is not the most prestigious area of legal practice, but Foreman had successfully represented some very distinguished citizens. By all accounts she was not liked by her colleagues in this male dominated world. Her very success in such an emotionally charged field of practice militated against popularity. And, as was to become clear, she was not liked by the other senior partners in Clayton Utz. Foreman was a highly successful woman in a field where few women were tolerated. Her fame made Foreman a marked woman.

One of her clients had brought an action against Foreman for gross overcharging in the carriage of the young woman's divorce and property settlement matter. Both the woman's wealthy connections and the legal fees charged ensured extensive media coverage. The case was settled, but Foreman's partners moved against her and demanded her resignation. This move damaged Foreman and put her at the centre of the scandal about gross overcharging by big city lawyers. Could she be laden with the burden of overcharging and carry the trouble away?

As has been told, her former partners brought a complaint against her, the Law Society commenced its investigations and filed five separate complaints. The Tribunal proceeded with great deliberation and examined each exhaustively. The Legal Profession Disciplinary Tribunal, unlike other professional tribunals, must observe the rules of evidence, framed on the basis of a presumption of innocence. The proceedings are adversarial. The two senior lawyers and one layperson hearing this matter were assiduous about fair play and attended to arguments about natural justice (most notably in determining whether supplementary complaints might be brought). The Tribunal reserved its decision and one month later found professional misconduct proved. It reviewed all aspects of the matters of complaint and in the light of these ordered a substantial fine—but not the deregistration of the solicitor. Entering into its deliberations was a recognition of the extreme stress under which Foreman had been working up to the day of the misconduct. Not only had she worked excessively long hours for many months, but these had been sustained under the threat of the closure of her department and her relegation to a diminished and, to her, an ignominious position. And she had suffered intense isolation during that period. She had erred and had suffered extensively on that account. She was not likely to err again. The principle of protection of the public was not at issue. She was castigated, incurred a heavy financial penalty and was to be allowed to continue in practice.

But the Law Society was not prepared to let her go, punished yet free, to continue in the profession. It again moved against her.

At the first disciplinary hearing the complaint of gross overcharging had not been demonstrated. But the media reports had tarred her reputation with that brush. In the public view she had charged half a million dollars for a divorce, she could typify the worst evils of the legal profession. Furthermore, the hearing had found in her a fatal flaw which opened under awesome pressure, a flaw which brought her down. Foreman had been marked before she was brought before the Tribunal and, although it had acted fairly and, some thought, too gently, the outcome crippled her.

After the Law Society appealed against the Tribunal's lenient orders, the Supreme Court viewed her misconduct more severely. She had misled the Court; her action struck at the trust which sustained the operation of the law and its Courts. Their penalty was heavy and exemplary. Only one of the three judges did not favour banishing her from practice, but he did not carry the day.

Writing for a national daily, the *Financial Review*, shortly after the Appeal Court handed down its judgment, Richard Ackland found in the Foreman case 'a devastating condemnation of commercial lawyers, firms' (11 Aug. 1994, p.16). Perhaps the charge of gross overcharging was brought to the wrong quarter, but it had stuck with her. And the issue troubled the Appeal judges who used the occasion to again ask the Law Society to address the issue. But it could not be imposed on Foreman or, indeed, at this stage, her former firm Clayton Utz.

The Law Society had taken action to deal with the scandal of gross overcharging which was bringing the profession into disrepute. It had seized on a highly successful female solicitor, but a woman resented for the aggressive brilliance and persistence with which she represented wealthy women seeking divorce and settlement of property. Foreman had fallen out with her colleagues, been ousted from the firm and set up her own independent practice. She was distinguished, but she stood alone. She had been at the centre of the scandal about the $500,000 divorce, and the criticism in the Family Court hearing had marked her deeply. She could carry away the burden of disgraceful overcharging of an injured public. But she walked clear of the complaint of overcharging. It might have fallen elsewhere but the only valid 'carrier' was her firm. It was not marked, not marginal, not even extraordinary. It stood among the 'top ten' firms, and was in no way different. If it had been brought down, the others could have fallen with it. But, Foreman had been sufficiently implicated. To the public she

was the archetype of the barbarously aggressive, viciously greedy lawyer—
'The Piranha in a Power Suit'. She was shamed and pilloried and thrown out of
the profession.

Foreman's case is riddled with contentious issues. Here was a woman highly
reputed in her profession who caved under pressure, and falsified a document.
That count felled her. Here was a woman whose excellence was edged with
arrogance and assertion, a most aggressive advocate, the lawyer who demol-
ished the husbands of women seeking their share of the wealth. She was disliked
and feared in the offices and courts of family law. Here was a woman prominent
in her exalted position as senior partner in an elite, metropolitan law firm which
had demonstrably grossly overcharged one of her clients; her firm, found by the
Family Court to have overcharged a wealthy young woman, typified the best
and most feared of the big city firms. She could be loaded with the mischief of
habitual exorbitant charges. The newspapers had so labelled her; she could be
driven out of the profession with great fanfare. And so she was.

The scapegoating did not succeed. Legals costs continued to rise inexorably
and ordinary people felt that justice was denied them. In March 1994 eight Supreme Court judges agreed to speak publicly and denounced charges 'which
increase the price of justice for ordinary Australians' (*Sydney Morning Herald*,
p.1A). The issue, however, did drop from political agendas. Thus, for a little
while the gods of public opinion were appeased. But fear and anger returned.

The judges began again to castigate the profession. In 1995 Sir Justice Daryl
Dawson of the High Court of Australia resounded themes raised by Sir Anthony
Mason, then President of the High Court, in his 1989 address to the Australian
Legal Convention (reported in *Australian Law News*, Sept. 1989, pp.11–13).
Dawson J reviled lawyers' 'preoccupation with the making of money' (*Austral-
ian Lawyer*, Nov. 1995, p.10). Complaints about overcharging continue to rise;
40 per cent of client complaints now relate to overcharging. To this day newspapers are still documenting the issue: 'Damning Verdict on Lawyers' (*Sydney
Morning Herald*, 2 April 1997, p.1); 'Clients in the Dark on Legal Costs' (*Daily
Telegraph*, 2 April 1997, p.9). The Legal Services Commissioner denounced the
soaring legal fees which now place access to law beyond the reach of 'the
common person'. That one aspect was what the reporting journalists gleaned
from the *Annual Report of the Legal Services Commission of New South Wales
1995–96*. Overcharging is just one of many causes for complaint against legal
firms, one that does not seem to diminish.

The Commissioner's primary message in the 1995–96 report however differed
from the much emphasised issue of overcharging: 'People seeking the help of a
legal practitioner are almost always seeking justice, and are often disappointed
when what they actually receive is the law' (p.3). In interview with me shortly
after his appointment Commissioner Stephen Mark declared, 'what people have

to understand is all they can get is law; law is not about justice'. The pity of it all is that this self-styled 'consummate bureaucrat' could be right.

Notes

1. Recent legislation in some states has vested the authority of Tribunal in senior members of the profession, but appeal in all aspects of law and fact, lies with the Supreme Court of the state.
2. My research associate and I observed and took notes throughout the Tribunal's hearing over 13 days in August/September 1993. This account relies substantially on the judgment handed down by the Tribunal and our observation of events recorded in contemporaneous notes taken during proceedings.
3. In court proceedings character references typically go to sentence not to the question of guilt or not.
4. The decision of the Appeal Court some years later was to constitute another significant attempt by the judiciary to address the scandal of lawyers, i.e. solicitors' and barristers' fees.
5. Courts in other states, at this time, had begun to deal with gross overcharging by legal practitioners.
6. The issue of professional misconduct inherent in gross overcharging taken up in detail by the judges in *Veghelyi v. Law Society of New South Wales* (CA 40257/91, October 1995, unreported) has relevance to the overall concern of this study about the safeguards against injustice in the Courts. The judges, two of whom had heard the appeal against the Foreman decision, took the opportunity to deliberate at length on the problem of gross overcharging. In this case other procedural justice issues of relevance to the subject matter of this book were addressed (see Chapter 7). These include:
   a) The onus of proof on the professional body was reaffirmed as the civil standard. Mahoney J found a matter proved 'if I were comfortably satisfied of it bearing in mind the gravity of what was sought to be proved' (Priestley J at 3).
   b) Appeals can be of three kinds: (1) appeals involving a hearing *ab inititio* (all aspects reheard); (2) appeals both upon fact and law, but limited to those facts before the court or tribunal appealed from; and (3) appeals only on questions of law. Appeals against a decision of a Medical Tribunal can only be on basis of law. In contrast appeals against a Legal Profession Disciplinary Tribunal can be of any of those types and are often of the first *ab inititio* character. The reasons advanced for this are firstly that a disciplinary proceeding against a lawyer can destroy personally, professionally and financially; 'That is essentially the reason why the legislature enacted that such appeals shall be dealt with by this Court' (Mahoney J at 4.)

CHAPTER 5

*A S*candal of *C*hurch and *S*tate

Members of a profession live quite intently within that group and assume unreflectively its identity along with an assimilation of its values, ideas and ways of thinking and acting. But, very few people live their lives in one sphere only. For most of us the spaces of our belonging and becoming are multiple, like circles or ellipses overlaid and merging and centring on the self, the project of our own becoming. Most people have separate lives at work and with family and friends. For some their training and experience take them into different fields of work and allow additional occupational identities. These people can identify with more that one profession; an academic lawyer, an engineer manager, or an actor/director exemplify such roles. The men, whose stories are told in the next two chapters, moved in more than one professional sphere and could identify with two professions. They appeared to have more options and could feasibly find acceptance in one profession to obviate the antagonism of the other. They had a part in their fate, but the groups to which each belonged determined much of what occurred.

Events placed Harry Whelehan at the centre of a crisis which brought down the Irish Government in 1994. Whelehan is a barrister of distinction, a Senior Counsel, and for three years the Attorney General of Ireland. He was a curious candidate for sacrifice to the twin gods of public opinion and political expediency. Whelehan is set centre stage in this interpretation of events as the unlikely hero of this drama.[1]

Irish Public Life

The elements woven into the fabric of public life vary from one country and culture to another. Invariably, however, these include a commitment to family and the wellbeing of children, an anxiety about persons in positions of trust, and a demand (sometimes unmet) for the integrity of the law and its judicial and administrative officers. In many nations religion is also tightly enmeshed in the prevailing political culture. In Ireland the Catholic Church retains a pervasive influence on the practices, morality and laws of the nation. Although it is widely believed that the Church's conservative hold on the character of Irish life has been slipping throughout this century, Catholicism is incorporated in the national identity and the Church is its most respected public institution. Religion and politics are linked in the public life of this country. Its citizens rejoice in a reputation for eloquence and wit, a sheer intoxication with the word, written and spoken. This delight in 'the good talk' is filled out by an enthusiasm for knowing and analysing events as they occur and as they are played out in the public arena.

A long history of British colonisation and suppression, the continuing troubles in the north of their island, and the proximity of Great Britain have undoubtedly served to intensify the sense of national identity and solidarity of the Irish Republic. Ireland is a small nation of just over three million people; they are well educated and most take a keen interest in politics and religion. The ruling elite of the country are well known, their activities chronicled by a press intent on investigation and analysis for an avid readership. This small nation of educated citizens, firmly set on being informed and vigorous in voicing their views, is as close an approximation to the ideal of the Greek *polis* as is likely to be seen in the late twentieth century world.

The growth of strong professional elements in the nation states of the twentieth century ensure that the members of any profession assume significant roles in the public life of a country. In all countries where the legal profession flourishes many of its members are invariably drawn into the business of politics as legislators, advisers, managers and administrators and as members of Parliament. So much of the business of government is legislative and lawyers are skilled in its formulation and essential to its drafting. And, as highly educated and active citizens trained in matters germane to parliamentary process, lawyers who enter politics assume key positions in Cabinet or Executive with relative ease. Lawyers are, and have long been, prominent in public life in Ireland.

The ordering of public life depends critically on the authority of the Irish Constitution. The Constitution of the Irish Free State was approved as the first legislation passed by *Dáil Eireann* (the lower house of parliament) in 1922. When Ireland moved to full independence in 1937, a new Constitution, *Bunreacht na hÉireann*, was put to the people in referendum. In a manner reflecting its intellectual inspiration from the eighteenth century revolutionary thinking of France and the United States, the Irish Constitution, like the Australian Constitution, enshrines the separation of powers to ensure freedom from arbitrary power. Additionally the Constitution guarantees basic protection for fundamental human rights. Although the designers of the 1937 Constitution were intent on breaking free of any perceived connection with British rule, the shadow of Westminster does fall across the Irish system of government and the traditions of common law remain apparent. Generations of Irish lawyers trained in London, Edinburgh and Dublin had mastered that intricate model, and much was carried into Ireland when the emancipatory legislation was drafted. As with other countries' constitutions, they imported what they thought best from around the world and most readily used the materials with which they were familiar.

As elsewhere, this expression of the will of a Sovereign People is the source of power for legislature, executive, and judiciary. The Constitution is the sole legal basis for the validity of the institutions of the State. Specifically these are the judicial system of Courts, the parliamentary system, that is the *Oireachtas* consisting of the *Dáil Eireann* and *Seanad Éireann* (the Senate), and the Executive or Cabinet. The head of the executive, *An Taoiseach*, is in Australian terms the prime minister and the second-in-charge, *Tanaiste*, the deputy prime minister.

Central to the events in this chapter is the office of Attorney General described in Article 30 of the Constitution as the legal adviser to the Government. The central significance of this office is apparent from Article 30 which specifies the office-holder's responsibilities. (Only two other offices within the legislature and executive are detailed in the Constitution, those of the Taoiseach and of the Comptroller and Auditor General). The Attorney General is appointed by the President of Ireland on the nomination of the Taoiseach and the Government. The Attorney General is not a member of government and reports to the Taoiseach not the Parliament. One of the several conventions of the office insists that the Attorney General be a member of the Bar, a senior counsel and the leader of the Bar on all ceremonial occasions. As legal adviser to government, the Attorney General examines all proposed legislation to be drafted from that office, represents the State in constitutional matters (upholding the constitutionality of any legislation being challenged), and, since 1987, scrutinises and acts on extradition requests from foreign governments.

The powers, authority and responsibilities of the Taoiseach are set out in Article 28 sections 5–11 inclusive, of the Constitution, and include the conditions which may give rise to the Tanaiste's deputising for the Taoiseach. The powers of the Taoiseach are extensive and at law the Tanaiste is only a minor player—a condition that would frustrate an ambitious and energetic leader.

As a visitor to Ireland I was struck by a universal reverence for the Constitution as the sacred text authorising rights and governing Irish society. The Constitution, born of centuries of struggle, proclaims the sovereignty of the Irish people as ultimate temporal authority in that land.

Politics and Religion

In the late 1980s the Catholic Church was making headlines when a number of scandals about the sexual activities of its priests and bishops titillated the public's imagination. These scandals concerned heterosexual affairs between adults and, although there was evidence of abuse of power and position, these could be seen as a human frailty, as sins to be forgiven. Sexual abuse of children, however, is quite another matter and stories about the incidence of this type of crime greatly agitated the public conscience. The emergence of the details of the nefarious career of Father Brendan Smyth, a priest of the Norbertine Religious Order, crystallised the issue of clerical sexual abuse of children. Smyth was to be the focus of a scandal that dismayed the Irish people and plunged its political life into turmoil.

The evidence of Smyth's continuing child abuse over several decades invoked a horrifying scandal which shook public confidence in the integrity and trustworthiness of the Catholic Church. The account of his many years of sexual molestation of children had been the subject of an Ulster Television feature entitled 'Suffer the Little Children' shown on Irish Television on 2 October 1994.[2] The reporter, Chris Moore, went on to publish a full account of his investigations in the book entitled *A Betrayal of Trust: The Father Brendan Smyth Affair and the Catholic Church.*

As in other countries in recent years the Irish people had already been dismayed to hear of cases of child sexual abuse involving clergy and religious. Other clerical sexual misdemeanours had made headlines: the Catholic Bishop whose affair had left his lover with no moral support and meagre financial assistance for rearing their child; the priest who suffered a fatal heart attack while engrossed in unpriestly conduct in a gay bar. But the uncovering of Father Smyth's continuing sexual abuse of the children of friends and parishioners in Ireland and the United States provoked a storm of adverse publicity. The scandal increased when it appeared that the priest's offences and proclivities had long been known to his religious superiors at the Norbertine Abbey in County Cavan, Northern Ireland. For over thirty years Father Smyth had been indulging an unnatural attraction to children. For more than twenty-five of those years his abusive activities were known and arrangements were intermittently made for his treatment—the treatment of the day being aversion techniques. The Catholic Church in Ireland, it was claimed, was covering up his offences and shielding him from the reach of law. Subsequently it became apparent that the Norbertine Abbot, arguably in the belief that religious rigour and psychiatric therapy could cure the man, had been complicit in hiding the offences and protecting the offender. When complaints arose Father Smyth would be reassigned to another area and further treatment ordered. The Norbertine Order is one of the several religious houses which answer directly to Rome and lie beyond the authority and control of the local bishops of Ireland. But such structural subtleties were ignored, and newspaper headlines told of the shocking extent of the sexual abuse and the scandal of the Church's cover-up.

Troubles in Government

Controversy was already centring on the government of the day over the pending appointment to the Presidency of the High Court. The Government had been formed from a rather awkward coalition of *Fianna Fail* and the Labour Party in 1992. This liaison of convenience was negotiated when Fianna Fail did not secure a sufficient majority to govern in its own right. It had not been an easy joining. After the election had been declared the parties had moved back and forth over seven weeks before agreeing on the basis for becoming government. Memories of each sides' hostile criticism of the capability and integrity of the other before and immediately after the 1992 election still rankled, but the leaders of each Party eventually had agreed to coalesce and form government. The coalition continued to be subject to internal tensions. Hints of scandal, common enough in politics, surfaced intermittently.

During the life of this coalition government concern about corruption in the Beef Processing Industry had led to the establishment of a Tribunal of Inquiry, over which the President of the High Court, Justice Hamilton, had presided. The resulting report had been completed by the end of July 1994. The Taoiseach and leader of Fianna Fail, Albert Reynolds, had appeared to be implicated in corrupt behaviour which favoured particular pastoral interests. The Tribunal of Inquiry cleared him of these imputations. But Reynolds' handling of the release of the report, when he triumphantly declared his personal vindication, marked a dangerous deepening of the rift between himself, as Taoiseach and leader of Fianna Fail, and the Tanaiste and leader of the Labour Party, Dick Spring. On the night when the report was handed to the Government, Labour Party officials found their entry to the offices of the Taoiseach blocked. Observers reported Tanaiste Spring's anger at hearing that his officials were barred from entry to government buildings (i.e. the section housing the Taoiseach's office) on the evening the Tribunal's report was made available. The report was scanned prior to its sighting by Cabinet and the Tanaiste. Excerpts of the report were 'selectively leaked to the media' (Spring in statement to the Dáil Sub-committee on Legislation and

Security, reported in the *Irish Times*, 18 Jan. 1995, p.6. See also *Irish Independent*, 1 Aug. 1994, p.1, 10). The Taoiseach issued a public statement claiming that the report completely vindicated his integrity. This forestalling of a full Cabinet review and response dashed a relationship of trust within government and between the two Party leaders.

Further tension emerged in September of that year when it appeared that the Taoiseach Reynolds was proposing to nominate the Attorney General, Mr Harry Whelehan, as President of the High Court. In subsequent evidence to the Sub-committee of the Dáil Commission of Inquiry into Security and Legislation Spring was to say that he believed that Taoiseach Reynolds had agreed to postpone any nomination for the High Court position, and that Reynolds had told him that he had informed Whelehan of the lack of agreement. As became clear during the Dáil Sub-committee hearings, Reynolds had not informed Whelehan of this. Spring put forward a surprise proposition that Supreme Court Judge Mrs Justice Susan Denham be appointed to Presidency of the High Court. There were sound arguments to support either distinguished nominee for the office. Mr Whelehan had served for some years as Attorney General, the senior legal adviser to government and the chief law officer of the country. Justice Denham enjoyed an outstanding reputation for the intelligence, courtesy and progressiveness which she brought to her judicial role. As was soon known, she had not, however, agreed that her name should go forward. And many feared that her liberal perspective and vision would be lost to the most senior court were she to move from the Supreme Court to the High Court.[3]

Within a few days Tanaiste Spring had withdrawn his insistence on the appointment of Justice Denham and asked for a compromise candidate, not Whelehan. The reasons for Spring's unwillingness to endorse a Whelehan appointment were not at any stage made known. There was speculation that Spring was simply standing firm against Reynolds' authority over the coalition. The rift between Taioseach and Tanaiste had now become public and neither was prepared to back down. The Labour leader's opposition was perplexing because he had brought his party into a coalition government where Whelehan was serving as Attorney General, a position of great trust and confidentiality in matters affecting the government of the country.

During this contretemps Reynolds was in Australia as the guest of the Victoria University of Technology, headed by a noted Irish–Australian, Professor Jarlath Ronayne. There he was awarded an honorary doctorate, an addition to a number of such distinctions awarded to him in the United States. Communication between the leader and his deputy in government was becoming curiously dislocated. Subsequent analyses suggest that the disagreement over the appointment to the High Court was symptomatic of deeper divisions between the two men, neither of whom wished to lose face in the confrontation. The newspapers had been pointing to and exacerbating the two leaders' conflicting opinions over the appointment of the Attorney General for some two weeks when the pair met for the first time in three weeks after Mr Reynolds returned to Dublin. At this stage the Taoiseach had publicly endorsed the nomination of Whelehan for President of the High Court and the Tanaiste was reported as 'not going to roll over' (*Irish Independent*, 5 Oct. 1994, p.1) and accept the nomination.

In filling senior judicial office Ireland observes a long-standing convention that the Attorney General has 'first refusal' of any judicial vacancy, and if that is refused, plays an important part on behalf of government in the 'sounding out' process (see Byrne & McCutcheon, p.38). In editorial *The Irish Times* made the same point and wondered about the Labour Party's objections which were becoming public (21 Sept. 1994, p.6).

For some weeks newspaper commentary had been mounting and had been canvassing a view that this disagreement could lead to a break in the coalition which would precipitate a general election. It was alleged that the Taoiseach's tendency to act without consultation with his coalition partner had eroded trust, and that this disagreement over a judicial appointment was an issue over which the Tanaiste was determined to force a compromise. Trust between the leaders had worn away when the two men met on 11 October to discuss a compromise which would obviate the need for an end to the coalition and a subsequent general election (*Irish Independent*, 11 Oct. 1994, p.1)

The Peace Process in Northern Ireland

The repercussions of a breakdown in the Government partnership, now on the agenda for public discussion, went further than a general election and possible change of government. Reynolds as An Taoiseach of his country had been negotiating with the then British Prime Minister, John Major, towards a settlement of the troubles in Northern Ireland. The issue of peace for all Ireland and thence cessation of the Irish Republican Army (IRA) aggressions in England and Northern Ireland had long been a most distressing sequence in the unhappy relations between Ireland and England. The opposing counterpart to the IRA in Northern Ireland continued to respond with equal disregard for the complicity or innocence of their victims. The present phase of those troubles might be dated either from the assertion of the Irish Free State in 1917 or from the 1937 promulgation of the Irish Constitution and the independence of Ireland. This had left the six counties in the North to continue under English sovereignty as part of the United Kingdom. Much of the violent protest has been carried on by the political arm of the IRA, Sinn Fein. Critical to any peace talks was the involvement of Sinn Fein, which was long opposed by the British Government and the Ulster Government in Northern Ireland. Sinn Fein leader Gerry Adams' participation in all-party negotiations was central to Reynolds' dealing with Britain's Tory Government. He was to come close to success and was instrumental in achieving a cessation of hostilities that lasted two years.

In telling of the events of 1994, however, it must be recognised that Reynolds and his advisers, with some collaboration from the British Prime Minister and his negotiating team, had been instrumental in moving the peace process forward to an unprecedented extent. As well as being in close communication with Major, Reynolds had forged a close and amicable relationship with Adams. This exchange between Sinn Fein and the Irish Republican Government had not been achieved before and was roundly criticised by some Irish commentators. Within two years communication at that level could continue without any adverse comment. So much had been achieved. Reynolds is a talented deal-maker and to this cause he had brought patient skills of a remarkably high order: 'Reynolds is a "wrangler", that is a wheeler-dealer, a go-between. He did very well in the peace process. He and Major are grey men and they understood each other; they knew how to make a deal—it was a most fortunate conjunction' (Mr Justice O'Flaherty, pers. comm., 17 July 1996).

On 31 August 1994 the IRA agreed to cease military operations. Reynolds received congratulatory phone calls from US President Clinton and British Prime Minister Major (see Duignan, 1995, p.149). One week later Adams and Reynolds met publicly; Tanaiste Spring's prior arrangements to visit Germany prevented his attending. On 14 October 1994 the IRA and Ulster Volunteer Force (UVF) acted to effect a ceasefire. The IRA had earlier suspended hostilities and at this point their antagonists in Northern Ireland, the Loyalist UVF, agreed to halt. Peace talks could begin with all parties including Sinn Fein, the Loyalists and the Governments of Ireland and England. A successful culmination of the peace process was Reynolds' great hope and objective. This would be the legacy of his time at the head of the Irish Government. The significance of this magnificent obsession in the events that unfolded should not be ignored.

Political Troubles Intensify

In the meantime Taoiseach Reynolds and Tanaiste Spring were still caught up in their disagreement over the High Court appointment. Spring did not (then or subsequently) produce adequate reasons for his opposition to the Whelehan appointment. There was talk of Whelehan's lack of judicial experience and his presumed conservatism. Much later information about scurrilous talk circulating in government circles spoke of Whelehan's membership in *Opus Dei*, a secret and ultra-conservative Catholic society. At the time Whelehan heard nothing of these and related rumours. Only when they were voiced during the Dáil Subcommittee's investigations was he able to know of the accusations and refute them. There was open speculation in the press that Spring was tired of Reynolds' dictatorial style of leadership, and that he had felt humiliated and overridden by Reynolds' handling of the partial release of the Beef Tribunal Report—a report that Reynolds had declared totally exonerated him. Spring, the press speculated, had concealed in the past and was not going to be beaten on this issue.

The October 1994 meeting of the two political leaders, Reynolds and Spring, had been preceded by the mediation of a Cabinet sub-committee established for this purpose. The two men met at Baldonnel, a military aerodrome south of Dublin, which their separate journeys back from overseas made convenient for a joint discussion late on the evening of 11 October. As told by the Government Press Secretary, Reynolds agreed that there would be changes in the judicial appointments system and believed that he had agreement that Whelehan would be appointed to the Presidency (Duignan, 1995). The system whereby the government of the day made judicial appointments had been criticised for some time as detracting from the 'separation of powers' implicit in the Constitution; the legislated reforms were to establish a more independent judicial appointments board. The Labour Party was subsequently to deny that their leader, Spring, had agreed to such a deal. The legislative change to the procedure for appointing judges and the establishment of a Judicial Appointments Committee was, however, put in motion during October. Reynolds could claim that he had met his side of the agreement.

Paedophilia Scandal Resurges

A few days before the October meeting Ulster Television had shown the program 'Suffer the Little Children' that detailed Father Smyth's 'career' as 'paedophile priest' (Ferguson, 1996). The priest had been convicted a few months earlier of sexually abusing eight children over a period of twenty-four years and in June 1994 had begun a four-year prison sentence in Belfast. He had given himself over to the Northern Ireland police while the extradition order still lay in the office of Attorney General. Outrage about the case redoubled when information about Smyth's recent period as chaplain to a children's ward in Tralee became public. Smyth had served intermittently as acting chaplain to Tralee General Hospital in the South of Ireland over three years, 1990–93, and had access to the children's ward at that time. His appointment was agreed and facilitated by the Abbot of his Order. Allegations of a Catholic Church cover-up of his behaviour gathered force. Anxiety about paedophilia involving priests and religious had turned to panic in many countries, including the United States, Great Britain, Australia and Ireland. The sense of betrayal in Catholic Ireland was most acute. Smyth acted as a lightning rod attracting the anti-clericalism of the disaffected and the grieving reproaches of committed Catholics. This priest had taken positions of trust and had abused that trust. Now the Catholic Church was seen to be complicit by simply reassigning him when complaints surfaced and protecting him from the authorities (*Irish Independent*, 24 Oct. 1994, p.1, 13).

When it was reported that the request for Father Smyth's extradition to answer charges in Northern Ireland had lain unnoticed in the Attorney General's office for seven months, allegations of the Government as well as the Church being engaged in a conspiracy to cover-up the offences were raised (*Irish Independent*, 24 Oct. 1994, p.1). Before the extradition request was brought to the Attorney General's attention Father Smyth had voluntarily surrendered himself to the authorities; Attorney General Whelehan had not known of the request for his extradition before this occurred. But in response to questions in the Dáil, the Minister for Justice, Mrs Geoghegan-Quinn, had explained that the case was complex and would be the first to be considered in the light of certain (1987) amendments to the extradition legislation. The government opposition and the media took the view that the delay was at best a 'foul-up in the Attorney General's office and at worst a policy decision not to act against a person accused of serious paedophile offences' (subsequently reported in the *Irish Independent*, 27 Oct. 1994, p.7). The Labour Party now had a rod with which to beat their Fianna Fail coalition partners who were intent on the appointment of the Attorney General, Whelehan, as President of the High Court. The appointment had yet to be decided by Cabinet. That agenda item was set down for the meeting of 11 November 1994. For weeks the media had run stories about the Father Smyth case, the delay in his extradition blamed on the Attorney General's office, and the dispute between the two political leaders in government over the appointment of the Attorney General to the High Court. Still the Labour Party leader gave no reason for the dissent attributed to him. Nor was Whelehan, secure in his standing as the legal adviser to Government and leader of his profession, given any inkling of the grounds for Spring's resistance to his appointment. Three months earlier Whelehan had mentioned to Spring his interest in the coming High Court vacancy. Spring had noted the matter, but made no response. Now the only place where Whelehan gleaned information about Spring's reservations was in newspaper speculation. The legal advocacy responsibilities of his position had involved him in controversies debated in the media and had schooled him in a firm imperviousness.

The Labour Party determined that the appointment could not be decided until the report on the Father Smyth case and the related delay in his extradition to Northern Ireland had been dealt with in the Dáil . (The Attorney General is not a member of the Dáil and reports directly to the Taioseach and the Government.) Reynolds did not agree with the Labour timetable and was determined to take his recommendation to the Cabinet meeting of 11 November 1994. The Attorney General's report on the matter was first to be presented to Cabinet and the report dated 9 November was made available at the Tanaiste's insistence before the meeting.

At the meeting of 11 November, Attorney General Whelehan presented his report and was questioned at length by members of Cabinet. He addressed the delay of extradition proceedings against Father Smyth, a matter of which he had not been informed by his staff, but one which he properly assumed responsibility for. He stated that he investigated the delay during which a member of staff had intermittently dealt with and shelved the file. The work load of the Attorney General's office was extremely heavy at the time, and the request for Smyth's extradition had been taken up by one of the office's senior legal assistants and was being worked on in intervals between more pressing cases. The nine alleged offences, committed between 29 and 5 years earlier, raised complex issues under the 1987 legislation, specifically section 50(2)(bbb) where extradition was held liable to be 'unjust, oppressive or invidious' by reason of the lapse of time since the specified offences had been committed. This in large measure had delayed the completion of the process set in motion by the request for extradition received by the relevant official in May 1993, and the briefing on this matter which the Attorney General would in due course receive. In the meantime (December 1993), the official in the Attorney General's office was informed by the UK Attorney General's office that Father Smyth was returning voluntarily to surrender himself to the Northern Ireland police authorities. Whelehan's report satisfied the Fianna Fail members of the probity of his handling of his office. It appeared, however, that the Labour members were not to be satisfied.

The conflict between the leaders of the two parties in coalition, which flared with publication of the Beef Tribunal Report in August 1994, had been subject to running news commentaries over several weeks; it had become a fight where the loser stood to lose in a most public fashion. Two days later the *Irish Times* was to editorialise that the Attorney General's response was 'not good enough' (14 Nov. 1994, p.19). Anger over the scandal of the paedophile priest was being displaced, at least in part, on to the Attorney General and Fianna Fail in government.

Having delivered his report and answered any questions raised in Cabinet Whelehan left the meeting. The issue of the nomination for the Presidency of the High Court was then raised. The Labour members were not willing to proceed and walked out of the meeting. The Taioseach persisted and Whelehan was nominated by the remaining majority in Cabinet. Spring and his Labour colleagues had been frustrated, they had lost face.

To a committee of inquiry set up the following year, subsequent evidence given by Fianna Fail Minister Geoghan-Quinn, asserted that Labour opposition to the Whelehan appointment to the Bench was limited to their leader, Spring. In the days leading up to the crisis she had conferred with several Labour members of Cabinet. It could be claimed that a Committee of Ministers, including Labour Ministers, had earlier withdrawn any objections to the nomination in return for further additions to judicial reforms to be legislated through the Courts and Court Officers Bill (evidence before the Dáil Sub-committee, 10 Jan. 1995, reported in the *Irish Times*, 18 Jan. 1995, p.6.). Of the fifteen Ministers present at the beginning of the Cabinet meeting of 11 November 1994, only one, Spring, had objected to the Whelehan appointment. The other four Labour Ministers, however, left with their party leader when the agenda item, regarding appointment to the Presidency of the High Court, was reached. The account pieced together from Geoghan-Quinn's evidence is corroborated by Duignan's participant record of those days. But others, particularly Spring, contradicted these recollections. As disaster slides into chaos rapid impressions crowd the mind and clear recollection is often neither possible nor desired.

The Appointment and the Fall-Out

The Taoiseach took the approval of Cabinet to the President, Mrs Mary Robinson, late on the same day and Whelehan received his seal of office as President of the High Court that evening, 11 November 1994. Upon Whelehan's resignation as Attorney General Mr Eoghan Fitzsimons was appointed to that office.

Over the following weekend the sense of impending crisis intensified as politicians met to seek a way to save the Government.

Fianna Fail members of Cabinet gathered to draft Reynolds' report to the Dáil on the Father Smyth case and its handling by the Attorney General's office. This procedure accorded with the order of things: the Attorney General is accountable to the Executive and the Cabinet, and the Taoiseach is accountable to the Parliament. Nonetheless the fault for the delay in handling Smyth's extradition lay in the Attorney General's office and the Taoiseach was first inclined to blame the senior legal assistant who had handled the extradition request. Reynolds instructed the newly appointed Attorney General, Fitzsimons, to seek the removal of the legal assistant. Some preliminary discussions about their removal took place, but other events overtook this move.

By the early hours of Tuesday the 15th the leader of the leading opposition party, *Fine Gael*, had tabled a motion of no confidence in the Taoiseach over his handling of the appointment to the High Court and over the delay in the Attorney General's office on the Father Smyth case.

Later that morning at 11.00 a.m. in a packed Court before all five Justices of the Supreme Court, Harry Whelehan took his oath of office.

That afternoon Taoiseach Reynolds addressed the Dáil. He informed it that Whelehan (now the former Attorney General) had not been informed of the extradition order which had lain waiting to be processed in his, then, office. An outsider might hazard that extradition of persons to answer charges in the British territory of Northern Ireland was not a high priority in the law office of the Republic of Ireland and that more significant matters awaited attention. This apparently was not so, but rather in the overworked and understaffed office the matter had not been brought the matter to the Attorney General's attention. The Taoiseach, relying on the Attorney General's report to Cabinet, did volunteer in his speech to the Dáil that such an extradition request was a complex matter and it was the first to be considered under the 1987 amendments to the extradition legislation. He expressed deep regret over the delay of extradition procedures in the Father Smyth case, acknowledged that Attorney General Whelehan had not been aware of the extradition request earlier, pointed to the way the Northern Ireland peace process might be jeopardised, and, paying tribute to Spring, declared that the Labour Party and Fianna Fail were the 'right partners' to succeed in the peace process. The most telling question put to the Taoiseach asked why he risked the break-up of the Government for the sake of a judicial appointment. Reynolds replied that the public nature of Labour opposition made acquiescence in the violation of an established convention (Attorney General's first claim on any judicial appointment which might arise) would imply that the Attorney General, law adviser to the Government, was not to be trusted and consequently his position would become untenable.

Already the newspaper columnists were howling their disapproval of all these events. The crisis now threw Fianna Fail into panic.

Government in Crisis

As was to become known, the night before his Tuesday 15th speech in the Dáil, the Taoiseach had been aware of another extradition matter involving a monk, John Anthony Duggan, also accused of paedophilia and whose extradition to England was sought. This was the first time that the case of this monk had been raised. In the agitation about this matter involving a Catholic seminarian accused of a similar crime, no attention was paid to the way it pointed to the Attorney General's fair and equitable dealing with issues involving Catholic clergy. In a later interview with senior members of the Dublin Bar, I was to be told that this case should have been seen as a vindication of Whelehan, unjustly accused in the newspapers of being partial in his office's treatment of clerical members of the Catholic Church (James Nugent SC, pers. comm., 17 July 1996). But in the hubbub of allegation and accusation no notice was taken of the earlier child sexual abuse case involving the clergy. The troubles besetting the Government were piling high and seemingly driving out rationality. The survival of the Government now needed the catharsis of a great sacrifice.

The Taoiseach later claimed that on the Monday night he had not thought the matter of Duggan's extradition in 1992 could bear significantly on the Smyth extradition required in 1994. He had asked his new Attorney General, Fitzsimons, for a written opinion on the relevance of the earlier case and had urged him to call on the former Attorney General to canvass his view that same night. Additionally Fitzsimons was to ask Whelehan, now appointed as President of the High Court, to consider his position. Whelehan responded in a letter to Fitzsimons the next day (Tuesday 15 November). On that morning Fitzsimmons' written advice had not come to the Taoiseach before he left for the Dáil. Not having any definitive advice the Taoiseach addressed the Dáil on the Tuesday afternoon and omitted any mention of the earlier Duggan case. In fact he stated that the Smyth extradition on charges of sexual abuse going back over many years was the first of this nature affected by recent (1987) legislation. He had exposed himself to the charge of misleading the Dáil.

Later on the evening of Tuesday 15th, the Taoiseach consulted the information about the earlier extradition case involving the accused monk Duggan. Now, it was asked by the Labour politicians, was it not incorrect to say that the Smyth extradition was the first of this type under amended legislation: the Duggan case predated it by two years. Attorney General Fitzsimons was despatched again by Reynolds to acquaint the President of the High Court, Whelehan, of the Taoiseach's serious criticism of him for not taking this into account in a previous explanation for the delay in the Smyth extradition. Fitzsimons did so and, as directed by the Taoiseach, put to Whelehan the possible danger to the peace process if the Government were to fall—a danger which might be averted were the Judge to resign. In subsequent evidence Fitzsimons reported that Whelehan had not been interested in his representations.

If Fitzsimons was able to fully acquaint Whelehan of the Taoiseach's withdrawal of confidence it is unlikely that the newly appointed judge would have contemplated the gravity of his own position, much less tacitly acknowledge some misconduct by resigning. The first warning is said to have come the evening before Whelehan's swearing into office after receiving the seal of office three days earlier. The second warning was delivered on the evening following his taking the oath of office before assembled judges of the Supreme Court. Secure in the probity of his actions, Whelehan appeared not to contemplate that his political colleagues could turn on him. Looking back one can marvel at his naivety.

By the next day, Wednesday 16 November, Fitzsimons had become convinced of the significance of the Duggan case despite the opposing views of the former Attorney General and the senior legal assistant who handled the matter. This shift in Fitzsimons' legal opinion impugned the honesty of the Taoiseach's address to the Dáil on the previous day. Subsequent evidence shows that the Taisoeach and several of his Ministers had had their attention drawn to the Duggan case on the night of Monday 14 November. But, it would be claimed, its significance was not apparent at that time. The document showed that a previous extradition request for another cleric (Duggan) had been processed two years earlier by the Attorney General; subsequently Duggan had been speedily extradited to England. It was soon assumed that this earlier case had raised the same questions in law said to be considered for the first time with regard to the priest Brendan Smyth. Subsequent analysis would show this assumption to be wrong. On the basis of information received and now becoming public knowledge, it appeared that the Taoiseach had known about the Duggan case before he made his 15 November speech to the Dáil. He had misled the Dáil.

The opposition in the Oireachtas had seen the widening split in government ranks. The politicians heard the public uproar over the Father Smyth case, the complicity of the Norbertine Abbey and, by extension, the Catholic Church, and now the assumed involvement of Fianna Fail in a scandalous cover-up. Fine Gael's motion of no-confidence in the Taoiseach was on the order paper for the Dáil of Thursday 17 November.

The Labour Party Ministers had earlier urged the Taioseach to repudiate the nomination of Whelehan for President of the High Court. On that basis they would vote against the no-confidence motion and continue in government with Fianna Fail.

At a stormy meeting in Reynolds' office the Labour Minister for Finance, Mr Ruari Quinn, declared 'Taioseach, we've come for a head—yours or Harry's' (Evidence by Spring before Dáil Sub-committee reported in the *Irish Times*, 18 Jan. 1995, p.6.) (See also Casey, 1996, p.222).

The Taoiseach did not hesitate. He gathered his ministers and together they drafted a speech.

The Denunciation

Through the night and into the early hours the members of Fianna Fail worked together to finalise their leader's speech for the next day. According to later evidence the atmosphere of crisis and impending crisis thickened intolerably, 'the members of Fianna Fail were running round like headless chickens' (*Irish Times*, 21 Jan. 1995). The next morning at 10.22 a.m. Tanaiste Spring signed the agreement to maintain coalition with Fianna Fail—to continue in government.

To deliver his part in the deal the Taoiseach turned on Whelehan. On the morning of Wednesday 16 November he arose to address the Dáil, stating that the former Attorney General's advice on the Father Smyth case was:

> seriously misleading ... Had my colleagues and I been aware of these facts last week we would not have proposed or supported the nomination of Harry Whelehan as President of the High Court ... If the former Attorney

General still held the position of Attorney General he would, in my view in the circumstances, have had no option but to resign.

Moreover, the Taoiseach admitted that:

reservations voiced by the Tanaiste are well founded and I regret the appointment of the former Attorney General as President of the High Court. I also regret my decision to proceed with the appointment against the expressed opposition of the Labour Party.

Reynolds' personal abnegation and Fianna Fail's condemnation of Whelehan were complete. Reynolds continued by enumerating the successes of his government beginning with 'the biggest breakthrough towards peace in Northern Ireland in 25 years'. Hence there was every reason for the partnership of Fianna Fail and Labour to continue in government. There was no hint of resignation in this speech. But matters were now out of his control.

The Dáil rang with the denunciation of the newly appointed judge. Rumours of outside interference, through Whelehan in the Attorney General's office, were voiced: the former Attorney General was alleged to be a member of the secret society Opus Dei; he had conspired with Cardinal Daly, head of the ecclesiastical hierarchy, in the cover-up; the senior legal assistant had been complicit in the cover-up; and there was a letter from Cardinal Daly on the Attorney General's desk. All such stories were later to be dropped for want of evidence and on the denial by all so accused. The newspapers, however, took up the cry questioning how the Judge might be forced from his post.

Some minutes after reaching agreement with Fianna Fail on how the crisis could be averted, the Labour Party decided not to proceed with the deal. Reynolds had not been informed of this turnabout and was proceeding to the speech which would repudiate Whelehan. Shortly after the '10.22 a.m. agreement' Spring, as he later reported in evidence, received a phone call informing him that the Taoiseach had known of the earlier Duggan case at the time of the Monday 14th speech when he had informed the Dáil that the Father Smyth case was the first of its type and therefore unduly complex. The Labour leader refused to reveal the source of this information beyond stating that it did not come from 'the Law Library [the Irish Bar], the Attorney General's office, the public service nor any party in Leinster House, either in Dáil or Seanad' (evidence to the Dáil Subcommittee on Legislation and Security, 17 Jan. 1995, *Irish Times*, 18 Jan. 1995, p.6.).

Reynolds' denial and denunciation of the Judge had not availed. The Dáil continued through 16 November and late in the day Tanaiste Spring set out his reasons for leading his Party out of Government. All the Labour members, he said, would 'resign from their offices before the vote [of no-confidence] is taken'.

There was still time to save the Government.

The rumours mounted that the Catholic Church had conspired with the legislature and the judiciary to suppress the Father Smyth case. At the centre of the chaos stood Whelehan. As Sean Duignan, who later wrote the story of the Reynolds Government from the inside (*One Spin on the Merry-Go-Round*), commented: 'It began with Harry, and it ended with Harry. For such an amiable fellow, he attracts trouble like a lightning conductor draws electricity' (1995, p.1). Now he had been put to sacrifice by his Fianna Fail colleagues, but he was still there as their appointee to the High Court.

On the evening of Wednesday 16 November, Justice Whelehan listened on radio to the Taoiseach's denunciation of him in the Dáil. His own position had been made untenable. That night he consulted with family and legal advisers. Shortly after noon the next day his letter of resignation was delivered to the President of Ireland. He had resigned just six days after being appointed President of the High Court to prevent the office being 'further embroiled in public controversy'. He went on to state:

> The judiciary must at all times enjoy total and unquestioned public respect and its reputation for absolute independence and integrity is of paramount importance under the Constitution ... The vindication of my own good name in the light of recent unjust attacks and the feelings of my wife and family must yield to these considerations to prevent the office of the President of the High Court being further embroiled in this controversy (*Irish Times*, 18 Nov. 1994, p.3).

The Chief Justice of the Supreme Court, Justice Hamilton, spoke of Whelehan's great courage 'motivated by the concern for the role and integrity of the judiciary and he placed that above his own personal career' (*Irish Times*, 18 Nov. 1994, p.1, 8).

The expulsion and the sacrifice of Harry Whelehan, however, was not enough.

Later that week the Tanaiste and five Labour Ministers tendered their resignation from the Government. Faced with the immediacy of the Dáil's vote of no-confidence in his Government, Reynolds announced to the Dáil that he intended to resign as An Taoiseach. In the early afternoon of 17 November he travelled to *Arras an Uacharain*, the official residence of the President, to tender his resignation to the President of Ireland. He continued as Acting Taoiseach pending further events. That evening he informed his Fianna Fail colleagues that he was stepping down as Party leader. The newspaper declared this his finest hour as Reynolds departed with 'great dignity and honour' (*Irish Times*, 18 Nov. 1994, p.12). But some commentators were not so kind: 'Now to undo the damage Reynolds has done' (O'Toole, *Irish Times, 18* Nov. 1994, p.18).

For a few hours Reynolds had wavered, but then he determined he would not continue as leader. That step might avoid a general election which 'would endanger the peace process' (Duignan, p.166).

After the Fall

On receipt of Reynolds' resignation as leader of the party (Saturday 19 November), Fianna Fail elected Mr Bertie Ahern[4], to replace him. In a curious way Ahern had been clear of the debacle of that chaotic week. Pressure of other duties had prevented him from taking part in Fianna Fail's drafting of the leader's two fateful speeches. Negotiations could begin to re-form the coalition with Labour. By the end of the month the renewed coalition was near.

Before the end of the month Fitzsimons' report on the communications between himself, the Taoiseach and Fianna Fail during the fateful November week leading to the resignation of Taoiseach Reynolds was presented to the Dáil. It now was made known that Fianna Fail members of Cabinet were aware of the Duggan case on Monday 14 November, the evening before Reynolds' speech in the Dáil which had omitted facts known to him and his Cabinet, and so he was judged as misleading the Dáil. Fianna Fail was wholly complicit in their leader's actions. The possibility of a renewed coalition with Labour was now lost. The Government plunged deeper into crisis.

By mid December a different coalition was forming. Fine Gael, the Democratic Left and the Labour Party were talking their way towards a 'rainbow coalition'. The Labour leader was moving his party away from any taint over its actions when the Whelehan affair had culminated in tragedy for Whelehan—and for Reynolds. Statements by the former Minister for Justice, Geoghegan-Quinn, put Spring in jeopardy. In response to questions put in an interview she replied that the Labour leader, Spring, had also known about the approach to Whelehan to comment on the relevance of the Duggan case before Spring entered into the doomed agreement with Fianna Fail on Wednesday 16 November. Spring denied that he had any such knowledge.

On Thursday 16 December the three-Party coalition Government elected Mr Bruton as Taoiseach and Spring as Tanaiste. A Bill to establish a Select Commission on Legislation and Security of the Dáil was introduced and quickly passed into legislation. The Dáil Sub-committee with carriage of the business quickly commenced hearings which continued into January 1995.

The Law Library Acts

When Whelehan resigned from the High Court he could not have seen a return
to the Bar as a likely possibility. There was the rule of the Bar Council's Code of
Conduct which states that a retired judge may not practice in a court of equal or
lesser jurisdiction than the court in which the judge had served. Therefore
Whelehan, who as President of the High Court had been *ex officio* a judge of the
Supreme Court, was prevented from appearing before any Court. He could not
earn a livelihood as a barrister. He had served on the Bench for one and a half
days—heard one case and part-heard another.

His application to the Council for readmission to the Law Library (the formal
organisation of practice at the Irish Bar) prompted the calling of an extraordinary
general meeting of the Bar. At the meeting on Friday 2 December over 400 barristers crowded into the Law Library to discuss one motion:

> Notwithstanding the terms of paragraph 5.21 of the Code of Conduct, and in
> the exceptional circumstances scheduled hereto, Harry A. Whelehan, senior
> counsel, is deemed to be a practising barrister and entitled to all rights and
> duties of a practising barrister, including the right to practise as a barrister in
> all courts (*Irish Times*, 3 Dec. 1994, p.5).

The schedule attached to this motion set out the circumstances of this excep-
tional case. The issue was whether a person, who had served only six days on
the Bench, had sat for only a day and a half and heard only a case and a half,
could practise at the Bar without restriction. The question before the meeting
was narrowed further: 'if a High Court judge should resign without hearing
cases of substance within a specified (6-day) time of being appointed he might,
notwithstanding the Code of Conduct, be permitted to return to the Bar' (James
Nugent SC, pers. comm., 17 July 1996).

The vote at the meeting showed 352 in favour of the resolution, 37 absten-
tions and none against. Several barristers proposed that a poll should be taken
and, when the requisite 50 barristers supported this recommendation, the vote
by show of hands was set aside and a secret postal ballot ordered. The decision
in favour of Whelehan's re-call to the Bar, which needed a two-thirds majority
under regulations, was carried by an overwhelming majority.

On requesting a copy of the minutes from this extraordinary general meeting,
Mr James Nugent SC (the current President of the Bar Council), explained to me
that there were no minutes taken on account that these were extraordinary circumstances (11 July 1996). It was agreed that if a man had taken up a judicial
appointment to a court for a specified (very limited) number of days, had heard a
specific and extremely small number of cases, and had then resigned from the

Bench, that such a person might return to practise as a barrister. There was no precedent for this, and this was not to serve as precedent. Thus a decision was not minuted and did not pass into the regulations.

Review

This case study has followed the events as they occurred. Although, in the months which followed, many were called to say what they knew, contradictions and omissions remain. All is still not clear. Much later an astute judicial observer spoke of the fall of the Government as 'a very complicated matter. We didn't understand it at the time. Perhaps we don't properly understand it yet'. There was, the Judge continued, the clash of personalities: Fianna Fail and Labour were most unlikely partners to form a government. Reynolds, a man of quick decision and determination loved a deal, that was his strength in the peace process. His sudden turning on Whelehan can be seen to be in character—he would have seen it as necessary. But, it was a terrible thing that he did. 'It was very painful for a good man and his family. But, I think he's doing all right now' (Mr Justice O'Flaherty, speaking on Whelehan, pers. comm., 17 July 1996).

Several parts of this drama were played on the public stage, as the news media reported much of what was being done, said and planned. In Ireland Church and State exert distinct and different lines of authority, but the Church's influence on the political continues. The affair of 'the paedophile priest' (Ferguson, 1996) brought scandal upon two great institutions of Irish life.

At that time Fianna Fail had more than enough troubles in its fractious partnership with the Labour Party. The partnership which had brought the two parties into Government in 1992 had become increasingly strained, and by the latter half of 1994 rumours of its untimely end were circulating. The personal antagonism between Taoiseach and Tanaiste, exacerbated over the former's handling of the aftermath of the Beef Tribunal Report, was pulling the two parties to the coalition apart. Tanaiste Spring appeared determined to assert his position through opposition to the Taoiseach's decision to have the Attorney General appointed to the vacant position on the High Court. Reynolds, believing he had a *quid pro quo* agreement, ignored hints of dissent. It was shaping into a contest of tactics. Of the situation Professor James Casey commented:

> It seems probable that once the dispute between Taoiseach and Tanaiste came into the public domain, Mr Reynolds would not have contemplated urging Mr Whelehan to withdraw, or have permitted him to do so. The media, suitably briefed, would most certainly have interpreted this as a victory for Mr Spring; and even an unforced withdrawal by Mr Whelehan would have been open to a construction adverse to the Taoiseach (1996, p.206).

Mr Whelehan did not contemplate withdrawing. He was the leader of his profession and legal adviser to the Government. To withdraw would infer that he was in some wise unworthy of the office. The very distinction of his judicial appointment increased his visibility and vulnerability.

The consternation about the clerical sexual abuse case grew sharper when it appeared children in hospital might have been exposed to the danger. Then came the story that the Church's presumed cover-up of the Smyth matter was aided and abetted by the Fianna Fail Government; the order for the priest's extradition had lain in the Attorney General's office for seven months. The detail contradicts this simple construction, but scandal always simplifies.

The allegation gave Tanaiste Spring strategic leverage to publicly defeat Taoiseach Reynolds over a prominent decision. It is doubtful whether Spring commanded the consensus of his Party colleagues, but, in compliance with their leader's directions, they left the Cabinet meeting before the critical agenda item was discussed. Labour seemed to be intent on leaving the coalition and so bringing down the Government. Political strategies then spun out of control.

The Greek chorus of media editorialised:

> The Fianna Fail party now in government, even at this mortal hour in its
> own fortunes, appears to be devoid of any sensitivity to the principle [of
> accountability] (*Irish Times*, 15 Nov. 1994, p.6).

Following the first of the Taoiseach's fateful speeches to the Dáil on November 15, attention shifted to the discovery of an earlier case which might have been taken as precedent for resolving the Father Smyth extradition. The Duggan case, as the two senior legal assistants of the Attorney General's Department later stated, was not relevant to the Father Smyth case and would not have provided any precedent for untangling the complexity of the Smyth extradition. These lawyers, with the greatest expertise in extradition matters, had been appalled at the incongruity of the Duggan case turning alarm into panic as that case was seized as a device for capping a longer history of distrust in Fianna Fail's integrity in government. Technically, however, it was not correct to say that the Father Smyth case was the first time that the 'lapse of time' aspect of an extradition had been considered. Time elapsed since Duggan's alleged offences had been briefly considered by the responsible legal assistant and had been decided to be not of substance. Then Duggan's extradition had been speedily executed over Attorney General Whelehan's signature. Two years later when the British Attorney General's office requested Smyth's extradition, it was rightly regarded as unprecedented in raising the lapse of time and possible contravention of a section of the 1987 legislation. The senior legal assistant in charge of Smyth's file was researching it whenever more immediate tasks permitted. Then he was informed that Father Smyth had voluntarily surrendered himself to the Northern Ireland Police and so no further action was needed. He had not referred the matter to his boss, the Attorney General, because his own work on the file had not been completed. As in so much else Whelehan was taken by surprise when asked, early in November 1994, to explain the delay of Father Smyth's case to Cabinet—a case he knew nothing about.

It is remarkable that in the alarms and excursions over the alleged complicity of Church, Parliament and Judiciary in subverting the course of justice no attention was paid to the substance of the Duggan case, of a monk extradited to answer charges of child sexual abuse. That case should have dispelled the allegations of an Attorney General using his office to hide a priest from justice. But, that exculpatory aspect was not aired and Whelehan had not remembered the matter.

After the Taoiseach presented to the Dáil the facts as set out in the Attorney General's report it appeared momentarily that he could avert the crisis. The request for extradition had suffered a regrettable and inexcusable delay. The man had given himself up and no further harm had ensued. Then came the argument about whether the Taoiseach and his Cabinet colleagues had, contrary to the statement in the Dáil, known of the earlier, purportedly relevant, extradition of a cleric accused of child sexual abuse.

This scandal was a device used by Labour to force its Fianna Fail partners in government to back down: 'Labour wanted to remain in government. They wanted simply for Albert Reynolds to say that he was wrong about Harry Whelehan and Dick Spring was right' (Browne, *Irish Times*, 11 Jan. 1995, p.14)

In the confusion of issues the scandal grew monstrously. Heaped onto concern about the integrity of government was grave worries about the fall from grace of clergy and Church. Fianna Fail plunged into crisis as its Cabinet Ministers panicked over how the Government might remain standing. The current troubles had been slated to the Attorney General's office; his report to Cabinet had responded to assertions of complicity in an alleged Church cover-up. The deep split in the coalition opened further and threatened to scuttle the Government. The repudiation of Harry Whelehan newly appointed President of the High Court might allay the storm blowing within the Government.

Harry Whelehan is first and foremost a lawyer with a deeply held commitment to the law, the law of Ireland. He enjoys the staunch collegiality of the Bar. As a lawyer with firm political affiliations he had readily accepted appointment as Attorney General in a Fianna Fail majority government. In doing so he did not leave the Bar, but his immediate professional community became that of government, of politics. His colleagues were now politicians and the Government became his milieu. But, as a barrister his links into the Law Library, the world of his profession, held, except for those few days of appointment to the Bench.

Whelehan enjoyed a distinguished career as barrister, became senior counsel in 1980, and was appointed Attorney General first by the Haughey (Fianna Fail) Government in 1991, and then reaffirmed in office by the Reynolds Government which followed in 1992. As Attorney General he had argued a number of cases touching on the Constitution before the Supreme Court. Early in his period of office he acted in the controversial case of X, a 14-year-old girl who sought to travel to England to terminate a pregnancy, the result of a rape. The argument before the Supreme Court hinged on provisions in the Constitution, but feminist and liberal antagonism had focused on Whelehan. A few months later, early in the proceedings of the Beef Tribunal, Whelehan had successfully persuaded the Supreme Court that Cabinet confidentiality was essential to good government and could not be breached. A couple of years earlier in a case, *Sankey v. Whitlam*, brought before the High Court of Australia, the court had ruled on the same principle, that is, in favour of the confidentiality of matters discussed in Cabinet. The advocacy of the Attorney General in these Irish cases attracted severe criticism from some quarters, but in both instances his actions were commended by the Supreme Court. There were more controversies; these are merely indicative and most quoted. A reading of Casey's *The Irish Law Officers*, which recounts the careers of a line of Attorneys General, suggests that controversy is endemic in that office. But, Whelehan's term of office was particularly contentious.

Most characteristic of the man and his handling of the responsibilities of his office is a commitment to the law: '[H]e is the representative of the State in constitutional actions and in this regard his function is to uphold the constitutionality of any challenged legislation' (Byrne & McCutcheon, 1990). Whelehan's reputation for conservatism derived, at least in part, from his office and his role as advocate for the Constitution and adviser to Government. He is a committed Catholic, but did not bring a dogmatic Catholicism to the law. (One could argue that Catholic morality had already been made integral to the Constitution.) In 1986 he was chosen by the Bar Council to present the pro-divorce argument on television during the referendum to permit divorce in Ireland.

Significantly for what was to happen, Whelehan immersed himself in his work as attorney for the State and seemed unaware of the troubles swirling around his office and himself. He certainly did not hear the stories circulating in Leinster House linking him as a member of the secret society Opus Dei. He was to deny such allegations when it was put to him by the Dáil Sub-committee in December of that year. At the time he was oblivious to the 'rolling snowball of vilification against me' (evidence given by Mr Whelehan before the Sub-committee of the Dáil Legislation and Security Commission, 21 Dec. 1994). Dr Mansergh, a senior adviser to Fianna Fail had earlier noted 'Mr Whelehan's apparent imperviousness to the turmoil around him' in an earlier case where he felt obliged to take a very unpopular stand in defence of a section of the Constitution. Newspaper columnist Deaglan de Breadun likened Whelehan to 'a man who went walking in tiger country, armed only with an umbrella' (*Irish Times* 13 Jan. 1995, p.10).

Whelehan had been a supporter of Fianna Fail since his university days and had run for office as chairman of the *Fianna Fail cuman* in University College Dublin. He was of the Party, but he had never sought election to the Dáil. As Attorney General appointed by Fianna Fail and adviser to that government he was, nonetheless, at the centre of the political scene.

As Attorney General he had first option on judicial office when a vacancy arose. He had not, however, sought a judicial appointment to the High or Supreme Court when such a position arose earlier; nor did he seek the position of Chief Justice of the Supreme Court when Finlay CJ had retired because he believed that the appointee should have prior judicial experience, preferably on the High Court. There had been no response when he broached his interest in appointment to the High Court with Tanaiste Spring. At no time did Spring reveal his objection or the grounds for objecting to Whelehan's aspirations. Not knowing of any objections Whelehan was prevented from confronting either the criticism or the critic.

Whelehan's position was simultaneously central and marginal to the troubles which enmeshed Fianna Fail as it tried to hold on to government in November 1994. The delay in handling the Smyth extradition and then Whelehan's judicial appointment were the pretexts for the failure of trust and the slide into conflict between the two leaders and their dazed parties. Whelehan was at the point of contention. But, although he was adviser to the Government, he was not of it. He could be expended if need be. And the need was soon declared. Whelehan was distinguished by his difference: a man of the law; adviser to Cabinet (appointed not elected); a long-time supporter of Fianna Fail, but not of its central core; the counsel of politicians, but, by all accounts, no politician. In the past two years he had been marked by a series of controversies. And there were those stories that turned his firm Catholicism into affiliation with secret societies and involvement with ecclesiastical-political deals. Then during those days when the Government spun out of control he was poised in the liminal phase of leaving one status and about to enter another. As he assumed high judicial office, the denunciation struck at him. Whelehan made a grand scapegoat. He was central to the events which had thrown the Government into chaos. Standing in the high office of Attorney General he had been marked by the conflicts where the law must be advocated and decisions reached. And yet the Attorney General is not a member of the Government. A longtime supporter of Fianna Fail he necessarily remained marginal to the Party. He was not quite one of them. The Fianna Fail members of Cabinet met through the night and together wrote the speech of denunciation.

Stepping from his position as the leader of his profession and the legal adviser to Government into the second highest judicial office in the land he was pulled out and offered up to appease Fianna Fail's erstwhile allies and to allay public alarm over perceived failures in government and abuses in the Church. Scandals enveloped all, chaos was palpable and Whelehan, innocent lodestone of troubles, stood high in the midst. He was set to be pulled down and driven out.

Serving up Whelehan's head might have satisfied many calls for vengeance against the Government, against the Church, against Fianna Fail, and against the desperate figure of the Taoiseach. The speech that brought him down had been composed by the Fianna Fail Cabinet. All had a hand in denouncing and driving him out. As Sean Duignan, government press secretary at the time, tells it:

> Finally it was time for the Taoiseach to go to the House ... I had no concep-
> tion of how to advise him, and merely asked if he still intended to disown
> Harry and apologise to Spring. He said: "I have to play the hand I've been
> dealt" (1995, p.163).

Whelehan, who had just resigned as Attorney General, stepped down from his new position on the Bench. Having been driven from judicial office he faced a bleak future in Dublin. After all that had happened he had no hope of an office in government or its Public Service. Regulation prevented his return to the Bar. The Bar Council called an extraordinary general meeting of the profession to consider how he might be returned to its midst. A way that would allow no repetition was devised and Whelehan resumed his life as senior counsel and membership of the Law Library, the institutional home of Dublin's barristers.

The remarkably astute journalist, Vincent Browne, anticipated the event:

> It is also likely that he will resume his successful practice and perhaps again
> be a candidate for judicial office for he has many of the qualities required/
> expertise in the law, scrupulous courtesy and an integrity which, his friends
> believe, will survive the buffeting which recent events have inflicted (*Irish
> Times*, 17 Nov. 1994, p.14).

But judicial office requires government appointment. Were Fianna Fail again in government it would not look to him again. Scapegoats never return. But now Fianna Fail itself has toppled.

Notes

1. Some of the detail of this chapter has been drawn from recorded evidence of political and administrative players who were caught into the events leading to the fall of the Reynolds Government.
2. 'Suffer the Little Children' was shown on the Counterpoint program.
3. The Supreme Court is the final court of appeal in the Irish legal system and its time is largely devoted to constitutional matters.
4. In 1997 Mr Bertie Ahern became An Taoisearch (Prime Minister) of the Irish Republic Government.

CHAPTER 6

The Longest Trial:
William McBride

The events that bring down people are invariably complex, multifaceted and deceptively inconsequential. The more often a story is told the more the variations; its significance alters with the perspective of the storyteller. The story of William McBride has been told in many ways: as denunciation, as cautionary tale, as tragedy of a fatal flaw, as a David and Goliath myth. He had his detractors and his defenders, and he told his own story in the thematically titled *Killing the Messenger*. There were other accounts including Bill Nicol's *McBride: Behind the Myth* and that of Norman Swan, as well as the many volumes of the Medical Tribunal and the three judgments emanating from the appeal to the New South Wales Supreme Court. The case was also cited in a number of journal articles decrying scientific fraud. The account presented uses a different theme to unravel the events and knit together a theory of how it all turned out the way it did.

Like most people William McBride belonged to more than one community. Foremost for him was the professional community of specialist obstetricians within the circle of medical practitioners. He also identified with the community of biomedical scientists, a group where his early scientific observations marked him out for great distinction. As well there was the community of women constituting his specialist practice of obstetrics. For many years Dr William McBride enjoyed honour and applause for his achievements in all three spheres. Until all slowly turned against him.

Intervention in Childbirth: Conflicting Ideologies

By 1980 feminist consciousness in many western countries had begun to critically appraise male intervention in childbirth, an elementally female domain. Such
continuing concern about barriers to women's entry to traditional male worlds of
professional and managerial authority had widened to take up a zealous antagonism towards male expertise in the women's world of childbirth and related health
issues. This critique initially emanated from feminist literature (see Daly, 1978;
Kitzinger, 1978; Kitzinger & Davis, 1978; Oakley, 1976; 1979; 1984; Peterson,
1983: Rothman, 1982, 1983; Weitz & Sullivan, 1985), with social scientists and
policy analysts in public health joining the debate (Taylor, 1979; Opit & Sellwood,
1979; Learoyd, 1985).

   In Australia popular concern about intervention in childbirth and interest in
the mounting female demand for access to safe homebirths, prompted a plethora
of newspaper articles variously advocating for, and cautioning against,
homebirths and the independent midwives who practised during the decades
1970 to 1990. Sixty-one such articles were counted in the ten years to 1979, 170 in
the following seven years to 1986 and, evidence of declining interest, 48 articles
in the next seven years (Noble, 1997). The goal of the homebirths movement was
to put women in charge of their own childbirth, free of medical domination.

   At the same time that women and their feminist protagonists were voicing
stringent criticism of the extent of clinical intervention in childbirth, obstetric
journals continued to applaud the better outcomes produced by improved techniques, particularly the surgical techniques used in caesarean section (Sutherst
& Case, 1975; Correy, 1977; Broe & Khoo, 1989). Rates for caesarean section as
well as other less dramatic interventions in childbirth had been noted as rising
for some years (Taylor, 1979).

   A study of trends in obstetric practice over twenty-five years found that
during the period from 1950 to 1975 clinical intervention by caesarean section,
epidural anaesthesia and augmented labour with oxytocin had risen steadily
(Correy, 1977). In particular caesarean section had increased three-fold from
2.4% of all deliveries in 1950 to 8.25% in 1975. The median for length of labour
appeared to have diminished significantly from a median of 8 hours in 1950 to 5
hours in 1975 (in round figures). The author of this paper, published in the
Australian and New Zealand Journal of Obstetrics & Gynaecology, viewed
these trends positively:

> The ultimate aim in obstetrics … is not only to prevent perinatal mortality
> and morbidity in all treatable conditions by more sophisticated methods of
> investigation and treatment, but also to diagnose at an early stage of preg-
> nancy. And so reduce or abolish … perinatal mortality by timely intervention
> early in pregnancy (Correy, 1977, p.88).

A Sydney-based study, published in the same journal six years later, found a three-fold increase in caesarean section rates in the decade 1971 to 1981. It appeared that privately insured patients were more likely to enjoy the assumed benefits of advances in obstetric technology (Blumenthal et al., 1984). Again such intervention was associated with improved outcomes and clinical indications were cited: 'the increase in the caesarean section rate for dystocia[1] contributed 33.2% of the increase ... fetal distress 23.8%, repeat caesarean section 16.9% and breech presentation 13.3%' (1984, p.248). A study of changing obstetric practice over forty-four years in Melbourne (1939 to 1983) reported a seven-fold increase in caesarean section rates, from 2% in the period 1939–47 to 14% in the years 1980–83. Over the same four decades forceps delivery had doubled from 10% in the 1940s to 20% in the 1970s. Again the author's comment were approving (Ratten, 1985, p.243):

> the dangers of forceps and caesarean delivery have been minimized and since 1970 the maternal and perinatal mortality ratio associated with these types of manipulative delivery are less than those in the overall hospital population.

The reasons for changes in obstetric practice are many, and include the improved safety of the operation, the extension of the clinical indications for surgical intervention, a trend for women to have their first baby at a later age, avoidance of prolonged labour for vaginal delivery, fears of malpractice suits should the baby be 'damaged' when obstetrician did not intervene, and the emphasis on the production of a 'perfect baby' (Biggs, 1984). Public health literature also noted that interventions, including induction of labour and caesarean section, can be more convenient for both practitioner and patient, and produce a larger fee for the practitioner.

Australian obstetric literature of the time did not unilaterally favour surgical intervention as a general practice, but attention was consistently directed to the largely positive outcomes of sophisticated obstetric techniques. Alternative views, while recognised, still invited qualification. Editorial comment in the *Australian and New Zealand Journal of Obstetrics and Gynaecology* exemplifies this cautionary response. An adverse review which stated that there was 'no corresponding fall in perinatal mortality rate associated with primary caesarean section' (Murray-Arthur & Correy, 1984, p.243), was prefaced by an editorial note, which sounded caution: 'Perinatal mortality rates are easily calculated but the justification of an increased caesarean section rate is likely to be an improved quality of survival of the infant—this information is not readily available but must not be overlooked in the caesarean section argument'. The editorial comment observed that caesarean section is used in cases where the foetus is at greatest risk. It should be noted that the obstetric profession did not view surgical intervention as routine procedure. The clinical papers invariably insisted that each case required careful judgment based on all assessable factors. The long-term outcome for children delivered by caesarean section was being studied and reported positively (see McBride et al., 1979).

Obstetricians in the 1980s were reassured and encouraged in therapeutic intervention by the clinical literature. The good practitioner read the journals and the best practice reflected the recent research. In a busy professional life very few would have known of, or adverted to, alternative opinion being raised in other disciplines. Increasing medical intervention, however, was generating concern in the relevant government departments anxious to reduce the level of elective surgery throughout the hospital system. Higher rates of active intervention in childbirth were widely noted and deprecated (Muhlen & Nordholm, 1980, 1981; Lumley, 1980a; Learoyd, 1985; Pryke, Muhlen & Wade, 1986). In 1979 Richard Taylor published a detailed critical analysis of what was being categorised as unnecessary surgical intervention under the title *Medicine out of Control: The Anatomy of a Malignant Technology*. His was an Australian rendition of Ivan Illich's trenchant thesis on the damage wrought by medical technology first voiced in *Medical Nemesis* (1975) and *Limits to Medicine* (1976). In Taylor's account clinical intervention in childbirth is described as part of the 'diseasification of pregnancy and childbirth' (1979, p.133).

These two powerful lobbies were deeply disturbed about increasing clinical, especially surgical, intervention in childbirth. While the public health advocates attacked such intervention as an unwarranted and potentially dangerous expenditure of public funds, feminist resentment gathered force to counteract a predominantly male intrusion in what was claimed as a uniquely female event. Public health and feminist concerns were taken seriously by the Complaints Unit of the New South Wales Health Department. For this community of interest the ever increasing rate of caesarean section and the near routine clinical intervention in childbirth assumed scandalous proportions. It had to be stopped.

The larger society did not share the concerns of the feminist or public health lobbies. Feminist antagonism towards the developments in obstetrics practice did not prevail among pregnant women generally. The majority came to hospital to have their babies and were grateful for any measures which might diminish any pain and danger which, they believed, threatened themselves and their babies. Natural childbirth was desired in most cases, but the safety of the mother and the delivery of the 'perfect baby' were paramount. Specialist obstetric practice flourished. Where advised (by the practitioner), surgical intervention was welcomed in the labour wards of the large maternity hospitals. Nonetheless, while patient compliance in pregnancy and childbirth remained the norm, the feminist critique was mounting and declaring their resistance to 'medical domination' and the 'medical model' of childbirth. Some resorted to homebirths assisted by a midwife or other non-medical attendant. Many more were attentive to the critique and the later establishment of birth centres (characterised by 'care but no intervention') at all major maternity hospitals evidences the strength of that critique. In public health journals feminist critics voiced their disapproval of obstetrics as widely practised and sometimes their criticism hit the popular press. This resistance fitted comfortably with public health advocates' deprecation of 'unnecessary medical procedures' and the worry about the 'escalating cost of health' (Learoyd, 1985).

Scientific Research

The work of scientists is systematically exposed to the scrutiny of peers and competitors. Publication in journals was a significant bastion against researcher dishonesty (Gaston, 1980, p.485). Many scientists have been confident in the strength of training for a science career whose integrity is fiercely guarded (see Fuchs, 1992, pp.34–43). There emerged in the 1980s some reason to repudiate this simple faith. For example, the controversies around both primacy of discovery and integrity of research on human immunedeficiency virus (HIV) (Patton, 1990; Rawling, 1994), or the purported African origins of HIV including Louis Pascal's account of international journal editors' continued rejection of his review of evidence pointing to the virus's accidental introduction into human subjects by a mass inoculation program in Central Africa. At the heart of science the canker was growing.

In the past two decades allegations of fraud have disturbed science and scientists to an extent not acknowledged before. These accusations were investigated and the results published in journals and, sometimes, the popular press. Hersen and Miller reflect on the contemporary prevalence of fraud in biomedical and social science research and recollect the stories of fraud had even implicated such famous scientists as Newton, Bernouilli, Dalton, Mendel, Peary, Millikin (1992, p.226). Policies to deal with allegations of fraud were being framed in several scientific arenas. Exemplifying this development the Institute of Medicine in the US published a lengthy report on responsible conduct in health research. At the same time a US government committee had examined ten cases of scientific fraud in major US universities and been highly critical of these institutions (Hersen & Miller, 1992). Denunciation of research fraud was universal, but, at the empirical, that is the specific level of individual matters, there was uncertainty and prevarication. In 1976 a scandal was raised regarding English psychologist Sir Cyril Burt, who had allegedly fabricated evidence to support his theories about inherited intelligence (see Hearnshaw, 1979; Joynson, 1989; Fletcher, 1991; Jensen, 1992). In this case, as in others, it is sometimes not clear where the fault lies or what it may be. Often issues are complicated by misconception and inadequate communication. Too often the trouble is systemic in origin. As such, blame is not easily attributed.

Nor was it always the case that it was the lonely scientist toiling alone, who was tempted and fell into fraudulent practice. As Robert Bell documented, large research institutes ('big science') and the large pharmaceutical companies could be guilty of fraud and criminal negligence. He investigated and reported on the making and selling of the pharmaceutical drug Zomax by McNeil Pharmaceutical (owned by Johnson & Johnson), and Versed by Hoffman-La Roche—both non-steroid anti-inflammatory drugs available and widely used in the 1970s despite occasional lethal side-effects. An equally compelling analysis of dangerous bias among industry and government scientists appeared in the highly regarded British journal *Sociology* (1994, vol.28, no.3). There Abraham presented a case history of Opren, a non-steroid anti-inflammatory drug used in the treatment of arthritis. It was strongly promoted by its manufacturer, Eli Lilly, and used widely by elderly people after its launch in the UK in 1980. Shortly afterwards individual scientists warned of the potential cumulative toxicity of the dose, but these small-sample studies were not published until two years later. By 1982 several elderly patients had died from hepatic-renal syndrome whilst taking Opren, and the sequence of cases was reported in the *British Medical Journal*. Only after these deaths did the British Committee on Safety of Medicines demand that Eli Lilly change the recommended dose for the elderly. The scandal was reported in January 1983 on the BBC program *Panorama*, titled 'The Opren Scandal'.

These and other related controversies in the 1980s underline the extent of community anxiety about negligence and fraud in science, especially biomedical science. Such worries have prompted sociological investigations of science, accusations of fraud and the hazards of scientific dishonesty. Two recent books exemplify the multi-disciplinary strengths of such investigators: Evelleen Richards' *Vitamin C and Cancer: Medicine and Politics* on the Cameron and Pauling disputes about the efficacy of Vitamin C as cancer therapy, and Jan Sapp's analysis of allegations of fraud in Moewus's work in genetics and microbiology, *Where the Truth Lies* (1990). The US sociologist J.D. Douglas reflected on the extent of dishonesty and violation of property rights associated with scientific discovery, many of which, although illegal, do not violate the ethics of science itself. It is difficult, he claims, to establish a *mens rea* (intentional, knowledgeable wrongdoing) of actions in a field where are found so much 'mythical thinking' (theoretical bias, paradigmatic expectations), simple mistakes, as well as ambition, haste, premature publication. Despite the extent of the problem he cautions against bureaucratic controls as a response to 'an explosion of scientific deviance, a growing betrayal of truth that is the corruption of the soul of science' (1992, p.81).

The rush of books and papers examining scientific fraud in the past two decades heightened the science community's sensitivity, stimulated a rash of committees, policies and protocols, and produced an eruption of fear and anxiety which spread to the educated public. Australian scientists, perhaps a little later than colleagues elsewhere, were alerted to the spread of dubious or dishonest practice in their own institutions, and Australian cases were added to the catalogue of frauds occurring in the world of science (see Swan, 1988; Jones, 1991). During the 1980s several of Australia's larger research universities had their own scandals; some were publicised, some were hushed up, all presumably were 'rectified'.

The links between medical science and medical practice are patent, with most of these links forged by the major pharmaceutical companies. This is a relationship on which pharmaceutical companies lavish considerable care and expense. They are active in providing information, education and sponsorship to the profession and depend on the reciprocity of medical practitioners prescribing and promoting their products. McBride, like most medical practitioners, enjoyed a comfortable relationship with the pharmaceutical companies. Medical practitioners might be seen as honorary associate members in the international pharmaceutical community, valued for the synergy of their interaction.

The primary identity of specialist medical practitioners lies with their profession, particularly the collegiate of their specialty. Some, like McBride, also hold a place in the scientific community. Very important for medical practitioners, general and specialist, is their relation to the patients who constitute their practice. These connections can be strong and, usually in obstetrics, very supportive. In the company of their patients such doctors readily assume the status of the intellectual, sometimes eluding charismatic authority. McBride practised among a clientele which highly valued his services and accorded him an excellent reputation.

The Fame of William McBride

In 1950 William McBride graduated in medicine from the University of Sydney and commenced practice as a resident medical officer at St George Hospital in Sydney. The following year he moved to Launceston General Hospital in Tasmania, returning to Sydney as a resident medical officer at Crown Street Women's Hospital in 1952. Three years later he was appointed as the medical superintendent. In the interim he completed his studies in England and was admitted as a member of the Royal College of Obstetricians and Gynaecologists in 1954. His specialist career was in a gratifying ascendancy.

In 1961 McBride became aware of a number of babies born with strange disabilities. He himself delivered three severely deformed babies within a few months of each other. Their arms were grossly shortened and deformed, and each suffered from atresia of the small bowel. The babies died within a week of birth. When studying the clinical records McBride discovered that each mother had used Distaval, a formulation of thalidomide, to overcome nausea early in the pregnancy. Further investigation and reflection prompted him to write a paper warning of the dangers of thalidomide taken during pregnancy. At the same time he persuaded the Crown Street Women's Hospital to withdraw the drug from use pending further investigation, and contacted the manufacturers to warn of the damage the drug could cause to the foetus. His paper, sent to the *Lancet* on 13 June 1961, was rejected the following month. In the meantime he commenced experiments to determine if thalidomide damaged the rabbit foetus and found no such effects. More babies with the same deformities were being born, but for the majority born to mothers who had taken the drug in early pregnancy there were no ill effects. Thalidomide seemed to strike 10 to 20% of babies. McBride, however, remained convinced of its teratogenic effects. He wrote a report of his observations for Distillers Biochemicals, the company which marketed the drug and then sent a letter to the *Lancet* which eventually published it on 16 December 1961.[2] This letter alerted the world to the danger of thalidomide which was severely damaging some infants in a seemingly haphazard fashion.

In the meantime in Hamburg, Dr Widukind Lenz was following up his own suspicions about the effects of thalidomide, by undertaking experiments to determine its effects on animal foetuses. He added his warnings to McBride's, telling the German manufacturers of the potential teratogenic action of thalidomide on the foetus. McBride, as Lenz readily conceded, was the first to warn of the grim consequences of the drug if used during pregnancy. International recognition as the obstetrician who discovered the teratogenic effects of thalidomide encouraged McBride to continue research, alongside his work as a leading practitioner in obstetrics and gynaecology.

Fame came quickly to McBride. In 1962 Sydney University conferred on him a doctorate in medicine. In 1969 he was awarded the British honour of Companion of the British Empire. Two years later the *L'Institut de la Vie* in Paris awarded him the Gold Medal for services to medical science (his most highly valued award). McBride used the prize money awarded by *L'Institut de la Vie* (approximately A$40,000) to establish Foundation 41, a charitable research body dedicated to research into the first 41 weeks of life (conception to the first week after birth). Donations flowed into support the work, and a number of eminent citizens, including professors of the medical faculties of the two major Sydney universities, formed the Board, with McBride becoming the Director. Five years later he was awarded the Order of Australia, and in 1972, he was named Father of the Year.

McBride's position at Foundation 41 was honorary, and the time and energy he devoted to research without financial reward. During this time he maintained a busy and successful obstetric practice and sustained active involvement in research, publishing in national and international medical and scientific journals. His international reputation as an expert on the potential effects of therapeutic drugs taken in pregnancy determined much of his own research agenda in teratology. Years before such anxieties were accepted as conventional wisdom, he was deeply concerned about the effect on the foetus of drugs taken in pregnancy, and he has remained sternly critical of the lack of adequate trials of therapeutic drugs used to obviate the discomforts of pregnancy. In 1972 he observed, and had reported to him, a number of deformed babies who had been born to mothers who had taken the newly available antidepressant, impramine, early in pregnancy. But fears that the drug was the cause of malformation were dispelled with further review of the purported evidence.

The next drug to attract attention as potentially teratogenic was Bendectin (American tradename) or Debendox (Australian tradename). McBride had expressed concern about its safety shortly after its release, a concern which was being expressed in several quarters. By 1983 Merrell Dow Pharmaceuticals had taken the drug off the market, still maintaining its therapeutic value in pregnancy, but deciding not to expose the company to protracted legal argument about attempts to implicate the drug in adverse outcomes observed in pregnancy. Prior to that decision claimants against the company had secured McBride as expert witness in support of their case and he had flown to the US a number of times to give evidence against the interests of the giant pharmaceutical company.

McBride had been (and still is), of the opinion that anticholinergic drugs taken during pregnancy can adversely affect the foetal neurological system and so cause malformations. In 1979 he determined to experiment with Debendox to see if it caused malformation in the rabbit foetus. His offer to buy some of the ingredients of Debendox from the manufacturer in order to perform the experiments was refused. Not to be thwarted he crushed Debendox tablets and had these fed to the experimental animals. The results however were nil—none of the ten pregnant rabbits produced malformed foetuses. Nonetheless he remained convinced of the danger this category of drugs posed for the human foetus. A year later McBride, still unable to obtain samples of dicyclomine hydrochloride (the suspect active ingredient in Debendox), determined to experiment with a related chemical, scopolamine hydrochloride, whose action is similar to the synthetic compound used in Debendox. He set up an experiment to determine its effects on chicks, where the egg had been injected with scopolamine hydrochloride, and on rabbit offspring born after the mother had ingested the drug dissolved in water. The results were that from the six pregnant rabbits who had drunk water from containers in which scopolamine hydrobromide had been dissolved, one litter contained severely malformed foetuses.

The results were described in a paper titled 'Effects of Scopolamine Hydrobromide on the Development of the Chick and Rabbit Embryo' and submitted to *The Journal of Toxicology and Applied Pharmacology*. The paper however was rejected on the basis of criticisms received via the refereeing process. One referee stated that although it was an important result, a larger proportion of affected foetuses would be desirable for statistical significance, and that this malformed litter may have been a chance result. Another of the referees stated that the volumes of dissolved scopolamine could not be correct as animals under the same environmental conditions drink amounts of water proportional to their body weights, and two of the animals would have died if they had consumed so much of the drug. (These did not include the rabbit whose litter was malformed.) There was said to be a problem about how much water the animals drank, how much was spilt in their enclosure and how much had evaporated. Further criticism was directed at the failure to use contemporaneous controls.

In response to these criticisms McBride made a number of changes to the paper:

1. The estimate of the water, and therefore the drug ingested, by three of the animals was reduced.
2. The inclusion (or implication) of a contemporaneous control group of rabbits, not dosed with the drug who delivered normal litters.
3. The addition of data on two rabbits, increasing the sample to eight, thereby increasing the number of litter of deformed foetuses to two. (These additions were wrongly represented as being from the University of New South Wales animal colony.)
4. The record of the weight of one rabbit was reduced from 4.62 kg to 4.02 kg.

This version of the experiment was published by *The Australian Journal of Biological Science* in 1982 (Vol. 35, No.2).

McBride had listed two junior researchers, Philip Vardy and Jill French, who had assisted with the experiment and had requested recognition (thereby assisting in the development of their scientific credentials) as co-authors of the paper. Copies of the revised paper were, McBride stated, sent to his co-authors, and he had shown the manuscript and journal proofs to one of his research team, Vardy. Vardy later denied this. The repercussions of this paper were to hit McBride eight years later.

McBride as Medical Activist

McBride's international reputation had been built on the discovery of the tragic effects of thalidomide taken during pregnancy. He continued his laboratory research and, perhaps more importantly, he monitored the outcome for mothers and babies to detect any untoward effects of drugs taken during pregnancy. He became obsessive in his scrutiny of any links between pharmaceuticals and damage to the foetus. He was frequently called to give expert evidence for the plaintiff (i.e. children born with a disability or their parents) where prenatal medication was possibly implicated. And he answered such calls with alacrity. Most of these cases were in the US and were costing pharmaceutical companies dearly in legal defence and diminished reputation. In 1980, when the drug Bendectin became suspect, McBride accepted a request to serve as expert witness for the parents of a child who claimed his deformities were due to Bendectin. McBride based his opinion on two studies, a laboratory experiment and an epidemiological observation of some adverse effects associated with Bendectin. His evidence was rejected by the court because of the lack of documentation for these studies. The respondent in this case was the company Richardson Merrell who later, after a merger, became Merrell Dow Pharmaceutical.

Subsequently McBride appeared as an expert witness for the plaintiff in another US case. This time the prescribed (anticholinergic) drugs taken by the mother during pregnancy were Tigan, Dramamine, Butibel, Donnatal and Etrafon. His submitted report for the case stated that the drugs taken could cause birth defects, and that the prenatal disabilities of the child were probably caused by, or contributed to, by his mother's ingestion of these drugs singularly or in combination during pregnancy. He referred in his depositions to a large number of scientific papers, including his own research on scopolamine hydrobromide and doxylamine succinate (another anticholinergic drug), and based his opinion on his education, training and experience.

McBride's crusade continued, and in 1985 he gave evidence in support of parents' claim that their daughter's limb deformations were due to her mother taking a prescribed vitamin A derivative, retinoic acid, for acne during pregnancy. He described the case in an article sent to the *Lancet* later that year.[3] It was some years before women were being warned not to use the preparation in early pregnancy.

Questions about the Reliability of the Science

Phillip Vardy first voiced his dismay about the revised paper detailing the scopolamine hydrobromide experiment in 1982. (His objections only referred to the validity of the rabbit component of the experiment.) Vardy later claimed he was alarmed when, in June 1982, he read the revised paper published under the same three names in the *Australian Journal of Biological Sciences*. He said that he asked the secretary of Foundation 41 for the file of material pertaining to this publication but it was refused (the secretary denied that he requested the file).

Howsoever he gained possession of it and of the jars of rabbit foetuses which had not been sectioned as the paper had stated. He detected inconsistencies between that detailed in the published report and the original data. Jill French, the other research assistant involved in the experiment, resigned from the Foundation in September 1982, giving as one reason for her departure the appearance of her name on the article whose accuracy she disputed. Her resignation prompted other research assistants to raise similar doubts to the Foundation's Research Advisory Committee, calling for an investigation of the discrepancies.

Four months after reading the revised paper, Vardy, who had accused McBride of fraud, tried to persuade Foundation 41's Research Advisory Committee in a meeting to seek McBride's resignation as director. The Committee refused, but, after perusing the relevant materials, proposed that McBride write to the journal and state the errors in the report and indicate that the experiment would be repeated.[4] The minutes of that committee meeting on the 2 November 1982, state that this course of action had satisfied Vardy. However he resigned on 1 November 1982 and, when he left that week, he took a number of papers and documents with him.

Several years later Vardy repeated his allegations to Dr Norman Swan, at that time a paediatrician (he later became a journalist). Dr Swan took up the case, investigations taking three years. On 12 December 1987 Swan accused McBride of scientific fraud on *The Science Show*, a radio program put to air by the national broadcaster, the Australian Broadcasting Commission.[5] This program attracted intense coverage in the media. Two days later a newspaper headline read: 'McBride: Storm over Cheating Claims' (*Sydney Morning Herald*, 14 Dec. 1987, p.1).

In response McBride released a detailed statement rejecting the accusations of scientific fraud and repudiating many of the statements made during the program. He defended the change in dosage recorded for two of the rabbits as a correction of earlier an earlier miscalculation, and revealed that two of the rabbits included in the report had been subject to the same experiment, conducted at the University of Virginia by Professor Jan Langman. The experiment, he insisted (as he was to repeat many times in the future), involved scopolamine hydrobromide and was not connected to Debendox. Notwithstanding this disclaimer McBride's expert evidence in cases in the US had been blamed as a significant factor in the decision to withdrawal Debendox from sale in 1983. Many members of the medical profession had been angered by McBride's part in the alarm raised about that particular drug and its consequent withdrawal. There were calls from the Private Doctors' Association to have Debendox returned to the market (*Sydney Morning Herald*, 14 Dec. 1987, p.1). He furnished further details of the original report of his experiment with Langman's results. He pointed to the explanatory note published in a later issue of the journal which had published the first report. He particularly objected to the program's one-sided address to the allegations, particularly the refusal to include a more senior researcher, supervisor of the two junior research assistants, in the discussion of the facts of the case.

Foundation 41 initially stood firm behind McBride, with the Chairman expressing the Committee of Management's complete confidence in him. Nonetheless on 16 December 1987 the Foundation announced its decision to set up a private committee of inquiry, with which McBride agreed to fully cooperate. Recently retired High Court judge, Sir Harry Gibbs, assisted by eminent scientists, Professor Robert Porter of the Australian National University and Professor Roger Short of Monash University, agreed to conduct the committee of inquiry (to be known as the Gibbs Committee of Inquiry). A private inquiry is not open and McBride was not permitted to be present while others gave their version of events. Witnesses included Dr Norman Swan, the two junior research assistants, Philip Vardy and Jill French, officials of the New South Wales Health Department and, of course, McBride. The Inquiry gained much of its authority from the reputation of its presiding member, Sir Harry Gibbs, who had been President of the High Court of Australia and hence the leading jurist in the land. It was hampered, however, by its status as a private committee of inquiry. Hence, it could not compel witnesses to attend, to swear to the truth of their evidence or to submit to cross-examination. Because of the nature of the inquiry, McBride was not permitted to be present to hear the evidence against him, to confront his accusers, to query that evidence, or to have legal representation in what was to become the trial of his professional reputation.

On 2 November 1988, ten months after its establishment, the Gibbs Committee of Inquiry published its report.[6] The Committee admitted that McBride had been disadvantaged because of its legal limitations, but found him guilty of scientific fraud. The finding was based on:

1. the inference that the eight rabbits were the subject of experiment in New South Wales, whereas only six were the subject of experiment in that state;
2. the change to the dosages stated for 'oral ingestion';
3. the statement that the foetuses in the experimental group were sectioned;
4. the inference that eight contemporaneous controls came from the same supplier and were fed the same diet;
5. the experiment as published suggests that McBride was lacking in scientific integrity;
6. the experiment was not conducted in accordance with proper scientific method.[7]

McBride resigned from Foundation 41 later that same day stating, 'I don't wish that there be any doubt cast over the work that I, and the foundation, have done over the past 16 years' (*Sydney Morning Herald*, 3 Nov. 1988, p.1). Newspapers ran editorial and learned comment on the issue. The noted law commentator, John Slee, noted the lack of professional solidarity to support McBride accused of the 'theoretically serious but, in practical terms, not so devastating offence of violating the scientific method ... it is also hard to accept the double standards of professional accountability that his case highlights' (*Sydney Morning Herald*, 4 Nov. 1988, p.14). When a profession or academic community draws away from a colleague the lines are clearly drawn. No one objects to the ostracism lest they too suffer the same fate.

On the same day McBride decided to appeal to the Supreme Court claiming that he had been denied natural justice. But other events, anticipated in the media (*Sydney Morning Herald*, 3 Nov. 1988, p.1), overtook this action. The Complaints Unit of the New South Wales Health Department had been investigating his obstetric practice on the grounds that he had not exercised adequate skill and care, his was too interventionist a practice, and his caesarean section rate was too high. There had been no complaint of any adverse event, but every clinical record involving his patients for the previous ten years were taken, with proper authority, from the relevant hospitals and examined to probe for breach of good practice. Following its investigation the Health Complaints Unit submitted its complaints to the New South Wales Medical Tribunal.

Walton v. McBride

The New South Wales Medical Tribunal is presided over by a district court judge, on this occasion Judge B.C.M. Wall, QC. The two medical practitioners serving on the bench were Professor G.D. Tracy, a distinguished surgeon and former President of the Royal Australian College of Surgery, who had been awarded an Order of Australia for his services to medicine, and Dr E. Sussman a consultant gynaecologist whose practice was based at Royal North Shore Hospital. The layperson serving on the Tribunal was Mrs M. Brophy.

The complaints were set out in particulars for the Medical Tribunal, which moved first to clear some legal procedural points in dispute. These involved the criteria to determine firstly, professional misconduct, and secondly, the legality of the particulars of complaint which simply pointed to an unacceptable rate of the incidence of caesarean sections performed by the practitioner. McBride objected to a complaint which simply noted a rate of caesarean section significantly higher than the norm. A hearing before the Supreme Court directed that the complaint must be sent out in specific detail (particularised). The Complaints Unit investigated the records and provided specific cases. Some of the matters in question occurred before October 1987 when amendments to the legislation brought a definition of professional misconduct slightly different to the earlier 'test of misconduct in a professional respect' (*Qidwai v. Brown* 1984 1 NSWLR

100). The Tribunal decided that the legislated definition of 1987 should apply. The section, 27(1) of the Medical Practitioners Act 1938, as amended in 1987, states in part that professional misconduct, in relation to a registered medical practitioner, includes the following:

(a) any conduct that demonstrates a lack of adequate
    i) knowledge;
    ii) experience;
    iii) skill;
    iv) judgment; or
    v) care
by the practitioner in the practice of medicine.

This was a somewhat wider definition than applied under the older precedent-based determination, but the assessment of this lack was still to be such as would incur the strong reprobation of medical peers.

The complaints which initially referred to statistically excessive rates of caesarean sections were revised and then allowed after the Tribunal assured itself that the onus of proof to justify clinical procedures would not be put on the practitioner. Rather the Complainant, the Health Department, was required to demonstrate lack of clinical justification for procedure(s) as constituting professional misconduct. Hence these occurrences were to be listed in the particulars of complaint. This ruling ameliorated the original complaint which resonated with the public health literature about 'unnecessary surgical procedures' discussed earlier in this chapter. Nonetheless, that allegation claimed to be typified in McBride's practice remained in place and featured prominently in media discussions. This was the part of complaints about clinical practice most salient and readily understood in the public discourse.

In the opening proceedings both sides appealed against different aspects of these determinations to the Supreme Court. That decision did not effectively counter the view of the Tribunal. But the Tribunal reserved consideration of what constituted professional misconduct with regard to the particulars of this case until the end of the hearing. The Complainant[8] duly revised the complaints, as required, and lodged a new form of 15 complaints.

After these preliminary skirmishes the Tribunal commenced its hearing on 6 November 1989 in the expectation that the hearing would take six weeks.

The Obstetric Complaints

The Complaints Unit's investigation into the clinical practice of Dr William McBride had taken many months. Of the final fifteen complaints, eight involved fifty-five patients treated by McBride at three public hospitals over a period of ten years. These 'obstetric complaints' consisted of omnibus or composite complaints (1, 7 and 8B), alleging professional misconduct in the clinical management of thirty-eight patients in their first pregnancy. The Complainant maintained that these primapara (first baby) patients were delivered by caesarean section without clinical justification. Twenty were private patients at Crown Street Women's Hospital from September 1979 to March 1983, eight at the Royal Hospital for Women Paddington during the years 1983 to 1988; and ten at St George Hospital, Kogarah from 1986 to 1988.

A further composite complaint (8A) alleged that in the case of eight private patients treated at St George Hospital between 1986 and 1988, McBride had diagnosed placenta praevia[9] and managed each accordingly without clinical signs to support the diagnoses. Particulars of these cases were put forward to demonstrate a pattern of practice amounting to professional misconduct.

The remaining obstetric complaints (2, 3, 4, 5 and 6) support separate charges of professional misconduct in relation to clinical management of five patients treated at Royal Hospital for Women.

The Tribunal considered carefully current clinical literature which favoured surgical intervention for a wide range of risks to which mother or infant might be exposed. This review of the literature supported McBride's fairly activist style of practice as falling well within the norms of sound practice. In giving reasons for its determination the Tribunal cited extensively from the clinical literature which argued the wide and various indications for caesarean section, (i.e. the demographic, sociological and cultural factors increasing the frequency of this procedure as safer and easier for mother and baby). This perusal of obstetric papers published in that period and the authorities cited in the Tribunal proceedings, underlines the strong support for intervention in the interests of the mother and especially the baby, at that time. This obstetric paradigm runs quite counter to the model recommended in the literature published in the public health journals; additionally these practices offended feminists and other women intent in regaining control over childbirth. But it would be a rare obstetrician who perused such 'alternative' readings.

The Tribunal expressed concern about issues of privacy breached by the access taken by the Complainant (the officer acting with the authority of the Health Department) to hospital records of patients without permission or knowledge of those patients. This anxiety was allayed by advice from the Crown Solicitor that the Complainant as person, authorised by the Secretary of the Department of Health, was acting within powers given by the Public Hospitals Act 1929, the Health Administration Act 1938, and the Medical Practitioners Act 1938. The search of clinical records however occurred after the Complaints Unit referred its complaints to the Tribunal, not the chronology anticipated in the legislation where 'it is more likely for obvious reasons, that the intention of the legislature was to require the investigation of complaints prior to their referral to Tribunal or Court' (*Medical Tribunal of New South Wales in the Matter of William McBride and the Medical Practitioners Act*, Background paper, Book 1 at 16). It seemed that investigation was following after, not leading to complaint. The Tribunal noted that there had not been a complaint by any patient of McBride, and registered concern about a hospital patient's right to privacy and confidentiality: 'What happened in this case was a retrospective analysis of a clinician's practice in obstetrics in the last decade not based on any complaint by a patient of that practice' (at 16). In the course of the hearing, patients were subpoenaed to give evidence and forty-four patients were named in an appendix to the Tribunal's decision. Many protested to the intrusion on their privacy and responded favourably to questions about the quality of McBride's clinical services.

The Complainant had originally sought to base much of this part of the case on a statistical analysis of a caesarean section rate grossly in excess of McBride's peers. The Complainant planned to choose four specialist obstetricians whose patterns of practice could be compared to that of McBride. The Tribunal rejected this approach as one where too many variables could be subsumed into a simplistic model and variation from that predetermined norm deemed as misconduct. This rejection prompted further recourse to patient records at the three mentioned hospitals to identify cases where diagnosis and treatment deviated from the norm. As a consequence the review of McBride's clinical cases was the most extensive scrutiny ever undertaken.

Four obstetric experts were called by each side to assess the quality of treatment in the cases identified. The experts called by the Complainant had been shown the hospital records prior to commencement of the Tribunal. After this preliminary perusal fifty-five patient records were put forward to support the complaint that obstetric care had deviated from good practice. As each matter came before the Tribunal, and the total clinical picture appeared, the experts called by the Complainant withdrew most initial criticisms. Further documentation, including records from McBride's private practice, patients' hospital antenatal cards, and additional hospital records not previously included, were put before the Tribunal. Patients, as well as some of their partners, were called to give evidence or submit statements. A number of nurses and medical practitioners employed by the relevant hospitals also gave evidence. McBride was examined and cross-examined. Expert obstetricians called by each side discussed clinical features of every case. Over the months of the Tribunal it became apparent that the serious obstetric complaints did not hold. McBride's pattern of obstetric practice tended to be interventionist but with positive outcomes for mothers and babies.

The greater part of the hearing of the clinical complaints was devoted to

McBride's pattern of practice bearing on caesarean section, and to the other composite complaint about diagnosis and treatment of placenta praevia observed in eight patients. One by one the particular complaint based on each case was defeated as the experts agreed that the obstetrician's practice was sound and within the bounds of the conventional practice at that time. Similarly five individual complaints about management of labour were not substantiated. McBride's record and reputation had survived a gruelling inquisition.

One fault was uncovered on this unblemished record. McBride had apparently failed to make firm arrangements for the obstetric care of a patient to a covering obstetrician of comparable qualifications and experience when called to give expert evidence in a US court case. This carelessness was held to be inexcusable and a departure from acceptable standards of care. This misconduct, the Tribunal found, warranted a reprimand.

The Scientific Fraud Complaints

The latter part of the Tribunal proceedings did not go so well for McBride.

Seven complaints were detailed under twenty-four particulars. Two complaints related to particulars devolved from the publication of scopolamine hydrobromide experiment, which had been the subject of the Gibbs Committee of Inquiry one year earlier, and the published qualifying note some time later.

Claims that the article was false and misleading in regard to procedures and outcomes of the chicken component of the experiment were not upheld. It appears that the experiment and the adverse outcome of malformed chicks after injection of the drug was not in question as alleged. The Tribunal did, however, find that the paper was false and misleading in several statements about the rabbit phase of the experiment as follows:

1. that 24 specific rabbits (from the University of New South Wales animal colony) including contemporaneous control does were used;
2. that the treated does were killed and the foetuses sectioned to inspect the organs;
3. that the scopolamine hydrobromide was delivered by 'intramuscular injection' (Vardy gave evidence that the injections were 'intraperitoneal');
4. that six of the eight rabbits given injections survived and produced 38 foetuses (Vardy stated that only five became pregnant);
5. that the days cited when injections were given were false (injection of the rabbits was said to have been given 10–14 after mating and should have been cited as 12–16, 11–15 and 11–14);
6. that the 12-hour intervals between injections were falsely stated;

7. that the time of death for two of the rabbits is falsely stated;
8. that the daily doses of the drug estimated for three of the animals and the eight of one were falsely stated; and
9. that two of the rabbits given scopolamine hydrobromide were not of the New South Wales colony and subject to experiment with the others as implied.

On this last point the Tribunal stated that it did not believe that the data regarding the additional two rabbits came from Professor Langman as McBride claimed. It did not, however, make a finding on this point. (It is important to note that the listing does not distinguish between what was false and what merely misleading, what intentional and what careless in its misstatement.)

There is no doubt that the experiment in question was carelessly carried out and inadequately supervised. A major difficulty lay in the calculation of the water, and hence, quantity of drug, ingested by the rabbits. There were other inadequacies of which the lack of contemporaneous controls (subject to all conditions of the experiment except the injection of the drug) was regarded seriously. Records appeared to be poorly kept, blame for which usually goes to the chief investigator not the assistants. In response to these allegations McBride disagreed with the parts of the evidence given by Vardy and, on most points, stated that the disputed data did not go to material issues which could affect the interpretation reached in the publication. In the contentions about the rabbit component of the experiment the Tribunal accepted the evidence of the Complainant's witness, Vardy, and rejected that of McBride.

A further complaint arose from the note that Foundation 41 had requested McBride submit following disputes about the published paper. McBride's statements in this note regarding contemporaneous controls and the reasons for repeating the experiment were held to be misleading.

The other complaints concerned issues around McBride's 1979 experiment using Debendox and the evidence which McBride gave in court cases brought against the drug's manufacturer in the US. These complaints were not proved, but minor aspects of McBride's evidence given in those actions were held to be incorrect. The Tribunal found that in describing his experiments with Debendox McBride mis-described finer details of the experiment, but not however with intention of making a false statement. That mis-description, it was held, was caused by reckless indifference or inexcusable carelessness.

Towards the close of the evidentiary proceedings, the Complainant again applied to add further complaints to the list. The Tribunal gave a tentative ruling against this request, returning to rule definitively at the end.

The Tribunal's Decision and Orders

The disciplinary hearing lasted 198 days. Preliminary directions had been heard in July 1989. Then the inquiry commenced in November 1989 and completed taking evidence in June 1991. McBride gave evidence and was cross-examined from day 77 to day 113 on all aspects of the obstetric complaints having to recall in fine detail forty-four cases selected from the previous ten years of obstetric practice. This part of the proceedings ended in February 1991.

In March 1991 the Tribunal began hearing the scientific fraud complaints, and McBride was again examined and cross-examined, this time on research conducted eleven years previously. His memory was aided by some but not all of the records (Vardy had taken some of the records of data and some specimens when he resigned from Foundation 41 in 1981). This shorter part of the hearing ended in June 1991. Eighteen months later in February 1993 the Tribunal delivered its interim findings. There was a further hearing in May and June 1993 to consider if the additional allegations might be brought by the Complainant. The Tribunal formally ruled against admitting these matters.

Finally on 30 July 1993, two years after it had completed the main hearing, the Tribunal delivered its orders. A newspaper headline declared the verdict: 'Tragic, Deceptive McBride Struck Off' (*Sydney Morning Herald*, 31 July 1993, p.3).

As noted above, the complaints about McBride's obstetric practice were not substantiated in that they could not support a finding of professional misconduct in any respect. Five of the seven complaints of scientific fraud were not upheld, the remaining two found to be proved in most particulars. In regard to these two, the Tribunal found that McBride had published false or misleading statements which he knew to be false or misleading. This had been done, they stated, to strengthen the appearance of the experiment and enhance the 'publishability' of the article, and hence support for his hypothesis that scopolamine hydrobromide can be teratogenic. Additionally misleading statements were made in the note which followed the article in question. These statements were made 'with either reckless indifference to the truth or were the result of inexcusable carelessness' (Book 8 at 9). This determination pointed to the decision sought by the Complainant that McBride was not of good character in the context of fitness to practise medicine. The Tribunal deliberated over the legal interpretation of this phrase. McBride, it found, had held to the belief that scientific principles of experimentation and publication of results could be set aside if it was necessary to warn the public of the potential danger of a drug. (There would be many who would agree with him, but that is not good positivist science.) Accordingly the Tribunal decided 'he had crossed the line that separates error of judgment and moral turpitude' and had continued in that 'moral blindness' (at 12–13). Medical research, the argument continued, is critical for the practice of medicine. Much depends on trust placed in scientific researchers and McBride was in breach of the trust between himself and fellow researchers. This called 'into question his lack of good character and hence his fitness to practise medicine' (at 15). The Tribunal noted that McBride did not accept that he had included spurious data (the 'Langman rabbits') in the experiment. Although the Tribunal did not believe that the Langman rabbits existed, it did not rule on this. It was, however, undeterred by McBride's avowed concern about the potential for harm if purportedly therapeutic drugs are taken in pregnancy, and would not allow the misconduct to be diminished by claims of altruistic purpose. Arguments had been advanced by both sides about motivation, and hence intention—a difficult and contentious inquiry into *mens rea* (evil intention). The Tribunal decided the motive was zeal to publish and found a compounding of the misconduct in refusal to concede wrongdoing. The Tribunal decided to its 'comfortable satisfaction that Dr McBride is not of good character in the context of fitness to practise medicine' (at 20). The majority concluded that he must be removed from the Register of Medical Practitioners.

Professor Tracy however dissented, stating that McBride had attended to the most serious complaint of fraud identified in the article and, to a lesser extent in the note which followed. Tracy agreed that the falsifications, with which McBride persisted, demonstrated 'a serious lack of scientific rigour ... a lack of appreciation for scientific method and meticulous notation of records ... complete indifference to the principles of statistical inference' (at 24). He went on to highlight McBride's distinguished career as an obstetrician, his discovery of the effects of thalidomide, his honorary directorship and voluntary research work, the establishment of Foundation 41, the excellent testimonials by distinguished legal and medical referees, and the trust and loyalty of his patients. In his opinion McBride's conduct warranted reprimand, but any additional penalty 'would be both unmerited and excessive' (at 26). The other three members of the Tribunal did not agree. McBride's name was removed from the Register of Medical Practitioners that day.

The Tribunal was very critical of the Complainant's conduct of the case and noted:

> ... the inordinate time scale of the inquiry (particularly in relation to the obstetric costs), the multiplicity of issues of fact and law, the length of the evidence and the submissions, oral and written, and the lengthy retirement of the members of the Tribunal for deliberations required in consequence of these matters can only be described as oppressive. Oppressive to the practitioner, oppressive to the public purse and oppressive to good governance of medical disciplinary proceedings (at 26).

Accordingly the Tribunal ordered that the Complainant should bear McBride's legal costs in relation to the obstetric complaints. (The usual order is that the deregistered practitioner meet the costs of both sides to the action.) Because the Complainant had succeeded in part, but not all, of the scientific fraud complaints, each party should pay its own costs in relation to this latter part of the inquiry. The Complainant appealed these costs orders.

In reaching its decision on each complaint the Tribunal applied the civil standard of proof, that is proof lay in the balance of probabilities having regard to the seriousness of the facts if proved. This is considerably removed from the standard of proof in criminal trials where proof 'beyond reasonable doubt' is required, and conforms rather with the standard in deciding civil matters (quarrels between citizens) where the Court resolves where right lies on the balance of probabilities. The Tribunal looked in its decision to feel 'a comfortable satisfaction that [it] has reached both a correct and just decision' (Rich J, *Briginshaw v. Briginshaw*, 1938, 60 CLR at 350).

After receiving the orders of the Tribunal McBride appealed the decision.

The Appeal to the Supreme Court

Leave to appeal was granted. The case opened before Mr Justice Michael Kirby, President of the Appeal Court, Mr Justice Kenneth Robert Handley and Mr Justice Phillip Ernest Powell of the appellate division of the Supreme Court of New South Wales on 5 October 1993. Given that appeals from the decision of the Medical Tribunal may only be based on issues of law not of fact and/or as an appeal regarding exercise of disciplinary powers (that is, against the orders or penalty imposed), the Court of Appeal looked at four issues:

1. Whether the Tribunal erred in law in concluding that McBride was not of good character in the context of the practice of medicine by reason of the scientific fraud.
2. Whether the Tribunal erred in law in taking into account matters outside the complaints McBride had been called to answer.
3. Whether the order for his removal from the Register of Medical Practitioners should not have been some other such as a reprimand.
4. Whether the Court should disturb the order made for costs by the Tribunal (that is, the award of costs in the obstetric matters against the Complaints Unit of the Department of Health). (Cross-appeal brought by Complainant.)

There were important principles at stake. McBride's first point of appeal addressed the legal meaning of the term 'not of good character' in respect to medicine; the second to disregard for rules of procedural fairness (natural justice) in reaching that determination; the third contested the claims that public interest and public confidence in the profession were served by his deregistration and claimed that this order ignored the evidence that the conduct in question was uncharacteristic.

There were significant points of law to be decided in this case and the judges attended carefully to the reasons for the view each took. These bore on the outcome for McBride, but went beyond the specificities of his case. This was a significant decision which explored earlier precedent and sought to establish new principles for discernment in disciplinary matters.

These issues were argued before the Supreme Court for three days. On 15 July 1994, nine months after the hearing, the Supreme Court presented its judgment.

The majority held that the dishonest reporting of an animal experiment on a suspected teratogen established that the practitioner, even if otherwise of good character and reputation, was 'not of good character' in respect of his practice of medicine and so should be deregistered. On the issue of lack of procedural fairness before the Tribunal, the majority held that lack of procedural fairness would constitute an error of law (and so could be point for appeal), and so the Tribunal was not entitled to suggest dishonesty outside of the particularised matters which the Respondent was on notice to answer. But, the majority determined, any departure from procedural fairness did not go so far as to require that the Tribunal's orders, for deregistration, should be set aside. Consequently the majority held that the orders for deregistration were fitting. The Presiding Judge, Justice Kirby, dissented from the majority ruling on all points.

The leading judgment was delivered by Justice Powell who was critical of the handling of the obstetric complaints: 'this series of complaints, to establish which so much time and effort and, no doubt, expense, had been directed, was revealed, upon examination, to be almost completely devoid of substance' (*McBride v. Walton* in the Supreme Court of New South Wales, CA No 40436/93 at p.14). Nonetheless he found that the false and misleading publication of an experiment relevant to medical science showed the applicant was not of good character in regard to the practice of medicine. In support he quoted extensively and approvingly from the Tribunal's decision which pointed to the dishonesty and evidence of the practitioner continuing in his fault and, indeed, having no insight into its gravity. Coming to the point that McBride had been deprived of procedural fairness, the Judge pointed out that matters in question, not particularised, had come from the transcript of his submissions and evidence to the Gibbs Committee of Inquiry; these McBride's counsel had allowed into the Tribunal proceedings, so these features could be taken into account. He wrote that McBride's counsel had pointed to subsequent good conduct, therefore subsequent acts of dishonesty should also be admitted. The critical question of whether the misconduct could be construed as an isolated episode was one that the Tribunal had to address. He accordingly dismissed the point of appeal which claimed that the Tribunal had lacked procedural fairness in considering matters which it had excluded from those particularised. The third ground of appeal, the severity of the penalty, Powell J found 'very difficult and troubling' (at 83), but McBride's deception in a field of medical research had evidenced a 'trait of dishonesty' which had not been demonstrably reformed, 'the Appellant lacks any real insight into the gravity of what he has done' (at 85).

Justice Handley's judgment did not differ substantially from Justice Powell's. In relation to the issue of not of good character in respect to McBride's medical practice, Handley pointed to the close links between research into therapeutic drugs and the application of these in medicine, and the need for trust among scientist and practitioners. On the issue of procedural fairness he opined that the Tribunal was initially in error in ruling that it could not take into account the matters, not particularised in the complaints but arising from the earlier Gibbs Committee of Inquiry, and also in ruling that it could not use its observation of McBride's evasive and unresponsive evidence before itself. But in eventually taking these into account it 'cancelled or corrected the errors in those rulings' (Handley J at 21). He held that the Tribunal, having found that the doctor was not of good character because of the two particulars of scientific fraud, had to consider whether he remained not of good character. In a somewhat ambivalent fashion he decided that, if there were a denial of procedural fairness, it was nonetheless immaterial to the conclusion reached.

Justice Kirby also raised critical questions regarding the obstetric complaints: 'How could such a welter of misconceived charges ever have been brought? Is the correct test being applied to the prosecution of such charges by the Complaints Unit of the Department of Health?' (at 12). He reflected that 'in his daily work as a medical practitioner (for which he requires registration to protect the public) as distinct from his work as a research scientist (for which he does not) McBride came through his scouring test before the Tribunal almost wholly unblemished' (at 12).

In regard to the scientific fraud complaints, Kirby P noted that the charges were of 'substantial, repeated, multitudinous and deliberate scientific fraud' (at 14) in twenty-four particulars of the seven complaints, but that the proven complaints devolved from the one experiment with scopolamine hydrobromide (referred to as Hyoscine for the remainder of this judgment). There had been no other complaint of dishonesty substantiated. In the reporting of the Hyoscine experiment there was the finding of dishonesty: the Tribunal had decided that there were six rabbits not eight, one malformed litter not two and that there were not contemporaneous controls to ensure scientific accuracy of outcome. For the rest the paper was found to be misleading 'but short of the intentional desire to distort the true conduct and outcome of the experiment' (at 19). The evidence, at variance in the details given in different cases in the US, Kirby P noted, showed 'palpable negligence', but had not convinced the Tribunal of an absence of good character. That damning finding was based on the dishonest reporting of the Hyoscine experiment:

> ... a narrow, isolated, particular matter only in respect of which he was found to have published intentionally misleading scientific data. This demonstrated a failure on the part of the Tribunal to apply the correct standard as to what "good character" meant in the context of the legislation. This was not a "perverse" finding only (although it was that); it was also a conclusion wrong in law when the primary findings were fully accepted and then submitted to the application of the statutory language, properly understood (Kirby J at 21).

Contrary to Powell J's leading judgment, Kirby P found that the Tribunal erred in law in finding McBride 'not of good character'. The dishonesty and carelessness related to one scientific experiment; this warranted censure and reprimand but was irrelevant to his continued practice in obstetrics and gynaecology. That practice had been reviewed intensively and come through that testing remarkably well with only one minor deviation: failing to ensure proper arrangements for care of one patient in his absence.

Again in contradistinction to the majority, Kirby P held that the Tribunal had been correct in ruling that the original complaints should not be amended or extended at the end of the hearing, but unfortunately it did, in fact, rely on these further matters and the respondent, McBride, had no opportunity to answer these further allegations. These matters, described in the Tribunal's findings, refer to McBride's response regarding the Hyoscine experiment to junior colleagues, to senior colleagues, to Foundation 41's press releases, to the Gibbs Committee of Inquiry and before the Tribunal itself. The claim that McBride's lawyers would have been informed of this line of attack in written and oral submissions was rejected because the Tribunal had already ruled out bringing these fresh charges. Kirby P considered a wide range of precedent and opined that 'a breach of the rules of procedural fairness (natural justice) constitutes an error of law' (at 8). After a lengthy review of the way the Tribunal had ruled and then considered additional matters he concluded that the Tribunal's conduct was an 'established departure from the rules of procedural fairness' (at 41).

As to the orders which should be made, if the Tribunal's finding of dishonesty in the publication of the Hyoscine experiment and the misleading nature of the subsequent note would constitute 'not of good character' (and Kirby P insisted this was not his opinion) then the removal from the Register of

Physicians was still not warranted. Given such a conclusion, Kirby P would agree with the dissenting direction put forward by Professor Tracy of the Tribunal, that being an order of reprimand.

Given that Kirby P's opinion was the minority, the finding of the majority prevailed. The appeal was dismissed with costs—this time McBride was required to pay his and the Health Department's legal costs.

McBride sought leave to appeal to the High Court of Australia; this was not granted. The three judges on the High Court bench, Justices Brennan, Toohey and Dawson, were not in accord, but the majority held that there was not sufficient matter in the legal points of appeal to warrant a further hearing.

McBride's Autobiography

In June 1994, one month before his appeal to the High Court was not allowed, McBride's autobiography, *Killing the Messenger*, was published. The book was largely devoted to his life as a medical practitioner and scientist, and to his reflections on the events of those years. Included are the details of his discovery of the teratogenic effects of thalidomide, of his observations of damaging side-effects of therapeutic drugs, and of various experiments including the inconclusive Debendox experiment and the experiment with scopolamine hydrobromide.

Immediately after the Tribunal's orders halted his practice of medicine, McBride had turned to his papers, diaries and files and begun writing this book. As the title suggests, McBride believes that much of his persecution was instigated and funded by Merrell Dow Pharmaceutical, the manufacturer of Bendectin/ Debendox which was eventually withdrawn because of allegations of side-effects had prompted so many costly law suits. As mentioned, McBride had served several times as an expert witness on behalf of the applicant seeking damages for the drug's alleged teratogenic effects on foetuses. He writes that his was the longest disciplinary hearing in medical history and during those years his obstetric practice had been gravely hampered, his resilience sorely tested and his robust health diminished. The book reflects his anger and frustration, albeit coloured by a laconic sense of humour. There he tells his side of the story without interruption, a tale of persecution. After reading the Tribunal's voluminous findings (over nine hundred pages) he could not accept the probity of those findings. But, his attempt to set the record straight was to be turned against him when he came two years later to seek readmission to the profession. After the sustained drama of earlier battles this last contest sounded the pathos of scapegoat.

Seeking Readmission

With the failure of his appeal to the Supreme Court and the rejection by the High Court to granted leave to appeal further, McBride sought to be reregistered by the Medical Registration Board. Two years had elapsed since he was struck off. The proceedings were set for 28 October 1995. It was not until the beginning of March 1996 however that all necessary documents were submitted. The Tribunal hearing opened on 11 March. The members of this Tribunal were Justice Freeman (presiding), Dr Neridah Brinkley, psychiatrist, Dr Cotton, medical practitioner and researcher, and Mr Valentine, layperson. John Basten QC, who had appeared for the Complainant in the Supreme Court appeal, appeared for the Health Care Complaints Commission (the former Health Complaints Unit had become a statutory body). McBride represented himself.[11]

This hearing was remarkably short. On day one, Basten QC submitted further volumes of the original Tribunal decision for perusal and an adjournment was taken. The Tribunal resumed later that day and continued the following morning before the application was concluded, the Tribunal indicating that its decision would be delivered at a later date.

McBride had been advised by friends in the law that the Tribunal looked for declarations and evidence of the applicant's contrition that should include acceptance of the earlier Tribunal's decision, insight into the faults which had led to the finding of professional misconduct, and evidence that the defects of character had been overcome. This is a heavy imposition on practitioners who may, however vainly, have denied the misconduct in an earlier hearing or have variously claimed that there was no fault to answer.

McBride, as applicant, handed up his request for reregistration with eleven pages of supporting argument, appending a recent letter asking him to review scientific papers, recently published papers, and further character references. The objective was to show his good character and his standing among clinical and scientific peers. These had been provided to the Tribunal and the Commission's lawyers some weeks earlier—a usual requirement to save the time of Court or Tribunal. The Commission's barrister, Basten QC, opened with a mild statement that his own position was one of 'sceptical neutrality'. He then submitted Volumes 6, 7 and 8 of the earlier Tribunal's findings. The addition of Volume 8, not included in earlier submission relevant to the case, necessitated an adjournment for a couple of hours to allow the Tribunal to peruse the extra document. Volume 8 was the final phase of the Tribunal's decision which discussed the purported persistence of the flaw of character, set out its orders for deregistration and included Professor Tracy's dissenting opinion.

When the Tribunal returned after this adjournment, McBride took the stand for cross-examination. Questions were put about his application, the findings of scientific fraud, the events and evidence which led to that finding, the extent of his clinical practice up to deregistration on 31 July 1993 and his attempts to keep up with his specialty since that date. McBride told the Tribunal that he had practised up till the end of July 1993; he no longer belonged to the College so did not receive all that literature; he read the journals in the Library; and that he no longer went to conferences—'that would be too embarrassing'.

Cross-examination continued on the following morning. Then the counsel for the Commission produced another document, McBride's book *Killing the Messenger*. It had not been among the documents submitted and took McBride by surprise. The Tribunal adjourned for a reading time and returned after lunch. Counsel for the Complainant then took the Tribunal to various sections to deduce that McBride, at the time of its publication two years earlier, had neither accepted the Tribunal's decision, nor been convinced of his defects.[12]

McBride now with his back to the wall faced his nemesis and did as he had been advised to do, stated his contrition: 'I now regret the dishonest act regarding a scientific experiment. I now see I had done this to make the article publishable. I believed it was dangerous for pregnant women to use these drugs'. He stated that this act had cost him three years of his working life and caused him great distress for a much longer period: 'I would be very foolish to risk this again'.

McBride continued by going over earlier claims. He spoke of his association with Professor Langman who had had a part in the experiments with scopolamine hydrobromide and whose two rabbits in the University of Virginia laboratory had been added to the sample of six used in the New South Wales experiment. Langman, he added, had died before the Gibbs Committee conducted its inquiry and that Committee had not been prepared to conclude that there was no experiment involving the 'Langman rabbits'. McBride pointed to the quality of his obstetric practice which had been subject to extraordinary scrutiny and not found wanting:

> No patient complained, no patient needed a transfusion or suffered a wound infection, no baby died, and, despite the publicity, no patient came forward to make a complaint ... My peers and my patients respect me.

He noted that some of the research in question which he had conducted had been repeated and his results vindicated. He had since carried out further research in the US and in Australia. The penalty for scientific dishonesty had been excessive, much harsher than that meted out to doctors brought before the Tribunal for more serious complaints. He stated for the Tribunal the sorrow of being denied seven years of his life, spent in litigation, and three years of clinical work; 'I did a very foolish thing'.

This admission was not enough.

In response Basten QC reminded the Tribunal of its powers to dismiss, reinstate or reinstate with conditions. The Medical Board, and hence the Medical Tribunal, cannot register unless satisfied that the person is now of good character and the onus is on the applicant to satisfy on that. Reformation of character is not usual and, it was pointed out, there was legal precedent for this opinion. The applicant must accept the findings of the earlier Tribunal and this acceptance he had not substantiated. Indeed the evidence in *Killing the Messenger* showed the applicant attempting to justify what he had done. Basten cited page and sentence. If an applicant continues to assert that the Tribunal had erred then there was no reform. Counsel now posited that, as well as the inclusion of the 'Langman rabbits' in the experiments there was further dishonesty: in Foundation 41's press release of 1980; in expert evidence given in the US in 1988; in tendering to a US Court in 1989 an expert report which relied, at least in part, on his own tainted experiments; in discernible 'lack of candour' before the original Tribunal. (Listening in the Court I recalled that these were the particulars, advanced at the end of the original Tribunal hearing, which McBride had not been given the opportunity to answer and which, it was argued in the Appeal, had not been allowed by that Tribunal). The dishonest course taken in 1980, the barrister now argued, had continued in 1989 and, as shown by his book, was still evident in 1994.

After a short adjournment Basten QC continued. I listened as counsel for the Complaints Commission addressed the Tribunal. Basten stated that he recognised McBride's admission that 'a combination of pride and remorse had clouded my judgment', but felt that it was much more, that the strength of belief had led him to wrong, to inappropriate steps, and (later in this application), the need to justify his belief. Basten stated that McBride does not accept the link between his misconduct and 'fitness to practise medicine', and that his book shows him believing himself the victim of injustice and failing to appreciate the seriousness of the findings against him. Turning to the character references counsel observed that they were provided by worthy persons, but there were none from leaders of the organised profession, no one would speak from the medical colleges. This was a grave isolation—a significant observation.

Counsel continued sorrowfully. He appreciated that McBride had been caught up in this tragedy in 1987 when sixty years old and there was some urgency as time ran out to continue a lifelong career. Nonetheless the necessary understanding and insight of his defect was wanting, had not been demonstrated. The Tribunal should not be satisfied with the applicant's pleas and should dismiss the application with costs.

Finally counsel covered all eventualities. Should the Tribunal consider restoration to the Register of Medical Practitioners then his instructions were that the following conditions should apply: (1) McBride to assist only at operations; (2) his medical practice be supervised; (3) a clinical supervisor appointed by the College; (4) the supervisor to report on his practice to the College; and (5) that he not undertake research without an ethics committee approved by the National Medical and Health Research Council (NHMRC) and the Medical Board. (It is relevant to note that four of these five conditions related to McBride's obstetric practice where none of the multiple complaints brought against him had succeeded and about which no allegations had been made to this Tribunal. The Health Care Complaints Commission continued in its repudiation of his obstetric practice and the style of clinical care it represented right to the end; its exoneration in the most rigorous audit it has ever conducted notwithstanding. And the fifth restriction, to limit his research activities, was beyond the power of this Medical Tribunal or the Medical Board. It was not matter to which the Tribunal had to direct attention. The question of conditions or restrictions did not arise.)

In reply to the these submissions McBride observed that naturally he was hurt by the earlier Tribunal's findings. He had, he said, been further distressed when given the previous day reports of two cases said to bear on his case. Those doctors had been struck off for serious crimes, disgraceful conduct— McBride questioned the parallel with his case. From the Bench Freeman J gently explained that the cases simply illustrated points at law to be considered when assessing a person's remorse and reform. The disadvantage occasioned by McBride's lack of legal counsel was painfully apparent. He lacked a second keen mind to grasp the drift of evidence and argument, to peruse additional documents tendered during proceedings, to advise on how his adversary might be rebutted. This was David and Goliath (again?). The medical practitioner was floundering in an alien environment, outclassed by a master of legal discourse so foreign to his own. The presiding judge tried, but could not right the balance. The Tribunal rose and would bring in its findings in due course.

Some weeks later I watched the Tribunal bring in its finding. McBride stood alone on his side of the Court to hear the short determination of his continued exile from the profession of medicine.

Outside the media waited with microphone and camera. He walked past ignoring all questions. His wife met him across the street and heard the outcome in silence. She had followed and was not surprised.

Review

In the 1950s a number of pharmaceutical products were becoming available and used to alleviate various symptoms suffered in pregnancy. When the teratogenic effects of thalidomide became known all became suspect. In some respects these early studies might be compared to the research in psychopharmacology then assuming importance. This research field is also fairly new. In 1949 the anti-manic properties of lithium were discovered and a very few years later chlorpromazine was recognised for its alleviation of anxiety and depression. Gratz and Simpson comment that early research was 'totally lacking in methodo-logical rigour by modern day standards, nevertheless, resulted in one of the notable therapeutic advances of the century' (1992, p.309). A couple of decades later research on pharmaceutical products had become more rigorous and firm protocols were being urged for experimentation.

Among these studies those on the effects of therapeutic drugs on the foetus were a more recent development. After the discovery of the effects of thalido-mide and the tragedies which occurred before the damage was discovered researchers were anxious not to recommend where assurances might later be misplaced. Foundation 41 was set up to undertake such research on dangerous exposures during pregnancy and in the infant's first week of life. Although assisted by reputable academic researchers the Foundation relied largely on public benevolence and was run parsimoniously with straightened resources. Its senior people gave their time voluntarily and its staff researchers were junior in their careers. Enthusiasm and dedication go only some way towards compen-sating for the time and attention needed in large research endeavours. This is not to deprecate the work done by a research foundation supported by public donation and the devotion of time available by scientists hard pressed in their professional lives. It should not surprise that some scientific work was inad-equately supervised, records poorly kept and ordinary control of experimentation somewhat lax. The evidence before the Gibbs Committee of Inquiry reflects such conditions. This was a small group of people who fell out with each other. Any systemic inadequacies would have been better addressed by taking stock and planning rather than by bringing accusation and denunciation which reflected poorly on all concerned. I reflect for a moment on this situation because this is where the sad events began.

The initial inquiry by the Research Advisory Committee was intent on de-fending a situation which needed fixing and it stayed with a particular discontent instead of taking a larger view of what was needed to ensure supervision and adherence to the current canons of science. The discontent festered.

The Gibbs Committee of Inquiry was unable to rectify the problems. It had its terms of reference thrust on it from the investigative *The Science Show* program, which had started the scandal. Furthermore the Committee was severely limited in its powers because it was a private inquiry dependent on what people assist-ing it were willing to allow or do. These limitations prevented the person accused of fraud of hearing the particulars of accusations brought against him, of con-fronting his accusers, of cross-examining his accusers, or of having evidence, for and against, given under oath. By its very constitution the Committee was unable to provide procedural fairness. The Presiding Member recognised the disadvantages under which McBride suffered but could not avoid them. These limitations may not have mattered except that the preparation of evidence and the findings of the Committee generated the material for one section of the case against McBride before the Medical Tribunal. It did appear that these matters were to be a minor refrain and the main theme was to be carried in the obstetric complaints. But when the planned condemnation of his obstetric practices failed the scientific fraud complaint served to bring him down.[10]

I wrote earlier in this chapter of the growing concern in science communities about scientific fraud and the controversies this generated. The thrust of those observations is to point to the readiness of such communities to denounce any of their number implicated in crime against prevailing standards of good science. I have suggested that this was, and still is, a dangerous time to deviate from canons of best practice. When a highly esteemed radio program, like *The Science Show*, produced its investigation and findings of scientific fraud in animal experiments which bear on the clinical safety of new pharmaceutical drugs it would command attention and stimulate antagonism towards the erring scientist. Nor was McBride an unlikely victim, he was exactly fit for purpose of holding up and denouncing as a bad scientist. His discovery of the effects of thalidomide on the unborn had not endeared him to the pharmaceutical companies which fund much of the world's medical research and manufacture and market the product of that research. Nor had the honours which flowed to him as a researcher and clinician, ten years out of university, pleased his peers. McBride was, by all accounts, an ebullient young man of strong enthusiasms and bounding self-confidence. Father of the Year, receiver of the honour, Companion of the British Empire, of the Order of Australia, recipient of *L'Institut de la Vie* Gold Medal for services to medicine and now Director of the research foundation he had founded. Fame provokes envy and fall from fame satiates the pangs of envy. McBride would certainly do as an example to frighten any errant scientist.

McBride himself points to the antagonism he felt coming from pharmaceutical companies. Indeed as early as August 1980 he had warning from a friend, a former high-ranking naval officer, whose private security investigation practice in retirement led to his receipt of such intelligence; McBride was being investigated by agents delegated by a US source. I do not argue against McBride's analysis and imputation of blame for his troubles detailed in *Killing the Messenger*. He made powerful enemies. His diagnosis of pharmaceutical interests' efforts to destroy his reputation is persuasive and, indeed, the Tribunal noted that particular companies had ample reason to discredit him. But it is not sufficient. It needed a multi-factorial force to bring him down. His peers in the clinical research science community moved away from him and left him marked and unaided.

There is always a danger in small nations, like Australia, that our scientists are hostage to the international financiers of the research they do. National bodies, like the NHMRC can form a good source of research funds and a stout defence against being captured by tied research funds and their research dictates, but such resources are limited. McBride had fallen out with the pharmaceutical industry that sustains a synergistic relation with the medical profession—so often a mutually satisfying connection. After the savaging by the Tribunal's decision he was limping badly.

These aspects of McBride's research science career recognised, I would still relate his fate more strongly to his activist practice in obstetrics. It was on this aspect of his integrity and reputation that the Health Care Complaints Commission lavished most of its resources of time, money and influence. The rising levels of clinical intervention in childbirth were being treated as a scandal in the public health journals. Medical practitioners, it was declared, were profiting prodigiously. The extent of this 'elective surgery' was inflating health budgets, increasingly sensitive to the pressures that the national health insurance of Medibank and then Medicare could impose. At the same time women were raising questions about the wisdom of activist intervention in 'nature'. Obstetrics, feminists were belatedly declaring, should be a woman's domain and medical domination was to be resisted. The bid to resume control of childbirth stimulated a central movement calling for homebirths and midwife-practitioners. This vanguard epitomised a more dispersed sense of concern about 'medicalisation' of pregnancy and parturition, a concern with some connection with the romanticism and 'return to nature' sentiments of the 1960s. These communities of interest coincided in sectors of the health policy industry and the departments of health. The Complaints Unit, as watchdog on clinical practice and health and hospital services was well aware of the public concern and ready to act when occasion allowed. McBride's obstetric practice, already in the news for other matters, seemed to typify all that was criticised in feminist and public health discourses. Ironically, his campaign against the use of pharmaceutical products, and the consequent 'medicalisation' of pregnancy was ignored.

McBride's enthusiasm for his professional practice, his acclaimed skill as an obstetrician and the quality of the hospitals where he worked established for him an excellent reputation. Women who had cause to expect or fear difficulty in childbirth or problems in delivering a healthy baby consulted him. His was an energetic and inquiring mind and an activist personality; he gained a reputation for advanced skill and knowledge of obstetric techniques. His rates for caesarean section were much higher than the norm, he monitored his patients closely and was quick to intervene when problems threatened. He was an obvious figure who might be used to deter others from activist practice and adherence to 'the medical model' being denounced in healthcare generally and obstetrics in particular.

He served that purpose well despite the final decisions. The intensive investigation of the previous ten years of his obstetric practice yielded fifty-five cases which it was thought might attract reprobation. Months were spent before the Tribunal with legal teams on both sides intent on exploring the issues and examining and cross-examining expert witnesses. When that saga was ended McBride's reputation as an obstetrician held unsullied, but he was not to escape. He was caught by his Achilles heel of haste and carelessness in the important minutiae of experimental science.

In the methodological discourses of science, the acceptable margins for error are argued: should the scientist risk the Type 1 or Type 2 errors (accepting a false null-hypothesis or rejecting a true null-hypothesis)? McBride, convinced of the danger of many normally therapeutic drugs if taken during pregnancy, always opted to reject the possibility that they had no adverse effect. Schrader-Frechette has recently argued for that option in all research into the deleterious effects of chemicals on the environment (1994, pp.106–117). But, that was a later argument involving different interest-lobbies. In McBride's case the charge of falsity in reporting a scientific experiment was upheld. Those early proceedings had, I argue, been marred by a failure of procedural fairness that was implicit in the limitations of Foundation 41's own private inquiry. That decision was to cripple his defence when the matter came to Medical Tribunal. He was not to be hung on the obstetric charge, but the other served as well to deliver up a man once highly honoured in the medical community. That professional community was initially divided about the support owed to a fellow practitioner. Perhaps that division might be seen in the deliberations of the first Medical Tribunal and the dissent of Professor Tracy. But, when the time came for his last request for reinstatement in the profession, his submission was not supported by any practitioners of standing or official position in the collegiate of obstetrics and gynaecology. At that last hearing he stood quite alone, head forward listening to the decision. *Ecce homo.*

In this interpretation of the events of those ten years since *The Science Show* of 1987, I have dwelt on McBride's marked and vulnerable centrality in several communities of interest unsettled by troubles to be feared and covered. He has been harried and pilloried in all of them and is now exiled never likely to return. The forces of rejection remain too strong. And yet it was all done with the trappings of regulatory zeal and legal procedure. The rituals of Tribunal and Court were solemnly enacted.

But the voices of dissent suggest that history will honour the man of quixotic zeal who provoked pharmaceutical giants in his quest for safer outcomes for mothers and babies. Events, and his own personality, marked him as a sign of contradiction in his own spheres of action. In his decision in response to McBride's appeal against ejection from medical practice Kirby P wrote:

it must be said bluntly that Dr McBride's contribution to humanity stands higher than that of any other person involved in these proceedings (at 28).

Enough is enough. This man, to whom the world and unnumbered babies born without deformity, and their families, owe a considerable debt, has had the error of his found misconduct adequately brought home to him. He should be allowed, for his remaining days of practice, to return to his professional activities (at 48).

He was not. The scapegoat cannot return.

Surviving

McBride's resilience remains extraordinary. In a 1994 interview I asked him what effect of all has had on him. He replied, 'It has nearly killed me ... the most punishing ordeal ... I have been deeply depressed. It has gone on so long'. He had hoped for a reprieve when he petitioned to be readmitted to medicine in 1996. The Tribunal's continued rejection, despite his formal abnegation, nearly crushed him. A man of extraordinary hope for fair dealing, he puzzles over the vehemence of the forces ranged against him intent on casting him down. He follows, and comments on, changes in obstetric practice. He will not acquiesce in withdrawal from the world of the mind and heart.

Notes

1. Dystocia is broadly failure to progress in labour due to one or more factors including disproportion between foetal head and maternal pelvis, large baby, maternal exhaustion.
2. A letter from McBride carrying the same message was published by the *Medical Journal of Australia* on 4 December 1961.
3. This article was not published.
4. McBride's note published in the *Australian Journal of Biological Science* (January 1983) stated that in the repetition of the experiment different water containers provided accurate measure of the water and chemical ingested by each rabbit. In later experiments, published in the *International Journal of Developmental Neuroscience*, similar malformations resulted: 37% of foetuses in one doe were malformed and all the foetuses of a second treated doe were malformed. McBride still puzzles over the way subsequent research supporting his findings was not permitted any relevance in legal proceedings which hinged on that first experiment.
5. Swan won the highly prized Walkley Award for Journalism for this episode of *The Science Show.*

6. Gibbs Committee of Inquiry, *Report of Committee of Inquiry*.
7. Findings of the Gibbs Committee of Inquiry reported in the *Sydney Morning Herald*, 3 Nov. 1988, p.4.
8. In these hearings, the title Complainant refers to the Director of the Health Complaints Unit, Ms Merrilyn Walton, who was the 'nominal complainant' in proceedings before the Medical Tribunal.
9. Placenta praevia occurs when the placenta precedes or threatens to precede the baby into the birth canal, and so endangers the wellbeing and life of the baby and threatens haemorrhage for the mother.
10. Dr Norman Swan took a different view of the problems when he produced his acclaimed *The Science Show* program in 1987 and when he summarised this case among several others in a paper for later publication (see Swan, 1993). In this account 'the case of the missing rabbits' Swan states his doubt that Professor Langman, an eminent embryologist, at the University of Virginia, was conducting similar experiments. He rejects McBride's claim that Langman, as a terminal illness overcame him, suggested that McBride might include in his study two rabbits dosed with hyoscine from his unreported experiment. The jury on that issue is never likely to return.
11. McBride told me his reasons for self-representation was that his funds had been exhausted and that he believed there was little to be gained by having a barrister speak for him; he had been advised of what was expected of him (pers. comm., 12 Mar. 1996).
12. The book, written immediately after his deregistration in July 1993, had been delivered to its publisher at the end of that year and was published in July 1994.

CHAPTER 7

A Question of Justice

Communities have been central to all the case studies presented. They hold as powerful centres of being in people's lives and, over many years, form their ways of thinking and acting. The force of such communities is, in the most part, beneficent. They make a strong secure way of being that engenders confidence and comfort in what that person has become. Here is where the social, the vital force and energy of sociability, might be found. If, in Rousseau's aphorism, 'man becomes man amongst men', it is in such communities that the moral force of society can be studied.

When I began to contemplate the scapegoat, I focused my gaze on its formation in the community from which it sprang. Where it emerged I looked for the conditions which brought it into being. At the time I was pondering the processes of regulation by which professions sustained reputation and ensured trust in their practice. A range of regulatory practices could be invoked within a profession and beyond these tactics lay the law with the sanctions of legislation and regulation. A profession's disciplines imposed its norms and among those disciplinary practices could be found traces of scapegoating. I do not doubt that I might have found scapegoating elsewhere, but my research then took me among professions and professionals. The significance of the active involvement of professional communities in all these cases must be grasped, otherwise we cannot understand how such things can happen in honourable communities, under the full surveillance of the law and with the benefit of courtly process.

I do not claim that scapegoating was the only process running in the way events around the central characters unfolded. The contingencies that shape our lives are much more complex than that. Other themes can be followed to order the chaos of conflict and confrontation. But this is the Ariadne thread which I took up to reach an understanding of how such things could happen.

Communities create scapegoats to purge evils which threaten to overwhelm. Central to the creation of the scapegoat are the conditions which prevail within a community and the means to which that community may resort to rid itself of its troubles. These are troubles which threaten reputation, even identity. Collectively and individually the members of a community hold passionately to the status of their belonging. The integrity and status of community becomes all important. To ensure its survival any sacrifice can be justified.

Professional bodies are communities par excellence. They are solidary, binding and exclusive. They confer status and honourable identity on those who belong. That belonging is negotiated through years of training, surveillance, examination and then initiation, as novice, into the company of colleagues. The sense of belonging to an exclusive and privileged band is deeply instilled and remains throughout professional life and beyond. The exclusivity is important.

Boundaries between professionals and all others are firmly drawn and not to be transgressed. Such boundaries hold, especially between practitioner and client. The community at large and specifically the client, or patient, must be kept at a distance, must not trespass on the professional territory. Hence client–practitioner boundaries are carefully patrolled, most zealously in medicine where the practitioner is licensed to intrude and intervene on body and mind in a way forbidden to others. Powerful taboos operate, purportedly to protect the client/patient and to uphold professional authority. The professional must maintain the boundaries, respect the distinctions and know the difference.

Professions are similarly mindful of the distinctions among them. Although practitioners of every profession commonly share the same class and cultural background, there are deep antagonisms between one professional camp and another. Although it is possible for an individual to practise in two or more domains, crossing from one to another is not easy and regarded with unease by those who stay within one fold. Many lawyers enter politics and other fields where command of organisational policy and practice is critical. But the boundaries are clear. The lawyer in the organisation is marked as different. Their loyalties can tie them more closely to a profession rather than organisation or party, and they may at any time return to their profession—so long as their integrity and reputation for integrity remain intact. The academic lawyer is a highly regarded exemplar of the balance which must be achieved if good repute is to be maintained in both spheres. There is good reason, beyond the obvious financial one, for the lawyer employed in a university to maintain practice skills, particularly those deployed in the Court. The distinction between law and politics proved significant for Whelehan's fortunes. But McBride's intermittent movements from medical practice to scientific research was not so readily viewed as engaging in two separate and distinct zones of practice. The boundary between the practice of medicine and scientific research was blurred. The authorities were to be ambivalent about the difference.

The discipline of a profession encompasses years devoted to advanced education and training in preparation for entry. The shaping of the student into the practitioner calls for knowledge, intellect, diligence and endurance. The university oversees the submission of mind and will to the processes of socialisation. The student must take up habits of learning and practice, must submit to the surveillance of continuing assessment, must satisfy in examination and conform to the patterns of behaviour which distinguish the good professional. These processes found the profession's claim to reputation and legitimate its authority. Everyday practices and rituals endorse and celebrate those claims.

Reputation for high learning, proven skill and responsibility provides the grounds of a profession's claim to trust. This is trust of a high order because much is at stake. Trust is familiar to us as a generalised trust in persistence of natural and moral social orders. Without a measure of trust in other people we would not leave the shelter of our house. Trust makes possible human relations from the most casual to the most intimate and without it no cooperation can occur. Reliance on others is a continual experience of everyday. But it assumes greater significance in situations of danger and anxiety when we do not know how best to proceed.

This is the trust implicit in professional relationship, the fiduciary trust or expectation that partners to an agreement will carry out obligations and responsibilities and that they are technically competent to do that with which they are entrusted. Moral and cultural authority dependent on reputation underpins trust. Trust permits practice. The crucial trust appears to be that of client in practitioner. Jacob notes:

> The doctor wields authority within the doctor–patient relationship by means
> of the trust created ... This creation of dependence is central to the activity
> and not a mere strategy for monopolization. The trust ... is placed under
> strain precisely where the supposed expertise can be judged by results
> (1988, p.117).

But professionals are equally responsible to colleagues whose trust is necessary to continued belonging to the profession. This latter is usually a more informed disposition and, although not necessary in the short term, is essential to practice in the long term. The distrust of colleagues will eventually unseat the professional. As Jacob states:

> In great measure professional morality consists in the duties owed to these
> modern "guilds" and their members. ...[their] rules deal with mistake han-
> dling, they classify people, and they set up criteria for recognizing a fellow
> worker, for determining who is safe, and maybe even necessary to initiate
> into the in-groups of close equals and indicate who must be kept at some
> distance (1988, p.129).

The trust of the client is tentative and easily disturbed. Its bases lie in the conditions of uncertainty and apprehension which beset any person who, in a life-disturbing or threatening situation, seeks help from the expert (the knowledgeable and skilful in that field). The client, who distrusts the practitioner, may, if those feelings spread, disturb the reputation and standing of the whole profession. This is a worry to the group. Reputation is a crucial source of a profession and a professional's authority. If the good name is damaged the concession of authority to practise is lost. But when colleagues distrust a fellow practitioner, the disturbance goes deeper. Sanctions, such as hesitancy or denial of referrals, withdrawal of cooperation or overt criticism, can occur. This distrust is more serious, because it undermines the grounds of collegiality and cooperation.

When reputation fails the habitual orders of authority and compliance slip away. Such times are dangerous and the restoration of order, or the transition to a new order, is secured through ritual which publicly proclaims and celebrates a reintegration. Disorder is disturbing, unclean, 'matter out of place' which can disrupt the patterns of existence (Douglas, 1977). The accustomed patterns of action and behaviour are crucial conditions of group and individual existence. Disorder threatens powerfully. It brings strong influences into play because order, whether the old order or a new one, must be restored. Carnival and the pageantry of carnival, which overturns the usual order, is a safety valve letting off destructive energies. Carnival deconstructs and give space for celebration of the creative moment of disorder. Then, in the final repudiation of 'the lord of misrule', the rituals restore old ways, accustomed orders of authority at the end of the day.

There are many ways of dealing with the disorderly and the impure. The malaise can be treated, those infected can be cured or put away, lest the infection spread. This response has been formalised by some medical boards in procedures for the 'impaired doctor' where counselling, therapy, or further training can be ordered. For a while conditions imposed on practice reinforce the limits of permissible behaviours. If these supportive interventions do not avail then a quiet deregistration puts the disabled out of practice. The medical profession is more enlightened than others in its recognition and treatment where there is hope of a cure. Such remedies are not available to the impaired lawyer. The only supportive intervention is the prescription of further legal education. Socialisation, it is assumed, must have been inadequate and more might make up the deficiency in the person.

Professions impose a range of sanctions on the erring practitioner. The first response is to deal with the error or deficit within house. The 'quiet word', the informal counsel, the withholding of cooperation or referral, the summoning before internal committees can be effective tactics. But these remedies are for the sick, the failing or the addicted and are no cure for major upheaval and undermining of the profession's reputation. Where only one or two practitioners need discipline, punishment or threat of punishment such remedies can prove effective and are used despite a professional bodies' discomfort with draconic imposition of authority. The usual forms of association in such bodies are collegial not autocratic. If these informal approaches are ineffective the relevant registration boards can summon the offender to appear before committee or tribunal. These bodies take in the statutory provisions secured through the state. The legislative authority of such bodies reinforces the power of a profession to deal with transgressors in its midst and condition or remove their right to practice.

But the limit of such procedures' effectiveness is reached when scandals besetting a profession, and so diminishing its reputation, are endemic, irrational, or hidden from view. Psychiatry found itself falling into such trouble as the findings of the Chelmsford Royal Commission became public and the extent of its moral malaise was known. Such situations have provoked the urge to seize one who can stand for the group, and identify them with the troubles, lay the evils upon them, and publicly punish and expel them along with all the evils now become theirs to bear. If this is done publicly with due ceremony, all are warned, the punishment is exemplary and the infection purged from the professional body—or so it can be believed.

These scapegoats are not mere victims. It is not simply that they are blamed and punished for bad practices imputed to them. Scapegoats must be driven far away from the group never to return. If they were allowed back they could bring the contagion, the plague, the evils attributed to them back among their erstwhile people.

There are many more victims than scapegoats. Scapegoats are those who are punished unfairly or with an excess of vigour not commensurable with the offence. Victims are different. They suffer but not necessarily at the hands of their own. They are picked on and vilified. The punishment may or may not be legitimate. One widely publicised case concerned a practitioner whom many saw as a victim of forces and circumstances which implicated public policy intent on allaying fears of contagion. As was stated of this case, 'a Sydney doctor [who] has been reprimanded but no one is sure what, if anything he did wrong' *(The Bulletin* 27 Dec. 1995, p.24). The case involved four patients who underwent minor surgery on the same day in the rooms of Dr Todd Davis and subsequently became infected with HIV. The medical procedures followed were vigorously investigated. It appeared that his practice meticulously conformed with strict infection control guidelines. All manner of hypotheses to account for the spread of the infection were examined and no fault could be found in the doctor's procedures. The arguments of the accusers assumed that the medical profession must know all that there is to know about the transmission of HIV. So, if infection originated from his surgery, the practitioner must be responsible. Dr Todd Davis, the Tribunal found, had engaged in 'unsatisfactory professional conduct' (*re Davis, Dr TP and the Medical Practice Act 1992* (1994) at 33). He was reprimanded, his private practice closed and strict conditions imposed on any employment he might negotiate in a hospital setting. Patients involved in this matter subsequently brought actions for negligence against Davis. These were settled out of court with terms of settlement not to be revealed. Davis suffered severely as his reputation was dragged into infamy through the weeks of Tribunal and Court hearings. No misconduct or fault was found. The Tribunal determined that:

> we are satisfied there must have been some breach of proper procedures, or an intervening act ... any such failure must be classified as unsatisfactory professional conduct, even in the absence of the disapproval of the peers of the respondent (at 32–3).

The media denounced him. His profession, deeply disturbed by the complaints and the way they were investigated and prosecuted, remained supportive. Davis continues to practise medicine and enjoys the regard of his colleagues.

Scapegoating is a communal action of quite a different kind to victimisation. Picking on victim can come from many sides of the community as well as from inside.

Scapegoating is a cost-saving mechanism where an individual who can be representative of the tribe is selected ' to hide the flaws in the social structure and to distract public opinion—an expedient for delaying or avoiding structural change' (Bonazzi,1983). The scapegoat is a simplification, readily understood by the mob.

In the four stories presented, scapegoating appeared to allay public alarm but it did nothing to cure the evil the scapegoat was set to purge. McBride's tribulation continued over seven years from 1989 to the failure of his last bid for reinstatement in 1996. For much of that time his name was tied to the disorder of unwarranted intervention in childbirth. The high rates of caesarean section associated with his practice of obstetrics could incur an exemplary punishment which would warn any whose practice followed a like pattern. The irony implicit in McBride's case heightens the symbolism of his expulsion. He was the man who warned the world of thalidomide and continued to protest the dangers of pharmaceuticals ingested early in pregnancy. He was intransigent in his suspicion of foreign substances taken into the body of a woman during pregnancy. Yet the accusations were of his dangerous surgical intervention at the other end of pregnancy's term. Eventually after months of intense investigation and public prosecution these charges failed. But public opinion had been distracted and there was no structural change. There has been no diminution in the proportion of babies delivered by caesarean section in public and private hospitals throughout Australia. Recent audits indicate further rises.

The second category of charges against McBride were of a different order. They emanated from a successful exercise in investigative journalism and the tentative findings of a private committee of inquiry. The media investigation leading to the denunciation on the ABC radio program *The Science Show* shouted scientific fraud. The Committee of Inquiry held that the experiment in question was carelessly conducted and reported with a cavalier disregard for accuracy of detail. Perhaps it was worse than that. Neither investigation nor inquiry was conducted in public; McBride himself was not permitted or able to be present when evidence was given against him. Other events overtook any recourse to appeal before a formal Court. As to the fact of the experiment's results, subsequent scientific experiments have reinforced those earlier indicative but not conclusive findings. The chemical compound in question, scopolamine hydrobromide, when ingested by animals of several species during pregnancy, is associated with foetal deformities. The commercial variety of this compound now carries a warning that it is not to be taken during pregnancy. I am not arguing for or against the decision that McBride was guilty of scientific fraud. A careful reading of relevant transcripts convinced me that this episode in his scientific research was hasty and careless. However, I could not find the ground for a more damning imputation.[1]

In proceedings before the Medical Tribunal the distinction between medical practice and scientific research was invoked in McBride's defence. The authority of medicine is based on its science and the lines between research and practice are frequently crossed. Increasing division of labour, implicit in specialisation, has underlined the distinction. Expertise in each field demands an excessive devotion of time and energy which tends mutual exclusion. The codes governing practice in each field are quite different. Nonetheless, medicine's explicit appeal to the authority of its science has long persuaded the public of the close links of one with the other. A failure of honesty in one sphere could be symptomatic of lack of good character in the context of the practice of medicine. Of those sitting on the Tribunal only the medical practitioner, who was both a professor and a cardiac surgeon with an outstanding reputation as a researcher and a practitioner, could discern the difference. His opinion dissented from that of his medical colleague on the Tribunal, as well as the layperson and the judge presiding. Professor Tracy's opinion was followed by the presiding judge on the Supreme Court when an appeal was run. But again the majority could not recognise the difference.

The distinction between Whelehan's two fields of practice was clearly defined and his profession was not distracted by accusations brought against him in the field of politics. This is not a moot point. The reputation of the lawyer, solicitor or barrister, must be for honesty and integrity in every sphere of activity. Whelehan's political colleagues were clear about what they were doing. The catastrophe might be avoided. The Irish government might be saved if a suitable offering could be found to propitiate the Dail and the public: 'we've come for a head—yours or Harry's'. Whelehan could be found, innocent or guilty, at the centre of the crisis. He was, in some ways, at the margin of government. Appointed by Taioseach and government, not elected by the people, he could be distinguished from the elected government of Fianna Fail. All guilt, of the despised priest, of Church and of Government, could be lashed on to him and by his expulsion carried away. This spectacular scapegoating was publicised around the world, but it did not save the Fianna Fail government. Then, in sharp differentiation to the action of Whelehan's political colleagues, his former professional colleagues moved for his reinstallation into the profession. An extraordinary general meeting was called, a plebiscite ordered and the specific obstacle to his reintegration moved to allow a moment when he could pass back into the fold. Lawyers might take a place in politics, individuals could pass from one profession and back again, but there could be no blurring of the boundaries. The difference was clearly marked.

These questions of the boundary between professions did not arise for Childs and Foreman, but the issue of difference, and knowing the difference, surfaced in other guises. Childs, it was claimed had no respect for boundaries, those between patient and practitioner. In response to the Tribunal's question she argued for an alternative therapy. There are many such in psychiatry and skilled practitioners often draw on a range of modalities. Childs had developed a modality of 'humanistic psychotherapy', which began with an agreement between practitioner and patient on the goals of therapy and the strategies through which these might be attained. She spoke of 'partnership' between doctor and patient. In this context she had allowed a therapeutic relationship to shift into friendship and, at least in the case of a fellow practitioner *cum* recent patient, into a long-term de facto relationship. She rejected the clear differentiation between the authority of practitioner and the subordinate status of patient. When she would find no error in this approach and refused to express contrition there was no forgiveness for the fault found in her.

For Foreman the loss of balance and discernment occurred when she substituted a reconstructed document into the file required by the Court. Later she could not recall the details. She had been put under such emotional pressure to perform and reach the financial goals of the firm that she lost all sense of balance and of care. On that fateful Sunday when she made the 'terrible error' she was a creature driven to distraction and, much later, admitted the error but could not recollect its commission. For one short hour she had been oblivious to the difference.

I have dwelt in some detail on the character of the central figures. They were all closely identified with their profession, held valued positions and high status, so they could stand for their community. But they were marked by signs of marginality. Women who were not stereotypically female had succeeded in male domains. Foreman was aggressive, sharp, ambitious; a fighter who gave no quarter. Childs, popular with students and sought after as their supervisor, was sharply critical of established knowledge; she was a woman of the left in a conservative profession. And the male practitioners, one in law/politics, the other in obstetrics/science moved across two territories. Their personalities, likewise, did not conform to the stereotype. Whelehan of the conservative mien and religious reputation was chief legal officer in an Ireland turning secular and adopted by a populist government. McBride, so successful so early, appeared as benignly arrogant; he was intent on the mission which threw him into conflict with his profession's allies—the international pharmaceutical industry. He became Don Quixote with Sancho Panza standing by ready with quip and joke almost to the end.

These were persons marked by non-conformities and the mark turned to stigma when all manner of villainies were imputed to them. Childs, it was said, slept with students. Foreman was atavistic in her treatment of opponents in family law matters and relentless in the avarice of her charges. Whelehan, they claimed, had used the law to prevent a poor rape victim any recourse to abortion of the cruel aftermath of that assault; he belonged to an evil secret society and was in league with machiavellian church interests. McBride, it was reported, had been impervious to the danger to children's health of lead in the atmosphere; people commented that his science was always slipshod; and that he was arrogant and distant, always in too much hurry to listen. The rumour mills found little grist for their grinding in this man.

People who can be put at the margins are in grave danger when unmanageable crisis overwhelms their community. And it is these times which start the scapegoating process. Persons on the edge, for whatever reason, stand out and can easily be seized to take on the load of others' guilt. So laden such persons can be driven away from the community which once held them close.

Well-defined problems can be resolved in cautious times. Uncharted hazards in a turbulent environment are more obdurate. This is the threat of the unknown, the shapeless menace. When a community feels itself gripped by trouble, disaster, disease, disorder, or chaos, survival is all. The wellbeing and honour of the whole justify any sacrifice. The scandals which threatened the professions of these stories were public and unmanageable: sexual abuse in psychiatry and hints of all manner of dark practices exposed in Chelmsford; gross overcharging and consequent denial of access to justice; dangerous obstetrics practised on women in childbirth; malfeasance in science; malpractice in the administration of justice and government. At specific points in recent history these issues, always clouded in suspicion, assumed scandalous proportions and called out for remedying. To continue to ignore them could quickly poison the reputation of the professions in which they festered. Finding the one to blame, punish and drive out is not the only strategy available, but it is a relatively painless one for all, except the one chosen. And in the renunciation the community can demonstrate rejection of the appalling behaviour and publicly cleanse itself of the imputations of evil; 'It is expedient that one man should die for the people and not that the whole nation should perish' (High Priest Caippas, John 11: 50).

The parade of the scapegoat, its beating and exit were always ceremonial. These remain as public rituals of denunciation of sin and proclamation of salvation for all those delivered from sin. The procedures of tribunal and court, published in sound image and print media, become fitting ritual for a secular society. But how could this happen where the rule of law prevails?

The pathologies which throw up the scapegoat erupt every now and then in the body of the community. Our histories chronicle such events and looking back on past savageries we can safely denounce a community's rush to condemnation. But, surely matters are better ordered now. Modern law, the rational creature of the Enlightenment, would reject such primal emotions and withstand their visitation on due process and procedural fairness. The law, however, is not impervious to subversion and not immune to the hysteria of the mob crying for blood to obliterate its own sense of evil. The procedures of the Courts, shaped and informed by centuries of experience in the realm of common law can largely withstand the demands of the crowd. Tribunals, uneasy amalgam of common and civil law forged in the bureaucratic necessity for efficiency and expedience, have not that strength and stability. They are more susceptible to the cries of a powerful community calling for deliverance from an unholy condition. Tribunals are established by government to deal promptly and effectively with offences within a defined area of activity. In the interests of administrative efficiency and capability they are freed of many of the rules which operate in the Courts. Those appointed to Tribunals or Commissions are knowledgeable about the statute-defined field of operation and are not necessarily lawyers. These practitioners are often not imbued with the disciplines and traditions of the law. Tribunals put aside adversarial approaches and adopt inquisitorial modes.

They are not constrained by the rules of evidence and so may inquire as they see fit, call and question witnesses, allow hearsay testimony. Tribunals may not, however, ignore evidentiary rules to the extent of denying natural justice to the persons brought before them.

I will not here presume to enter the lawyers' learned debates over the merits and disadvantages of the summary justice dispensed by tribunals. But, it should be noted that tribunals as a creation of governments are outside the system of courts, have significant discretion in the way matters are handled and are not bound by the same rules which have evolved to protect the ideals of natural justice and the rights of 'the accused'. The words of Justice Evatt in dissent from the bench of the High Court in 1933 are often quoted in defence of the significance of rules of evidence (cited in Giles J, 1990, p.7):

> After all, they represent the attempt made, through many generations, to evolve a method of enquiry best calculated to prevent error and elicit.

The Medical Tribunal of New South Wales is typical of the many tribunals established by statute for specific purposes. The Legal Services Tribunal is significantly different. In the lawyers' tribunal the rules of evidence are observed. The decisive majority of this Tribunal are lawyers. Appeal from the decisions of the Tribunal can be made by contesting points of law or fact. The appeal to the Supreme Court provides for a hearing *de novo*; that is the whole matter determined by the Legal Services Tribunal can be heard again. These are strong and arguably expensive bulwarks to justice in a common law system. Despite an intense perusal of the reports of matters concerned with professional misconduct in the law I could find only one case where the processes of scapegoating could be discerned. My reading suggested that several lawyers had been victimised, but it seemed that appeal to the Supreme Court rectified matters. A number of these cases, and notably that of Malfantes in 1993, drew down from the Bench stern criticism of the professional body. But, in my relatively untutored view, natural justice was eventually served. I could not make that claim about all the matters brought before the Medical Tribunal. I have chosen the two most publicised cases of scapegoating to demonstrate my arguments. Others equally persuasive, if of lesser notoriety, could have been presented.

So, does scapegoating work? Does the purging cure the evil? Certainly talk and accusations of sex in the surgery, specifically the psychiatrists' exploitation of the sick and fragile, continued. More psychiatrists were led to the Tribunal. After Childs, Dr Allan Bowen-James was accused of like offences. They said he did not observe the boundaries: he continued psychotherapy in public coffee shops with patients nervous of the psychiatrist's couch; he kept long and unusual surgery hours working as late as 9 p.m. When one patient complained that her therapy had involved a sexual relationship these practices were drawn into the picture as demonstrating laxity in maintaining the doctor–patient distinction and corroborating allegations of sexual misconduct. The majority on the Tribunal accepted the patient's assertion over Bowen-James' denial. The two medical practitioners on the Tribunal did not believe critical parts of the patient's version of events; the presiding judge and layperson on the Tribunal thought otherwise. The judge in casting his vote tipped the balance and Bowen-James' deregistration was ordered. The appeal to the Supreme Court was necessarily based on points of law which did not go to the main issues on which the Tribunal divided and so that appeal failed. But this Court too was divided. The presiding judge dissented from the decision of his brother judges. Bowen-James has not sought the restoration of his name to the Register. To do so would require assuring the Tribunal of his contrition for previous misconduct. He continues to protest his innocence of all charges. He cannot in conscience offer true contrition.

A number of other psychiatrists have been arraigned before the Tribunal and met the same fate. Several are former professional associates and a few are former students of Childs. Their practice of psychiatry shared some common features of her humanistic psychotherapy. Was this 'a slaughter of innocents'? I do not know. That research has not been done and, without the most detailed inquiry, one cannot question the decisions of a Tribunal.

In 1993 the Royal Australian College of Psychiatry published its Code of Ethics, which it had prepared by a small team of consultants the previous year. Members of this profession now have an explicit guide which specifies what is permitted and what is forbidden. Despite the purge sexual misconduct remains the most frequently cited offence in matters coming before the Medical Tribunal. Certainly it is one of the easiest ways for a complainant to crucify a practitioner. The behaviour is rightly deplored by the profession of psychiatry and such matters are prosecuted vigorously.

And the other cases whose stories I have told? As noted at the end of each chapter the evils they were set to purge continue unabated. But they are not so publicly visible.

None of these scapegoats have returned to the community which drove them out. Only one, William McBride, sought readmission and faced again the humiliation of rejection. The one case which had a comforting outcome is that of Harry Whelehan SC. Perhaps it is fitting that the best story comes out of Ireland.

In all of this there is much to question and regret. The traces of scapegoating run right through human history. But ours is a civilization that holds to a promise that there should be no more scapegoats. There is a belief that our institutions have been profoundly influenced by the myths of a Judaic then Christian heritage. There had been one who stood for all and was worthier than all for his destiny, to take away the evil of the world. The pity of it all is that we have not heeded the promise and cannot leave well enough alone.

Notes

1. Years later during McBride's appeal to the Supreme Court he was not allowed to interrupt a judge's rhetorical question and draw attention to experiments conducted by the US National Toxicology Program of the National Institute of Environmental Health Sciences which concluded that scopolamine hydrobromide was linked to chromosome aberrations. Mine is not an argument about the merits or utility of these experiments; only a note about the distance between legal and scientific discourses. McBride's lawyers advised him that such an interjection from plaintiff, or defendant, legally represented was irrelevant and discourteous in the Court. McBride stayed silent and still does not understand why subsequent findings could not bear out his probity as a scientist.

BIBLIOGRAPHY

Academic Theses
Noble, Carolyn (1997) At Home in the World: A sociological study of homebiths and independent midwifery in Australia, PhD thesis, University of New South Wales.

Books
Abel, R. (1988) *The Legal Profession in England and Wales*. Oxford: Basil Blackwell.

Abel, R.L and Lewis, P.S.C. (eds) (1988a) *Lawyers in Society*, volume 1, *The Common Law World*. Los Angeles: University of California Press.

Abel, R.L and Lewis, P.S.C. (eds) (1988b) *Lawyers in Society*, volume 2, *The Civil Law World*. Los Angeles: University of California Press.

Abel, R.L and Lewis, P.S.C. (eds) (1989) *Lawyers in Society*, volume 3, *Comparative Theories*. Los Angeles: University of California Press.

Baldwin, J. (1965) *Going to Meet the Man*. London: Joseph.

Barber, B. (1983) *The Logic and Limits of Trust*. London: Longman

Barber, B. (1990) *Social Studies of Science*. New Brunswick: Transaction Publishers.

Bauman, Z. (1988) *Freedom*. London: Open University Press.

Becker, H.S., Geer, B., Hughes, E.C. and Strauss, A. (1961) *Boys in White: Student Culture in Medical School*. University of Chicago Press.

Bell, D. (1973) *The Coming of Post-Industrial Society*. New York: Basic Books.

Bell, Robert (1992) *Impure Science: Fraud Compromise and Political Influence in Scientific Research*. New York: John Wiley & Sons.

Berman, E. (1990) *Scapegoat: The Impact of Death fear on an American Family*. New York: BKS Demand.

Boreham P., Pemberton, A. & Wilson, P. (eds) (1974) *The Professions in Australia*. St. Lucia: University of Queensland Press.

Breggin, Peter R. (1993) *Toxic Psychiatry: Drugs and Electroconvulsive Therapy: The Truth and the Better Alternatives*. London: Fontana.

Brint, S. (1974) *In an Age of Experts: The Changing Role of Professionals in Politics and Public Life*. Princeton University Press.

Burrage, M. & Torsendahl, R. (1990) (eds) *Professions in Theory and History: Rethinking the Study of Professions*. London: Sage.

Byrne, Raymond & McCutcheon, Paul J. (1990) *The Irish Legal System* (2nd edn). Dublin: Butterworths.

Carr-Saunders, A.M. & Wilson, P.A. (1933) *The Professions*. London: Clarendon Press.

Casey, James (1996) *The Irish Law Officers*. Dublin: The Round Hall Press.

Collins, R. (1979) *The Credential Society*. New York: Academic Press.

Collins, R. (1990) 'Market Closure and the Conflict Theory of the Professions'. In *Professions in Theory and History: Rethinking the Study of Professions*, edited by M. Burrage and R. Torsendahl. London: Sage.

Daly, Mary (1978) *Gyn/Ecology: The Meta-ethics of Radical Feminism*. Boston: Beacon Press.

Daniel, A. (1990) *Medicine and the State: Professional Autonomy and Public Accountability*. Sydney: Allen & Unwin.

Davis, N.Z. (1975) *Society and Culture in Early Modern France*. Stanford University Press.

Derber, C., Schwartz, W.A. & Magrass, Y. (1990) *Power in the Highest Degree: Professionals and the Rise of a New Mandarin Order*. New York: Oxford University Press.

Douglas, M. (1977) *Purity and Danger: An Analysis of Concepts of Pollution and Taboo*. London: Routledge & Kegan Paul.

Duignan, Sean (1996) *One Spin on the Merry-Go-Round*. Dublin: Blackwater Press.

Durkheim, E. (1933 [1893]) *The Division of Labour in Society*, trans. G. Simpson. New York: The Free Press.

Durkheim, E. (1995 [1912]) *The Elementary Forms of Religious Life*, trans. K.E. Fields. New York: The Free Press.

Durkheim E. (1957) *Professional Ethics and Civic Morals*, trans. C. Brookfield. London: Routledge & Kegan Paul.

Dwyer, A.R. (1988) *Ethics and Psychiatry: Towards Professional Definition*. Washington, D.C.: American Psychiatric Press.

Eco, U. (1992) *The Name of the Rose*, trans. W. Weaver. London: Minerva.

Ellis, B.E. (1991) American Psycho. London: Picado.

Ehrenreich, B. and English, D. (1976) *Witches, Midwives and Nurses: A History of Women Healers*. London: Writes and Readers.

Etzioni, A. (ed.) *The Semi-Professions and their Organization: Teachers, Nurses, Social Workers*. New York: The Free Press.

Euripides (1981) *The Bacchants*, trans. Moses Hadas and John McLean. New York: Bantam Books.

Fletcher, R. (1991) *Science, Ideology and the Media: The Cyril Burt Scandal*. New Brunswick, New Jersey: Transaction Publishers.

Foucault, M. (1973) *The Birth of the Clinic: An Archaeology of Medical Perception*. London: Tavistock Publications.

Foucault, M. (1984a) 'The Means of Correct Training'. In *The Foucault Reader*, edited by P. Rabinow. Harmondsworth: Penguin Books.

Foucault, M. (1984b) 'Panopticism'. In *The Foucault Reader*, edited by P. Rabinow. Harmondsworth: Penguin Books.

Foucault, M. (1984c) 'The Birth of the Clinic'. In *The Foucault Reader*, edited by P. Rabinow. Harmondsworth: Penguin Books.

Foucault, M. (1991) 'Governmentality'. In *The Foucault Effect: Studies in Governmentality*, by G. Burchell, C. Gordon and P. Miller, pp.87–104. London: Harvester Wheatsheaf.

Foucault, M. (1991) 'Questions of Method'. In *The Foucault Effect: Studies in Governmentality* by G. Burchell, C. Gordon and P. Miller, pp.70–86. London: Harvester Wheatsheaf.

Frazer, Sir James George (1933 [1913]) *The Golden Bough: A Study in Magic and Religion* (3rd edn), Part VI, *The Scapegoat*. London: Macmillan and Co.

Freidson, E. (1976) *Doctoring Together: A Study of Professional Social Control*. New York: Elselvier.

Freidson, E. (1994) *Professionalism Reborn: Theory, Prophecy and Policy*. Cambridge: Polity Press.

Fuchs, S. (1992) *The Professional Quest for Truth: A Social Theory of Science and Knowledge*. University of New York Press.

Gabbard, G.O. (ed) (1989) *Sexual Exploitation in Professional Relationships*. Washington, DC: American Psychiatric Press.

Gaskin, Ina May (1978) *Spiritual Midwifery*. Summestown, Tenn.: The Book Publishing Co.

Gaston, Jerry (1994) Sociology of Science and Technology. In *A Guide to The Culture of Science, Technology, and Medicine*, edited by Paul T. Durbin, pp.465–526. New York: The Free Press.

Gellner, E. (1988) Trust, Cohesion and the Social Order. In *Trust: Making and Breaking Cooperative Relations,* edited by D. Gambetta. Oxford: Basil Blackwell.

Giddens, A. (1990) *The Consequences of Modernity*. Cambridge: Polity Press.

Girard, Rene (1986) *The Scapegoat*, trans. Yvonne Freccero. Baltimore: The John Hopkins University Press.

Gouldner, A.W. (1971) *The Coming Crisis of Western Sociology*. Cambridge: Cambridge University Press.

Gouldner, A.W. (1979) *The Future of Intellectuals and the Rise of the New Class*. London: Macmillan.

Gratz, Sylvia S. and Simpson George M. (1992) 'Psychopharmacology'. In *Research in Psychiatry: Issues, Strategies, and Methods*, edited by L.K.G. Hsu and M. Hersenm, pp. 309–29. New York: Plenum Medical Book Co.

Harris, John (1988) *Scapegoat! Famous Courts Martial*. London: Severn House Publishers.

Harrison, Jane (1960 [1903, 1922]) *Prolegomena to the Study of Greek Religion* (3rd edn). New York: Meridian.

Hearnshaw, L.S. (1979) *Cyril Burt, Psychologist.* Ithaca, New York: Cornell University Press.

Hersen, Michel & Miller, David J. (1992) 'Future Directions: A Modest Proposal'. In *Research Fraud in the Behavioural Sciences*, edited by Miller David J. and Hersen Michel. New York: John Wiley.

Hughes, E.C. (1958) *Men and their Work.* Glencoe, Illi.: The Free Press.

Hughes E.C. (1963) 'Professions'. In *The Professions in America* edited by *Daedalus* and K.S. Lynn. Boston: Beacon Press.

Hughes E.C. (1977) 'Professions'. In *The Professions in America* edited by ? Daedalus and K.S. Lynn. Boston: Beacon Press.

Ibsen, H. (1963) *An Enemy of the People*, trans. M. Meyer. London: R. Hart-Davis.

Illich, I. (1976) *Limits to Medicine.* Harmondsworth: Penguin Books. (Published in 1975 as *Medical Nemesis.*)

Illich, I. (1977) *Disabling Professions.* London: Marion Boyars.

Jackson, J.A. (1970) *Professions and Professionalisation.* London: Cambridge University Press.

Jacob, J.M. (1988) *Doctors and Rules: A Sociology of Professional Values.* London: Routledge.

Jensen, Arthur R. (1992) 'Scientific Fraud or False Accusation? The Case of Cyril Burt'. In *Research Fraud in the Behavioural Sciences*, edited by David J. Miller and Michel, Hersen. New York: John Wiley.

Jetter K. (1990) 'Kings and Scapegoats in Twentieth Century Families and Corporations'. In *Corporations, Businesses, and Families*, edited by R.S. Hanks & M.R. Sussman. New York: The Haworth Press.

Johnson, T. (1972) *Professions and Power.* London: Macmillan.

Johnson, T. (1982) 'The State and the Professions: Peculiarities of the British'. In *Social Class and the Division of Labour: Essays in Honour of Ilya Neustradt*, edited by A. Giddens and G. Mackenzie. London: Cambridge University Press.

Joyce, James (1937) *Ulysses.* London: Bodley Head.

Joynson, R.B. (1989) *The Burt Affair.* London: Routledge.

King, P.J.L. (1995) *Professional Practice Management.* Sydney: Law Book Company.

Kitzinger, Sheila (1978) *Women as Mothers.* London: Fontana Books.

Kitzinger, S. & Davis, J. (1978) *The Place of Birth.* Oxford University Press.

Larson, M.S. (1977) *The Rise of Professionalism: A Sociological Analysis.* University of California Press.

Lieberman, J.K. (1981) *The Litigious Society.* New York: Basic Books.

Ligermoet, Henny & Ireland, Margaret (1978) *Responsible Homebirth.* Shoalhaven, Western Australia: Midwifery Contact Centre.

Little, Miles (1995) *Humane Medicine.* New York: Cambridge University Press.

Malamud, B. (1967) *The Fixer.* Harmondsworth: Penguin.

Martin, B., Baker, A.C.M., Manwell, C. & Pugh, C. (eds) (1986) *Intellectual Suppression: Australian Case Histories, Analysis and Responses.* Sydney: Angus & Robertson.

McBride, William (1994) *Killing the Messenger.* Sydney: Eldorado Press.

MacDonald, K. (1995) T*he Sociology of the Professions.* London: Sage.

Maley, B. (1974) 'Professionalism and Professional Ethics'. In *Social Change in Australia*, edited by D. Edgar. Melbourne: Cheshire.

Miller David J. & Hersen, Michel (eds) (1992) *Research Fraud in the Behavioural Sciences.* New York: John Wiley.

Moore, Chris (1995) *Betrayal of Trust: The Father Brendan Smyth Affair and the Catholic Church.* Dublin: Marino Books.

Murphy, R. (1988) *Social closure: The Theory of Monopolization and Exclusion.* Oxford: Clarendon Press.

Nicol, Bill (1989) *McBride: Behind the Myth.* Crows Nest: ABC Press.

Oakley, Ann (1976) 'Wise Women and Medicine Men: Changes in the Management of Childbirth'. In *The Rights and Wrongs of Women* by A. Oakley and J. Mitchell. Harmondsworth: Penguin.

Oakely, Ann (1979) *Becoming a Mother.* Oxford: Martin Robertson.

Oakley, Ann (1984) *The Captured Womb: A History of the Medical Care of Women.* Oxford: Basil Blackwell.

Pascal, Louis (1991) What Happens When Science Goes Bad. The Corruption of Science and the Porigin of AIDS: A Study in Spontaneous Generation. Working Paper No.9. Science and Technology Analysis Research Programmes. University of Wollongong.

Patton, Cindy (1990) *Inventing AIDS.* New York: Routledge.

Perkin, H. (1989) *The Rise of Professional Society: England since 1880.* London: Routledge.

Pillari, U. (1991) *Scapegoating in Families: Intergenerational Patterns of Emotional and Physical Abuse.* Brummer Mazel.

Rich, Adrienne (1976) *Of Woman Born: Motherhood as Experience and Institution.* New York: Bantam.

Rosenthal, M. (1994) *The Incompetent Doctor: Behind Closed Doors.* Buckingham, Philadelphia: Open University Press.

Rothman, Barbara Katz (1983) *In Labour: Women and Power in the Birthplace.* New York: W.W.Norton.

Rueschemeyer, D. (1973) *Lawyers and their Society: A Comparative Study of the Legal Profession in Germany and the United States.* Cambridge, Mass.: Harvard University Press.

Rueschemeyer, D. (1986) *Power and the Division of Labour.* Cambridge: Polity Press.

Sapp, J. (1990) *Where the Truth Lies: Franz Moewus and the Origins of Molecular Biology.* Cambridge: Cambridge University Press.

Smith, Russell G. (1994) *Medical Discipline: The Professional Conduct Jurisdiction of the General Medical Council, 1858–1990.* Oxford: Clarendon.

Starr, P. (1982) *The Social Transformation of American Medicine*. New York: Basic Books.

Strindberg, A. (1967) *The Scapegoat*, trans. A. Paulson. New York: Paul S. Eriksson.

Swan, Norman (1988) Scientific Fraud, *58th Australian and New Zealand Association for Advancement of Science (AZAAS) Conference Proceedings*, pp.1–14.

Swan, N. (1993) 'Baron Munchausen at the Lab Bench?' In *Fraud and Misconduct in Medical Research*, edited by Stephen Lock and Frank Wells, pp.142–57. London: BMJ Publishing Group.

Taylor, Richard (1979) *Medicine Out of Control: The Anatomy of a Malignant Technology*. Melbourne: Sun Books.

Turner, B.S. (1987) *Medical Power and Social Knowledge*. London: Sage.

Vickery, John B. (1973) *The Literary Impact of The Golden Bough*. Princeton, New Jersey: Princeton University Press.

Vickery, John B. (1974) 'The Scapegoat in Literature: Some Kinds and Uses'. In *The Binding of Proteus: Perspectives on Myth and the Literary Process*, edited by M.W. McCune, O. Tickler and P.M.Withim. Lewisburg: Bucknell University Press and London: Associated University Presses.

Weber, M (1948 [1906]) 'The Protestant Sects and the Spirit of Capitalism'. In *From Max Weber: Essays in Sociology*, edited by H.H. Gerth and C.W. Mills. London: Routledge & Kegan Paul.

Weisbrot, D. (1988) Lawyers in Australia'. In *The Common Law World*, volume 1, *Lawyers in Society*, edited by R.L. Abel and P.S.C. Lewis. Los Angeles: University of California Press.

Weisbrot, D. (1990) *Australian Lawyers*. Melbourne: Longman Cheshire.

Willis, E. (1983) *Medical Dominance: The Division of Labour in Australian Health Care*. Sydney: Allen & Unwin.

Cases

re Arvind, Dr Balakrishnan and the Medical Practitioners Act (1994). Reasons for Determination, 27 June 1994.

re Beshara, Dr Atef and the Medical Practice Act (1995). Reasons for Determination, 24 November 1995.

Bowen-James v. Delegate of the Director-General of the Department of Health (1992) 27 NSWLR 457.

Briginshaw v. Briginshaw (1938) 60 CLR 336.

re Bowen-James, Dr Alan and the Medical Practitioners' Act (1992) Medical Tribunal of New South Wales. Reasons for Determination and Orders, 8 September 1992.

Buttsworth v. Walton (1991) Supreme Court of New South Wales Court of Appeal (unreported) CA 40520/91.

Buttsworth v. Walton (1991) Judgment in Supreme Court of New South Wales Court of Appeal. Appeal from Medical Tribunal. Unreported Judgment 40520/91.

Childs v. Walton (1990) Supreme Court of New South Wales Court of Appeal (unreported) CA 4025/90.

re Childs, Dr Winifred and the Medical Practitioners' Act (1990). Reasons for Decision, 9 April 1990.

re Childs, Dr Winifred and the Medical Practitioners' Act (1990). Orders, 8 May 1990.

Council of the Law Society of New South Wales v. Foreman (1994) 34 NSWLR 408.

Council of the Law Society of New South Wales v. Veghelyi. Determination of the Legal Services Tribunal, 8 March 1995.

re Davis, Dr TP and the Medical Practice Act 1992 (1994). Reasons for Determination and Orders, 9 December 1994.

re Edmond, Dr Edward and the Medical Practitioners' Act 1938 (1992). Reasons for Determination, 10 December 1992.

re Harrison, Dr John Wilkin and the Medical Practice Act 1992 (1994). Reasons for Determination and Orders, 9 December 1994.

re Jolly, Dr Hugh Morrison and the Medical Practice Act 1992 (1995). Reasons for Determination, 19 September 1995.

Law Society of New South Wales v. Malfanti. Legal Profession Disciplinary Tribunal. Reasons for Determination, 8 May 1991.

Malfanti v. Legal Profession Disciplinary Tribunal. Supreme Court of New South Wales Court of Appeal. Reported in *Legal Profession Disciplinary Reports* No.4, 1993, pp.17–23.

re McBride, Dr William Griffith and the Medical Practitioners Act. Reasons for Determination and Orders, May 1992.

McBride v. Walton (1994) Supreme Court of New South Wales Court of Appeal. CA 40436/93.

Quidwai v. Brown (1984) 1 NSWLR.

Richter v. Walton (1993) Supreme Court of New South Wales Court of Appeal CA 40309/93.

Sankey v. Whitlam (1978) 142 CLR 1.

R v. War Pensions Entitlement Appeal Tribunal ex parte Bott (1933) 50 CLR 228.

re Richter, Dr Martin Bruce and the Medical Practitioners Act (1993). Judgment, 5 May 1993.

Veghelyi v. Law Society of New South Wales. Supreme Court of New South Wales CA 40237/91. Reported in *Legal Profession Disciplinary Reports*, No.2, 1996, pp. 9–24.

Walton v. McBride Supreme Court of New South Wales Court of Appeal. Unreported, 3 October 1989.

re Woolcock, James Alexander and the Medical Practice Act 1992 (1995). Reasons for Determination, 14 September 1995.

re Zaidi, Mr M.H. and the Medical Practice Act (1994). Judgment. 31 March 1994.

re Zoglmeyer, Dr Brigitte and the Medical Practice Act 1992 (1995). Reasons for Determination and Orders, 22 December 1995.

Journal Articles

Abraham, J. (1994) Bias in Science and Medical Knowledge: The Opren Controversy. *Sociology* **28(3)**, 717–36.

Abraham, John (1994) Distributing the Benefit of the Doubt: Scientists, Regulators and Drug Safety. *Science, Technology and Human Values* **19(4)**, 493–522.

Adamson, G. & Gare, D. (1980) Hospital or Home Births? *Journal of the American Medical Association* **243**, 1732–6.

Andrews, Gavin (1991a) The Changing Nature of Psychiatry. *Australian and New Zealand Journal of Psychiatry* **25**, 453–9.

Andrews, Gavin (1991b) Psychotherapy: From Freud to Cognitive Science. *Medical Journal of Australia* **155**, 845–8.

Beumont (1992) Phenomenology and the History of Psychiatry. *Australian New Zealand Journal of Psychiatry* **26**, 532–45.

Biggs, John S.G. (1984) The Rise of the Caesarean Section: A Review. *The Australian and New Zealand Journal of Obstetrics and Gynaecology* **24(2)**, 67–71.

Blumenthal, N.J., Harris, R.S., O'Connor, M.C. & Lancaster, P.A. (1984) Changing Caesarean Section Rates Experience at a Sydney Obstetric Teaching Hospital. *Australian and New Zealand Journal of Obstetrics and Gynaecology* **24**, 246–51.

Boeker, Warren (1992) Power and Managerial Dismissal: Scapegoating at the Top. *Administrative Science Quarterly* **37**, 400–21.

Bonazzi, G. (1983) Scapegoating in Complex Organizations: The Results of a Comparative Study of the Symbolic Blame-giving in Italian and French Public Administration. *Organizations Studies* **4(1)**, 1–18.

Bremmer, Jan (1983) Scapegoat Rituals in Ancient Greece. *Harvard Studies in Classical Philology* **87**, 299–320.

Broe, S. & Khoo, Soo-Keat (1989) How Safe is Caesarean Section in Current Practice? A Survey of Mortality and Serious Morbidity. *Australian New Zealand Journal of Obstetrics and Gynaeclogy* **29**, 93–8.

Correy, J.F. (1977) A Review of Obstetric Practice in Hobart over 25 Years. *Australian and New Zealand Journal of Obstetrics and Gynaecology* **17**, 84–8.

Douglas, J.D. (1992) Betraying Scientific Truth. *Society* **30(1)**, 76–82.

Ferguson, H. (1985) The Paedophile Priest: A Deconstruction. *Studies* **84(335)**, 247–56.

Galletly, P. (1993) Psychiatrist–Patient Sexual Relationships: The Ethical Dilemmas. *Australian and New Zealand Journal of Psychiatry* **27**, 133–7.

Gandolfo, P. (1989) The Cost of Justice: What Price a Fairgo? *Law Institute Journal* **63(10)**, 953–5.

Gartrell, N., Herman, J. and Olarte, S. (1986) Psychiatrist–Patient Sexual Contact. *American Journal of Psychiatry* **143**, 112–31.

Giles, Justice (1990) Dispensing with the Rules of Evidence. *Bar News* (The Journal of the NSW Bar Association), 5–16.

Jones, June Rider (1991) Scientific Fraud–Researchers–Excellence: Is there a connection? Asian Pacific Special Law Librarians Conference, **4**, 448–93.

Joynson, Robert B. (1994) Fallible Judgments. *Society* **31**, March/April, 45–51.

Kardener, S.H, Fuller, M. & Mensh, I.N. (1973) A Survey of Physicians' Attitudes and Practises regarding Erotic and Non-Erotic contact with Patients. *American Journal of Psychiatry* **130**, 1077–81.

Kearney, R. (1995) Myths and Scapegoats: The Case of Rene Girard. *Theory, Culture and Society* **12(4)**, pp. 1–14.

Learoyd, Brian M. (1985) Unnecessary Surgery Debate. *New Doctor* **36**, 11–18.

Lumley, Judith (1980a) Patterns of Obstetric Intervention: Tasmania and Victoria. *New Doctor* **15**, 27–9.

Lumley, Judith (1980b) Foetal Monitoring: A Look at the Evidence. *New Doctor* No.15, 45–8.

Lupton, Deborah (1993) Back to Bedlam? *Australian New Zealand Journal of Psychiatry* **27**, 140–8.

McBride, W.G., Black, B.P., Brown, C.J., Dolby, R.M., Murray, A.D. & Thomas, D.B. (1979) Method of Delivery and Developmental Outcome at Five Years of Age. *Medical Journal of Australia 1979* **1**, 301–4.

McBride, W.G. (1961) Thalidomide and Congenital Abnormalities. *The Lancet* **2**, 1358.

McBride, W.G., Vardy, P.H. & French, J. (1982) Effects of Scopolamine Hydrobromide on the Development of the Chick and Rabbit Embryo. *The Australian Journal of Biological Science* **35(2)**, 3–8.

McBride, W.G. (1983) Note on the paper 'Effects of Scopolamine Hychobromide on the Deveopment of the Chick and Rabbit Embryo'. *The Australian Journal of Biological Sciences* **36(2)**, 171–2.

McBride, W.G. (1994) Thalidomide may be a Mutagen. *British Medical Journal* **308**, 1635–6.

Martin, B. (1992) Scientific Fraud and the Power Structure of Science. *Prometheus* **10(1)**, 83–98.

Medlicott, R.W. (1968) Erotic Professional Indiscretions, Actual or Assumed, and Alleged. *Australian and New Zealand Journal of Psychiatry* **25**, 27–30.

Muhlen-Schulte, Liselott (1987) Homebirth on Trial? The Facts: In Australia and Holland. *New Doctor*, no.46, 17–21.

Muhlen, L. & Nordholm, Lena (1981) Survey of Mothers' Experiences of Active Intervention in Childbirth. *New Doctor* **20**, 29–30.

Murray-Arthur, F. & Correy, J.F. (1984) A Review of Primary Caesarean Sections in Tasmania. *Australian New Zealand Journal of Obstetrics and Gynaecology* **24**, 242–45.

Opit, L.J. & Sellwood, T.S. (1979) Casesarean Section Rates in Australia. *Medical Journal of Australia* **2**, 706–709.

Parsons, Talcott (1980) Sociology of Modern Anti-Semitism. *Contemporary Jewry* **5(1)**, 31–8.

Peterson, Karen (1983) Technology as a last resort in Home Birth: The work of lay midwives. *Social Problems* **30**, 272–83.

Pinch, Trev (1993) Generations of SSK. *Social Studies of Science* **23**, 363–73.

Pryke, Margaret, Muhlen, Liselotte & Wade, Kenneth (1986) Childbirth and Surgery: the experience of an Australian sample of 120 women during birth. *New Doctor* No. 39: 21–4.

Ratten, Graeme J. (1985) Changes in Obstetric Practice in Our Time. *Australian and New Zealand Journal of Obstetrics and Gynaecology* **25(4)**, 241–4.

Rawling, A. (1994) The AIDS virus dispute: Awarding priority for the discovery of the human immunodeficiency virus (HIV). *Science, Technology, and Human Values* **19**, 342–60.

Richards, Evelleen (1991) Vitamin C and Cancer: Medicine or Politics? *Social Studies of Science* **23**, 363–73.

Sutherst, J. & Case, B. (1975) Caesarean Section and its Place in the Active Approach to Delivery. *Clinics in Obstetrics and Gynaeclogy* **2(1)**, 6–10.

Weitz, Rose & Sullivan, Deborarh (1985) Licensed Lay Midwifery and the Medical Model of Birth. *Sociology of Health and Illness* **7(1)**, 36–54.

Legislation

Bunreacht Na hÉireann (Constitution of Ireland). (In operation as from 29 December 1937 and including amendments to December 1992.)

Health Care Complaints Act 1993 (NSW).

Legal Profession Act 1987 (No.109), as at 1 July 1994 (NSW).

Legal Profession Reform Act 1993 (No.87) (NSW).

Medical Practitioners Act 1938 (No.37) (NSW).

Medical Practice Act 1992 (No.94) (NSW).

Newspaper Articles

Australian Law News
September 1989 'Chief Justice on State of Judicature', pp.11–13.

Australian Lawyer
November 1995 'New view of law puts money first', pp.10–12.

Bulletin
11 June 1991, 'People v Lawyers v Money', pp.28–33.

Daily Telegraph
2 April 1997, 'Clients in the Dark on Legal Costs', p.1.

Irish Independent
1 August 1994, 'Grin and Bear It: Pre-emptive Strike that left the Junior Partner Floundering', p.10.

5 October 1994, 'Judges Clash puts Govt on Brink of Election', p.1.

11 October 1994, 'Leaders left to sort out AG Row', p.1.

24 October 1994, AG accused over Sex Priest Extradition Delay', p.1.

24 October 1994, 'Paedophile Priests must be Reported', p.13.

27 October 1994, 'Paedophile: Dail "Not Misled" ', p.7.

14 November 1994, editorial: 'A Matter of Accountability', p.19.

Irish Times

1994, editorial: 'Picking the Judges', 21 September, p.6.

1994, editorial: Even at this Mortal Hour', 15 November, p.6.

18 November 1994 'Subdued Whelehan Resigns 6 days after Appointment', p.1.

18 November 1994, 'Great Courage Shown', p.8.

18 November 1994, 'Statement of Resignation', p.8.

18 November 1994 'Departure one of "Dignity and Honour" ', p.12.

18 November 1994, 'Now to undo the Damage Reynolds has done', p.18.

3 December 1994 'All Members of the Bar to be polled on Whelehan Issue',
    p.5.

13 January 1995, 'Who's on "The Street" to Compare with Harry?', p.10.

18 January 1995, 'Dail Sub-Committee on Leglisation and Security: I felt it
    unwise to appoint Whelehan', p.6.

21 January 1995, Browne, Vincent, 'Some of the Mysteries are likely to
    Remain', p.12.

Justinian

July 1992 'Carol Foreman's Family Law Special: A Story to Keep', p.1 and
    pp.5–7.

Sydney Morning Herald

14 December 1987, 'McBride: Storm over Cheating Claims', p.1.

10 April 1990, 'Doctor's Lesbian Encounter with Patient "Deplored" by
    Tribunal', p.3.

8 December 1990, (*Good Weekend Magazine*), 'Psychiatric Ouch: The
    Downfall of Dr Win Childs', pp. 57–67.

22 July 1991, 'Collins Review takes the Axe to Legal Costs', p.1.

13 August 1991, 'Winners and Losers in the High Cost of Justice', p.6.

10 September 1991, 'Legal Fees Distort True Value—says A-G', p.2.

17 October 1991, editorial, 'The High Cost of Lawyers', p.10.

5 November 1991, 'Top Lawyer Quits after Row Over Fee', p. 1, 6.

7 December 1991, 'Matrimoney: Our Million Dollar Divorce Law Debacle',
    p.35, 38 (journalist: Valerie Lawson).

9 March 1992, 'Cut Legal Fees for Blacks, says Law Society', p.2.

4 April 1992, 'Price of Justice is Too High, says Marsden', p.7.

5 December 1992, 'Struck off, but Mental Health Workers Back in Similar
    Business', p.9.

31 July 1993, 'Piranha or Pussycat?' Spectrum, p.39.

31 July 1993, 'Tragic, Deceptive McBride Struck Off', p.3.

3 August 1993, 'Lawyer Accused of Gross Overcharging', p.2.

3 March 1994, 'Judgment Day', Spectrum, p. 1A, 8A.

6 August 1994, 'Struck off: The Piranha in a Power Suit', p.1.
2 April 1997, 'Damning Verdict on Lawyers', p.1.

Reports

Health Care Complaints Commission *Annual Report 1994/5* and *1995/6*.
  Sydney: State Health Publication.

Legal Services Commissioner (1996) *Annual Report of the Legal Services
  Commission of New South Wales 1995–96.* Sydney: Office of the Legal
  Services Commissioner.

New South Wales Department of Health, *In the Public Interest: The
  Complaints Unit Annual Report 1989; 1990; 1992/3* and *1993/4.* Sydney:
  State Health Publication.

New South Wales Inquiry into Health Services for the Psychiatrically Ill and
  Developmentally Disabled (1983). Sydney: New South Wales Department of
  Health, Division of Planning and Research.

Richmond Report. *See* New South Wales Inquiry into Health Services for the
  Psychiatrically Ill and Developmentally Disabled.

INDEX

For Product Safety Concerns and Information please contact our EU
representative GPSR@taylorandfrancis.com
Taylor & Francis Verlag GmbH, Kaufingerstraße 24, 80331 München, Germany